To Minnet

from

Oct. 95.

GW00392652

EBB TIDE
The Story of a Family and a Boat

EBB TIDE

**The story
of a family
and a boat**

B. H. LePine-Williams

The Book Guild Ltd.
Sussex, England

The Book Guild Ltd.
25 High Street,
Lewes, Sussex

First published 1992
© B.H. LePine-Williams 1992
Set in Baskerville
Typesetting by Southern Reproductions (Sussex)
East Grinstead, Sussex
Printed in Great Britain by
Antony Rowe Ltd.
Chippenham, Wiltshire.

A catalogue record for this book is
available from the British Library

ISBN 0 86332 740 0

CONTENTS

List of Illustrations   6
List of Maps   7
Acknowledgements   8
Introduction   9
Chapter   1   1957/8 The Beginning   15
Chapter   2   1959-1973 The Rebuilding   19
Chapter   3   1960 Early Voyages   37
Chapter   4   1961 First seagoing – Jersey   42
Chapter   5   1962 La Rochelle; Acton Bridge   51
Chapter   6   1963 Upton on Severn; Ile de Ré; Acton Bridge   67
Chapter   7   1964 Upton on Severn; Ile de Ré; Acton Bridge   80
Chapter   8   1965 Upton on Severn; Lequietio;
              Acton Bridge; I.O.M.   95
Chapter   9   1966 Upton on Severn; Lequietio again;
              Acton Bridge   107
Chapter 10   1967 Bordeaux etc.   115
Chapter 11   1968 First Pavillon d'Or – Ramsgate   124
Chapter 12   1969 Second Pavillon d'Or – Kampen, Holland   136
Chapter 13   1970 The Faroe Islands   149
Chapter 14   1971 Third Pavillon d'Or – Cologne, Germany   161
Chapter 15   1972 Last Visit to St Martin   170
Chapter 16   How we came to go to Solomon Islands   177
Chapter 17   1973 Before the Voyage   181
Chapter 18   1973 The Voyage Part 1
              Birkenhead to the Panama Canal   191
Chapter 19   1973/4 The Voyage Part 2
              Across the Pacific to Solomon Islands   213
Chapter 20   The Years in Solomon Islands   234
Chapter 21   Farewell to Ebb Tide   249
Appendix: Statistical details of the voyage
              to Honiara   251

LIST OF ILLUSTRATIONS

The Skipper   10
The Mate in her galley   10
The new engine being lowered in - Acton Bridge   18
The forward cabin showing Spanish windlass   18
1968 Pavillon d'Or - at Ardrishaig   122
1969 Pavillon d'Or flying proudly   122
1969 Pavillon d'Or - being boarded by Dutch TV   134
1971 Pavillon d'Or - alongside coaster in Ilfracombe   134
1971 Pavillon d'Or - being chased up the Rhine   159
1971 Pavillon d'Or - sailing from the Hook
  to Ramsgate   159
1973 Before the voyage - Morpeth Dock Birkenhead   189
1973 The crew before the voyage - Birkenhead Dock   189
1973 Going through the Panama Canal   212
1973 Galapagos - Anne trying to make friends
  with a seal   212
1974 Nuku Hiva - towing the fuel out to *Ebb Tide*   227
1974 The one we threw back - Marquesas to Samoa   227
1974 Baddeley on the reef at Sikaiana before the tow   248
Honiara - 'Wild men' greeting the Archbishop of
  Canterbury   248

LIST OF MAPS

1960 – Early Voyages	36
1961 – Jersey	41
1962-67 Biscay Voyages	66
1962-66 Winter Cruises	94
1968 – Pavillon d'Or – Ramsgate	123
1969 – Pavillon d'Or – Kampen	135
1970 – Route to the Faroes	148
1971 – Pavillon d'Or – Cologne	160
1973 – Route of 'The Voyage'	190

ACKNOWLEDGEMENTS

As I have said in the Introduction, this book started out as a means of putting a log into my computer. Like Topsy 'it grew' and without the great help from my wife, who faithfully drew all the maps as well as proof reading many, many times, it would probably not have got any further than just being a 'log'.

I should like to thank the Cruising Association for their permission to reproduce chapters eighteen and nineteen which appeared in their journal.

I must too acknowledge the help given by many of our friends who contributed by proof reading, as well as making many helpful suggestions. Amongst these I must mention the names of the Rev Ian Beacham, who helpfully criticized the very early efforts, and the Rev Graeme Brady, who read it at a later stage and made many helpful suggestions.

Our children too have been helpful in filling in many gaps in our memories, after all it is nearly thirty-two years since we set out on this adventure, and one's memory tends to forget many things.

INTRODUCTION

Anne and I met during the war when I was in the army isolation hospital in South Wales suffering from a pretty severe attack of mumps in a most inconvenient place. We became engaged before I was discharged, some three weeks later, and were married in London three months after that. The old adage 'marry in haste and repent at leisure' has certainly not applied in our case.

Before I was demobilized from the RAF my father bought a factory in Coventry and both Anne and I decided we would not live close to where I would be working after demobilization, but well away. We drew a circle with a radius of twenty miles from the centre of Coventry and our honeymoon was spent house hunting. We finally found a house in East Haddon, Northamptonshire, which was five miles outside the circle, but we both fell in love with it and bought it. My father was horrified that we should live so far from work and made no bones about telling me on every possible occasion. In spite of the post-war petrol rationing, I always had enough to commute and almost without exception, as a matter of principle, was in the office before my father, who lived less than three miles from the works.

In the exuberance of youth we planned to have ten children, the doctor at the isolation hospital having told me on my discharge that 'you will be able to have children, do not worry.' In the event, due to changing circumstances in our lives, we ended up with six, three of each gender. The eldest, Vivien, was followed a year later by Simon; the next year Marion appeared; another year elapsed and Gillian came on the scene. Anne had a two year break before Neil appeared. He was followed two years later by Guy. Both Neil and Guy were born in Chester. I was in the same hospital as Anne when

9

The Skipper

The Mate in her galley

Neil was born, but I too was a patient, suffering from some sort of fever.

I had been brought up in the understanding that I would follow my father in our business and so was not able to follow the career I probably would have chosen if I had been free to do so. My inclinations would have led me to become an electrical engineer and much of my work reflects this.

Following a serious reversal in our business in Coventry, for which I was unjustly blamed, I left my father to his own devices and decided to farm. In East Haddon I had established a very small farm as a hobby and was keenly interested in this occupation. We sold our house and bought a farm in Kelsall, Cheshire, my home county, and set up there. My inbred engineering instincts, however, took over and I began undertaking repairs to agricultural implements for neighbouring farmers. This proved to be more profitable and interesting than farming. We finally sold the farm and bought a house and land in Tarporley, about five miles away. At the time it was not a particularly good move since we lost the majority of our customers who had sent in their machines for repair. However, we had built up a good reputation and our style of customer changed, so that eventually we became involved in the fabrication of steel framed buildings.

The fabrication side grew, rather like Topsy, and we built up a good reputation in the constructional engineering field, undertaking contracts for many well known architects and structural engineers. My aspiration of building a factory in what was little more than a village in those days, was to provide work for local people so that they did not have to spend time commuting. We built up a labour force from Tarporley and district, but had to import some skilled workers such as draughtsmen until we could train enough locally.

We ended up exporting a considerable quantity of structural steelwork to Baltimore in America with the result that our main customer, who wanted to have full control of our output to meet his building programme, made an offer for our business. The offer was eventually accepted and was one of the best decisions we ever made. We were in some financial difficulty at that time, as the result of over trading, coupled with over ambition, and we certainly would not have survived the Heath 'three day week'. Our factory continued for several years under its new owner but he had to pour so much money into it to keep it afloat that finally the burden became too great and he closed it down.

The net result of all this was that we finally ended up in the South Pacific, having sailed our own boat there. This story is a history of our lives from the time we began 'boating' as a means of taking holidays with our children, until some twenty-five years later when we had retired (well almost).

Obviously our hobby had an effect on our children. Two began their careers at sea, one in the Royal Navy and the other in the Merchant Navy. Both have, however, 'swallowed the anchor' and Neil, who holds a 'Master's Ticket', emigrated to South Africa, since he could not find a job in the UK, which would enable him to either pay his mortgage or 'live in the style to which he had become accustomed'; I am not sure which.

Our family has unfortunately followed the national average for the break up of marriages, ie. one third, but they are in the process of re-marrying or have re-married.

In 1982, having completed nearly nine years in Solomon Islands, the time came for us to leave and return home. Some years earlier, during a visit of one of the directors of the Bank Line to Solomon Islands, we had arranged with him to travel home on one of their cargo ships. Having sailed across the Atlantic and Pacific Oceans in *Ebb Tide* we wanted to complete our circumnavigation by sea. Bank Line vessels made the round trip from England on a monthly basis, travelling via the Panama Canal and various Pacific Islands, unloading and collecting cargo en route, and would carry up to two passengers in the 'owner's suite.' They returned through the Malacca Straits, across the Indian Ocean, via the Suez Canal and the Mediterranean, to England. I had always had a vague wish to sail through the Malacca Straits, probably as the result of reading some of Conrad's books, so this way of returning home was doubly appealing. In the event we went through during the night.

At the beginning of the year, when I had taken the decision to hand over my duties to the Solomon Islander whom I had been training for my position, I booked a passage on the August ship which was the *Corabank,* scheduled to arrive at the beginning of the month. As the result of the previous arrangement, we were allowed to board her in Honiara. This was a privilege, since Bank Line had by then ceased collecting passengers from Solomon Islands, and any from there normally had to join ship in either Port Moresby in Papua New Guinea, or Port Headland in Western Australia.

Due to bad weather on her way out, *Corabank* was delayed, so the agents in Honiara could not give us any definite sailing date. We were obviously keyed up to return home, having said our farewells and attended the various farewell functions. We were resigned to hanging about for a few more days when, without any prior warning, I received a telephone call to say that she would be docking that night; I was told that our personal effects must be taken to the port immediately, and we must board the following morning!

We spent nearly three months on the *Corabank*, during which time she called at the major ports in Papua New Guinea. This enabled us to have a look at the country and we visited the gigantic copper mine at Bougainville (at the time of writing, the subject of a certain amount of controversy), which was an experience in itself. I think I carried my personal 'hoodoo' with me since *Corabank* suffered quite a few engine problems on the return voyage. We had to wait at the southern entrance to the Suez Canal until we were the last vessel in the day's convoy because the chief engineer had used some pretty basic Anglo Saxon to a port official when he was questioned about the reliability of the engine. When we were off Hull the engine failed again, but the crew were able to drop anchor just before she was driven on to a navigational buoy.

While we were in Solomon Islands I realized that I had never set down a narrative log of our own voyage there and planned to do so on the way home. Part of the time on board the *Corabank* was spent in typing one, mainly for circulating round our family. Following our move from the Isle of Man back to Cheshire to a much smaller home, we had to sort out a lot of papers, when I found my original copy of the log, and noted that it contained plenty of typing errors. Having purchased a succession of computers I decided to type it into my current one so that I would have an 'error free' copy. This done, I then thought that it would be a good idea to build all *Ebb Tide's* logs into a book, since our incursion into 'yachting' had such an enormous influence on the life of all our family.

This has been done in the hope that others might be interested, and possibly their lives too be subjected to a similar influence.

Part of this book is of necessity fairly technical since Anne and I had taken an almost derelict boat and made her not only into an extremely comfortable home as well as an equally seaworthy vessel, but also a means of spending holidays with our family for the majority of their early lives, until they left the nest. I feel that those who may read it would like to have a certain amount of simple technical information; it may help them to avoid some of the problems we met.

The Rev Ian Beacham, a good friend of mine who does not have any knowledge of the sea, very kindly read through the proofs as the book was being developed. He gave me a lot of sound advice and pointed out that possibly those who read it later may not have any knowledge of the marine way of life. It is for that reason that I have added details of our watchkeeping, the cooking arrangements, and a short description of the Panama Canal.

1

1957/58

The Beginning

This story begins in 1957 when, not having had a holiday with my family for over sixteen years, I felt that it was long past time that I did. Anne and I came to the conclusion that with six children and a golden labrador, taking a holiday in a hotel was not on, and so we looked for an alternative. Caravanning did not appeal to us and 'boating' was the only alternative which did, so in 1958 we hired a cruiser named *Golden Eagle* from the boatyard on the River Avon at Tewkesbury, in Gloucestershire. We toured the rivers Severn and Avon as far as they were navigable in those days: the upper limit on the Severn being just above Stourport, while the lower limit was the entrance to Gloucester docks. On the Avon the limit was just above Evesham.

That summer the weather was superb; we all enjoyed the holiday so much that we decided we must own a boat of our own. We thought that it would be far cheaper in the long run than hiring; little did we know then that we would end up being hooked. The 'in' pop song that year was 'Lipstick on your collar,' and every time we hear this tune our minds go back to cruising up and down the Rivers Severn and Avon with the children stretched out sun-bathing on *Golden Eagle's* deck. Since we owned our business and ploughed back all the profits, our finances were somewhat limited, so we could not afford a great deal and looked for a 'conversion' rather then a purpose built boat.

Before we became hooked on boats and when we were at Tarporley, we bought a Burrell traction engine. Phil Archer, my partner, and I towed it home from a farm about three miles away. We tested the boiler to about twice the working pressure and then decided to 'steam it'. Before we could do this, however, we had to remove goodness knows how many dozen eggs from the firebox. We ran it a few times up and down the drive to the works before deciding to rebuild it. When it was stripped down we discovered that the smoke box was rusted through and so decided to rebuild it. Phil, however, decided to get married, so the poor old engine was left. Eventually it was cut up for scrap in order to make room in our yard for *Dolphin,* our first boat.

We had somehow decided that a thirty foot boat was the length we wanted, probably because that was about the length of the *Golden Eagle.* We searched high and low for one capable of sleeping eight. At the time we were told that it was impossible, but at the end of 1958, after a long search, we finally located one lying in the Heybridge basin on the east coast. She was a converted lifeboat named *Arthur David* by her original owner, but she could just sleep our family of eight. She had a double berth 'owner's cabin' which also had a small berth, the occupier of which had his feet in a wardrobe: a two berthed cabin forward and a 'saloon', the dining table which could be converted into two berths, but when our children were small, the three girls slept there.

The purchase was duly made and the first problem was to get her from Heybridge basin to Maldon in Essex, and the second, from Maldon to Tarporley in Cheshire, where we lived. The first was accomplished by engaging a 'professional' crew. Due to adverse weather conditions they met on that short passage they lost one of the two dinghies which came with her. The second task was accomplished by transporting her home on our own low loader. She had the distinction of being the first boat to travel on the newly opened M1.

She was unloaded in our works yard at Tarporley and set up on stocks. By then it was late autumn so the winter was spent in giving her a complete refit. This included the installation of a BMC diesel in place of the original petrol version. With six young children on board we did not want to have to cope with petrol as well. I installed a new radio telephone, a later model of which had a radio direction finding facility built in. In order to be able to use it legally, I had to pass an oral examination to obtain the necessary 'restricted operator's licence.' This was duly taken in *Dolphin* sitting in the stocks at Tarporley, the examiner coming from Liverpool for the purpose. He said that because it was so new, the radio telephone was not on the list of 'approved' equipment, however he accepted it and proceeded with the examination. During his visit I managed to trap his fingers in the wheelhouse door, which was a sliding one, but that did not affect the result and I was duly issued with a licence which I still have in my possession.

The previous owner was a printer and he had used old print metal for ballast. This was an unexpected bonus since we had plenty of heavy steel scrap in the works and so were able to sell the print metal. The money from this helped with the cost of the refit. We also sold the old petrol engine and much of the other surplus equipment through the medium of an advertisement in *Motor Boat & Yachting*.

After the refit had been completed she was taken to Sharpness on our low loader. Sharpness is at the Severn Estuary end of the Gloucester/Sharpness ship canal and was a thriving grain port. On this journey I was accompanied by Philip Archer, my business partner, Simon our eldest son, and Kerry, the low loader driver. *Dolphin* was duly launched by crane.

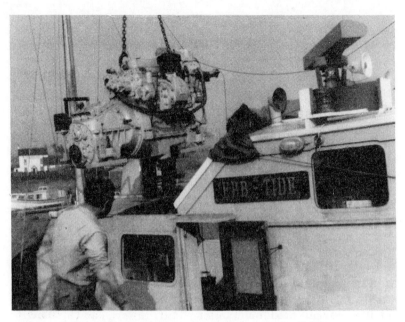

The new engine being lowered in – Acton Bridge

The forward cabin showing Spanish windlass

2

1959-1973

The Rebuilding

In spite of being double diagonal teak construction, having been on dry land for so long she leaked a fair amount, so we waited for the timbers to swell and 'take up' before we began her first voyage under new ownership. This passage turned out to be somewhat difficult. During the refit I had inadvertently connected the steering gear back to front, with the result that every natural wheel movement had to be mentally reversed before putting it into effect. Rather like driving a car backwards! We made our way along the ship canal to Gloucester, then up the River Severn to Tewkesbury where we locked into the River Avon and spent the night alongside the town wharf. The next morning we locked back into the River Severn and set off for Worcester where I had arranged for a mooring just above the racecourse. On our arrival at Worcester the gear lever in the wheelhouse broke off and Phil Archer had to sit on the engine and operate the gear lever on the gearbox as I manoeuvred on to our mooring. I note that we called in at Upton on Severn on the way up river. Little did I realize then that we would soon have a larger boat and Upton would be our summer mooring place for three years.

That summer we had a wonderful holiday and, apart from cruising up and down the Rivers Severn and Avon, we ventured out into the estuary to make a visit to Avonmouth. A Severn pilot was engaged for this short trip since it included passing through the tricky 'Shoots' at Aust. We spent the night in Avonmouth dock and returned the following day. During this short passage we found that we were making water at an alarming rate. An investigation indicated that this was due to the stern tube having become loose. At Sharpness we were advised to go up the canal to Bob Davies's shipyard at Saul. On arrival, and during the processes of mooring and pumping the bilges, when both Anne and I were fully occupied, Gillian, our youngest daughter, began demanding that Anne should cut her toe nails! (she was then eight).

We had a lot of fun with *Dolphin* during the short time we had her. She was well used for the purpose for which boats are built, ie. moving, rather than sitting in a mooring. We spent many weekends at Upton on Severn where the Severn Motor Yacht Club held its annual regatta. We had bought a Norwegian dinghy for *Dolphin* since the one which had survived the delivery trip from Heybridge Basin to Maldon was extremely heavy. We christened the Norwegian dinghy the 'banana boat' as it looked something like a banana. On one occasion when we were attending a Severn Regatta dinner, both Anne and I were appropriately dressed and as I stepped into the banana boat it sank! Luckily we were close to the landing stage and the water was not deep enough to do any real damage so we did not have too much of a problem. Unfortunately, the banana boat was stolen from our mooring at Acton Bridge some years later. During the time we had it, the children had a great deal of pleasure from it.

The enjoyment we obtained from *Dolphin* in the short space of time she was in use was such that we soon had the urge to own a larger boat. She was really too crowded with eight and a dog on board, so another search began. As I said earlier, we could not afford the cost of a purpose-built motor yacht, so we looked for something we could build up ourselves. The first one was an ex-Jersey fishing boat which had been used for scallop fishing in the Irish Sea, and was lying at Port St Mary, Isle of Man. I flew over to look at her but found that the owner had not only removed the engine, but the propeller shaft and stern tube as well. Quite apart from that there was no accommodation at all so that the conversion would have been a major undertaking.

We had been planning to carry out a conversion on the River Weaver at Acton Bridge where there is a motor boat club. Acton Bridge is not far from Northwich and our then home at Tarporley. The removal of the engine and stern gear would have meant towing her from Port St Mary to Acton Bridge, so she was rejected. In retrospect that was probably a good thing, we had little knowledge of seamanship and no knowledge then of dangerous currents which run in the Mersey, plus the fact that we were still extremely inexperienced. I had quite a problem obtaining the refund of the £50 which had been paid to the 'agent'. The only consolation was that the owner lunched me pretty well.

We continued our search, but in the meantime we moved *Dolphin* to the Severn Motor Yacht Club mooring at Kempsey, which is just south of Worcester. A fellow yacht member of the club, Wing Commander Harry Nunn, suggested that an ex-Admiralty fifty-two foot harbour launch would suit our purpose admirably. He was a staunch believer in conversion rather than building from scratch and owned an ex-Admiralty pinnace which he had converted himself. Again we scoured the yachting magazines and eventually located one in Perth, Scotland. We made arrangements for a trial run and Anne and I motored up there with another friend. We left Tarporley at about 3am and arrived at Perth in time for breakfast. On the way I dropped off a bag of bolts and nuts at a building site in the Lake District, where our company was working. A policeman who happened to be passing the site at the time was more then a little intrigued when I threw the bag over the entrance gate.

The trial run duly took place and we were suitably impressed; she handled well and we both felt that we could convert her to suit our purpose. However, when I was making a final check of the engine and discovered that the compression was so poor that I could spin the flywheel by hand, I decided that she was not for us and a couple of hours later we were on our way home.

In our innocence we had planned to take her from Perth, down the Firth of Tay, into the North Sea, up the Firth of Forth to Edinburgh, across Scotland via the ship canal (which at that time ran between Edinburgh and Glasgow), south down the Irish Sea, up the Mersey and the Manchester Ship Canal, then via the River Weaver to Acton Bridge. Again in retrospect, it was a good thing that the engine was in such a poor condition, otherwise goodness only knows what trouble we might have met had the planned delivery trip been undertaken.

The following weekend we went down as usual to *Dolphin* on her mooring at Kempsey. Across the river was a fifty-two foot harbour launch named *Ebb Tide* which belonged to another member of the club. During the weekend the steward told us that she had been put up for sale and gave us the key so that we could have a look around. Our first impression was that it was not for us. She was filthy, smelly and dilapidated. We came away with a smell in our nostrils which for years afterwards we always referred to as 'the *Ebb Tide* smell'. Incidentally it took many years of cleaning to remove the smell completely. Anyway, after further thought and negotiations, we finally purchased her and poor *Dolphin* was stripped of all the equipment we thought was better than that on *Ebb Tide* and then taken to the Worcester Canal Basin where she lay, unvisited by us, until she was sold. We had more than enough to cope with in getting *Ebb Tide* into some sort of shape. Having two boats is rather like having two houses, with one on the market.

Later on I joined the Admiralty Ferry Crew Association as the result of seeing a paragraph in *Motor Boat and Yachting* asking for recruits. This organization had its origins in the 'little ships' which had been to Dunkirk. It gave its members some privileges, one of which was that they could join in with the Royal Navy Auxiliary Service, 'Dad's Navy', when they were engaged in exercises with NATO. Later this service was amalgamated with the RNXS, since the powers that be decided that there was no room for a 'private navy' in the modern one. After attending a training course at *HMS Vernon* I obtained a skipper's ticket. Anne joined later, attended a similar course, and obtained a mate's ticket.

We had many trips with this service. In those days we crewed an inshore minesweeper, *XSV Puttenham,* from Birkenhead to Plymouth for her annual refit, and then back again after the refit had been completed. This gave us a fair amount of rough weather experience since these trips were always made in the winter and, as many readers will know, in those days minesweepers had open bridges. On one occasion, on the way back from Plymouth, we had a crew of fifteen, but only five of us were 'serviceable', the remainder being seasick. During the tossing about we were experiencing one of the engineers managed to trap his hand in between some gears in the engine room. The skipper decided to head for Fishguard to obtain some medical assistance. He was an ex-Blue Funnel officer and insisted on keeping five miles off all land. In consequence we had to go five miles north of Fishguard, turn south, and then head for the harbour. As I always believed that the shortest distance between two points is a straight line, my frustration can be imagined! All this time Anne was acting as ship's doctor and doing her best to cope with the injury while she and her patient were being flung about the mess deck. When we arrived at Fishguard a local doctor was called, who said he could not do any better than Anne and cleaned up the wound with Phisohex. After this we always had a bottle in our medical chest and it came in useful many more times than I like to remember. It was put to good use in Solomon Islands after I had been working on the little ships there. We still have a bottle in our medicine chest now.

On our return to Birkenhead I discovered that the skipper was subject to seasickness; the only thing which had kept him from suffering was a new version of that well known remedy Sea Legs. This too was added to our medicine chest.

Anne and I attended the yachtmasters' course at the Liverpool School of Navigation. We stayed for four years, up to what was then the 'ocean going' course, but did not take any of the examinations. This was mainly because with the pressure of work I could not spare more than one night a week dashing over to Liverpool; it was difficult enough to spare one evening, let alone two, and the road was very different in those days. On one occasion I had been unable to attend the 'signing on' evening so Anne signed on for me. She was somewhat shattered when Captain Twentyman, the navigation instructor, said, 'We will spend the evening revising spherical trigonometry,' She had never heard of this branch of mathematics! I had also received navigational training when I was a pilot in the RAF during the war and this stood me in good stead.

Having taken up boating as a means of spending our holidays with our children, it became almost an obsessive way of life for us. Our house was neglected and *Ebb Tide* always came first. When at long last we decided that we really must buy some new furniture and went into a shop in Chester to see what was available in three piece suites, we selected one and placed our order, fully expecting to be able to have it delivered immediately. To our disgust and surprise we were told that delivery would take sixteen weeks. We told them what to do with their furniture and returned home. It was after this that the really major change in our lives took place. We agreed to sell our business.

As can be read later, we made more and more passages, both in *Ebb Tide* and RNXS vessels. Little did we realize that there was a purpose behind all the experience we were gaining; everything was pointing to the voyage of our lives.

Ebb Tide was built for the admiralty in 1941 by Dickie of Bangor, North Wales. During a visit made many years later, we met one of the shipwrights who had worked on her. He told us that she was the last of the harbour launches they had built with pre war timber.

Harbour launches were originally built to take either steam or diesel engines, hence the large funnel. They did not have a deck house, only a small shelter or doghouse, set amidships for the helmsman and the steering wheel. There were no masts, other than a small upright steel post for signalling purposes. A raised steel trunking was set over the accommodation compartments and teak side decks about eighteen inches wide were set between this and the hull. There were no topsides, just deck then overboard. Two heavy rubbing strakes ran the full length of the hull, one just above water level and the other at deck level. A large bronze rudder was fitted outside the transom and it was the size of this rudder which made the vessel extremely manoeuvrable. Basically the hull was divided up into five watertight compartments, the forward one a chain locker, then a saloon, a large engine room, another smaller saloon, finally a self draining cockpit. The only means of access was through watertight steel hatches set in the steel deck. I assume that the forward saloon was for the use of ratings since it only had small portholes in the steel trunking, while the aft saloon had sliding windows. Needless to say in a seaway these leaked in no uncertain manner, so we replaced them at an early date as a matter of some priority.

The original owner had converted her by building a reasonably large deckhouse in place of the original doghouse.

This deck house was in two levels, the forward part having full headroom and forming a wheelhouse, the lower part forming a saloon in which it was not possible to stand upright. Access to the forward and aft saloons had been achieved by cutting openings in two of the water tight bulkheads, so that steep companionways could be fitted through the fore and aft engine room bulkheads. Part of the cockpit had been cut out and a washroom formed by building the sides of the hull up to the steel trunking height and then decking over with timber covered with canvas which was then soaked in paint, the traditional method at that time. The original large funnel had been retained and the wheelhouse built up to and partly around it.

From the time of purchase in 1960, until we sailed for Solomon Islands in September 1973, Anne and I completely rebuilt her, mostly by ourselves. We had to have a certain amount of professional assistance when the tasks were too large to be undertaken in spare time working, and also in our very early days, while we gained experience in boat building and its associated works.

Initially we had some of the work carried out by Bob Davies at his little shipyard on the Sharpness ship canal, where we had taken *Dolphin* to have the stern tube fixed. Amongst other work undertaken there we had the lower outside rubbing strakes removed in order to improve her appearance and also to stop the 'banging' which took place when she rolled in a heavy sea. During this operation one of the shipwrights said to me, 'I would not like to take this boat across the Atlantic.' Little did I know that we would be doing just that before we were many years older. She was what is called a 'floaty boat' which probably accounted for the fact that she could cope with bad weather as well as she did.

At a later date when we had moved our winter mooring to Acton Bridge we had to employ shipwrights in Cheshire to undertake underwater repairs and also to rebuild the bulwarks, which were pretty well rotten. At the end of all this work the only original part was the hull, stern tube and side decks.

We modified her every winter as we gained more experience and also to convert her to what we wanted. One of the first and important modifications was to make the wheelhouse watertight. The original up and down sliding windows were replaced with quarter inch plate glass. Since no provision had been made for keeping the windows clear, soon after our first 'seagoing' we fitted a Kent Screen in the one in front of the helmsman. These windows remained until we finally rebuilt the front part of the wheelhouse, when they were replaced with brass framed toughened glass. At the same time the upper part of the wheelhouse was rebuilt so that it was in a leaning forward position.

The hand-driven and worn out anchor winch which came with her was replaced in 1960 by a hydraulic one, and this survived until we had been in Solomon Islands for a couple of years. By then it was impossible to obtain spares, the manufacturer having built the winches with Government surplus aircraft hydraulic pumps and motors. When this supply dried up he sold out to another marine equipment company who discontinued their manufacture.

The foremast was rotten and after our first passage to Ilfracombe we returned minus the truck (or button). During the 1960/61 winter refit we removed the foremast and fitted a boom to the after mast, which was in good condition, so that we could raise and lower the dinghy instead of using the original heavy steel davit fitted on the after deck. It was extremely difficult to use and so heavy that it increased the top hamper far too much. Later, through an advertisement in *Motor Boat and Yachting*, we purchased a fifty foot mast. This lay on the Isle of Wight and so our lorry was sent down to collect it. Although the lorry was set up with 'horses' to carry long lengths of steel extended over the cab, the mast did not appreciate this method of transport and retaliated by snapping off over the cab. Both pieces were later used, the longer to make a mizzen and the shorter a boom. The original after mast was then moved to the foredeck as a foremast. Having two masts improved not only her appearance, but also the efficiency of the radio transceiver aerial.

As I said earlier, the wheelhouse, which had been built when *Ebb Tide* was originally 'converted', had two levels. This was corrected in 1960 when, after fitting the engine, we lowered the floor. In a spare space in our factory over the winter of 1961 Anne and I built a new after part for the wheelhouse, took it down to Stourport on Severn, where we wintered in the canal basin, and fitted it in March 1962 during a snowstorm. Before this she looked rather like a double decker bus, since we had fitted additional windows to the lower part of the deck saloon so that we could see out.

Although we carried out a great many alterations while we were in Stourport basin, we eventually found that the weekly journey was too time wasting, especially during the spells of bad weather which entailed motoring in difficult conditions. It was also hard on our children, so we decided to move up to Acton Bridge, on the River Weaver in Cheshire, which was only ten miles from home. This was where we had intended to convert the first boat looked at in the Isle of Man, or the harbour launch from Perth. The first voyage with *Ebb Tide* to this winter mooring is fully described in chapter five. We learnt a lot from that experience.

After we had moved our winter base to the River Weaver, we used the little British Waterways dry dock under the arches of the railway viaduct at Northwich. Incidentally this was a good example of how our forefathers had used natural resources. The dry dock was situated below the adjacent lock so that it could be filled from the upper part of the Weaver and then drained out into the lower part below the lock without the need of pumps for either purpose.

After dry docking, during the extremely cold winter in 1963, when the underwater checks and repairs had been completed, we moved her to below Hunts Lock, which is just by the dry dock. *Ebb Tide* was frozen in and had about ten inches of ice round her. This at least gave the part time shipwrights a good solid base from which to rebuild the topsides and did not appear to have caused any damage to her hull.

As will be read later, the engine installed at the time we purchased her was replaced early in 1961. The replacement engine gave us much more room below, so during the same refit, we took the opportunity to build a small cabin forward of the engine, in what had been engine room space. This gave us two additional berths. The original fuel storage had been two sixty gallon tanks fitted in the wings of the engine room. This capacity was hardly sufficient for serious cruising, so a two hundred gallon tank was made in our works and fitted in the aft cockpit. This was then covered over with a plywood deck painted with Dekaplex.

Originally the forward accommodation had been a large saloon. One of the previous owners had built a flimsy bulkhead to make a galley at the forward end but had not made any real provision for ventilation, other than the small portholes set in the sides of the steel trunking between the teak side decks and the raised steel one. This left a comparatively large saloon with two seats/berths. We purchased two teak skylights through another advertisement in *Motor Boat and Yachting,* and these were fitted in the steel foredeck, one in place of the steel hatch and the other further aft, which very greatly improved the ventilation and lighting in the saloon. It also gave us a supply of one and a half inch thick teak, since they were over two feet high and for our purpose did not need to be more than about a foot.

Apart from the engine change and making another cabin, our first major modification was to replace the original flimsy bulkhead with a more solid one and then build another, leaving sufficient space between the two to make a heads on one side and a wardrobe on the other. We then built four berths in the smaller cabin thus formed and four berths in the new saloon. We thus had two four berth cabins, one for the boys and one for the girls. The cabin in what had been the engine room was made into the galley.

The original engine room had six foot headroom, which was ideal for carrying out routine maintenance and repairs, but very space wasting. It had been designed for an engineer to sit in and operate the engine controls in true navy fashion. In 1961, following the engine problems we had met during our first trip to sea, the Gardner engine and gearbox was removed and replaced by a Grey Marine 6/71 engine. When we removed the steel deck over the engine room so that we could fit a new timber one at a lower level to make a new wheelhouse floor, Anne was unfortunate enough to slip through the opening in the steel deck and still bears the scars on her legs to this day, some twenty-five years later.

Originally, as I said in the previous paragraph, the gear lever had been operated by an engineer. When the Gardner engine had been fitted a large gear lever had been installed in the aft part of the wheelhouse, so that when manoeuvring it was necessary to dash from the wheel to the gear lever and back to the wheel. I think that in part this contributed to *Ebb Tide* being on the rocks at Gloucester, as described in the next chapter.

The fresh water system left a lot to be desired. A switch had to be turned on each time water was required. Sometimes a tap was left on at one end when the switch was operated at the other, so that quite a lot of water was wasted. We tried a simple electric pump fitted with a pressure switch, but this was also not very satisfactory. It kept switching on in the middle of the night and waking us up when the pressure dropped. A small Goodwin pressurised system was then installed which worked well and, apart from a pressure switch failure when we were in Solomon Islands, gave no problems at all.

The battery charging arrangements were far from satisfactory. The dynamo fitted to the original main engine would only charge when under way, since it was driven from the propeller shaft end of the gearbox. The auxiliary charging engine was a two stroke petrol one which was temperamental and very noisy, to say the least. During the first few months of our ownership I replaced this with a small single cylinder diesel I had bought back in 1946 and had not been used for many years. This drove a government surplus ex-aircraft dynamo which worked pretty well, although cooling was a slight problem since aircraft dynamos were designed to be force cooled. I more or less overcame this by fitting a small electric fan, also government surplus. The ex-aircraft dynamo I initially fitted to the Grey Marine main engine was replaced by an early version of a battery charging alternator, now standard fitting to all cars. This caused so much interference on the radio that it had to be switched off when the radio was in use. The manufacturers, CAV, sent an engineer to Upton on Severn over a weekend to fit a suppression box at no cost, for which I was grateful.

The bilge pumping arrangements were also primitive. A hand operated one was fitted in one of the side decks and drew from various compartments through a manifold. Unfortunately, due to the alterations made before we were the owners, this system did not work and was eventually removed. It was replaced by a gear type pump driven by an ex 'chore horse' dynamo used as an electric motor. This worked extremely well until the gears became too worn and it would not self prime. Several other types of pump were tried before a Jabsco, driven by the main engine, was finally installed. To overcome the problems with this type of pump when it was run'dry', an electric clutch was fitted so that when the bilges were empty, the pump could be turned off from the bridge.

In 1964 we installed a General Motors four cylinder diesel engine with a 3:1 reduction ratio gearbox, in place of the six cylinder one, fitted in 1961 which had a 2:1 ratio gearbox. This meant changing the propeller from the original thirty-inch diameter one, to a thirty-six inch diameter one, since it would be run at a much slower speed. The opportunity was also taken to use the extra space in the engine room, which had been made available by the shorter engine, to make and fit two one hundred and ten gallon wing tanks and fit two government surplus hundred and fifty gallon fuel tanks athwartships. This increased her fuel capacity to five hundred and twenty gallons. We finally installed fresh water tanks with a total capacity of two hundred gallons in place of the original rusty fifty gallon.

The midships cabin, which we built when the original engine had been changed, was later converted into the galley, thus releasing space forward. As I said earlier, this extra space was then converted into a small four berth cabin. As the family grew up and left the nest, we reduced the number of berths to make the remaining ones more comfortable. *Ebb Tide* finally ended up with a two berth forward cabin, our cabin and a saloon, which also had two berths.

Due to the rain water which had seeped through the decks, the elm deck shelves had rotted, so they were replaced. This repair was carried out during the 1966/67 winter refit. In order to do it, all the bulkheads in the forward part of the vessel were removed, which left the hull in an extremely flexible state. To overcome this the hull sides were pulled and held in with Spanish windlasses (that is a loop of rope with a horizontal piece of timber threaded through; this is then twisted so that the length of the loop is reduced), then five inch wide planks of half-inch oak were inserted, screwed to the hull. Further planks were laid on and screwed together, with liberal applications of glue, to build the deck shelves up to the original size. We also rebuilt most of the longitudinal stringers in a similar way, since many of these were also rotten.

30

Harbour launch hulls were of teak planks laid double diagonally and supported by horizontal stringers, so there were no hull frames in the accepted sense. Small frames from the keels on up to the lower horizontal stringers were fitted at two foot intervals, the hull being strengthened by four steel bulkheads. During this refit we also installed two wing fuel tanks in the saloon behind the berths. The final addition of a two hundred and eighty gallon tank in the stern increased our total fuel capacity to over a thousand gallons.

In passing I must mention that the original fuel tanks were found to have about two inches of sludge in them. This only came to light when one of them started dripping fuel from its bottom. It also explained why, when the Gardner engine had been fitted by the previous owner and the fuel system re-piped, the fuel tank outlets had been fitted three inches up from the bottom. Luckily for us this was discovered before we made any passages at sea, otherwise we would have had some really major fuel blockages to contend with instead of the comparatively minor ones which dogged us for many years.

In 1970, when a friend at the yacht club at Acton Bridge told us that he had bought a couple of General Motors diesels. I bought one from him. They had originally been used for research purposes in the Shell laboratories at Stanlow. The one I bought was a 4/71 model, and since it was turbo-charged, the scavenging blower only ran at one and a half times the crankshaft speed instead of the usual twice. It also had four valves per cylinder instead of two. I modified it by removing the turbo-charger, and fitting the latest cylinder liners and pistons, which increased the compression ratio, and also the smallest of the latest N50 injectors, which had been introduced by General Motors. These modifications reduced the final consumption to well below that obtained by other engines available at that time, and also at a fraction of the cost. For those who are interested in fuel consumption, I calculated that it was below .37 lb/bhp/hour.

Over the years we tried several different propellers in an effort to find one which was the most suitable. A firm loaned us one which at least gave the speed we were aiming for, but not much else since it churned up the water and used an enormous amount of fuel in the process. They were most indignant when I returned it as being unsuitable and said, 'Well it gave you the speed you wanted.' We found that one from Bruntons of Sudbury was the most suitable and was used until, on the recommendation of a friend, a nylon bladed one was fitted. We had hit the bronze one so often on odd submerged objects in the river and damaged the blades, that we followed the recommendation. The manufacturer's claim that the nylon ones were more efficient and that the blades could also be replaced individually if they were damaged was the major influence for this change. The first claim was incorrect and when I tackled them about it they admitted that the example quoted in their literature referred to a vessel which had been fitted with an incorrect propeller in the first place. On the voyage to Solomon Islands we found that the warm tropical sea water allowed the blades to distort and reduced their efficiency. This accounted for some of the poor performance on the last leg of the voyage. We only found this out after our arrival when *Ebb Tide* was slipped at the marine base at Tulagi. Then it was obvious to the naked eye that distortion had taken place. A replacement was borrowed from the marine department and a new one to the original specification ordered from Bruntons and fitted on its arrival some six months later. I wrote to the manufacturers of the nylon bladed propeller and complained about their misleading statements, but when one is 12,000 miles away it is impossible to thrust the Sale of Goods Act, or whatever was in force then, down suppliers' throats.

When in 1964 we fitted the first four cylinder engine, and since we did not want to have gas on board, I bought a 10 kva 240 volt alternator and built a compact diesel alternator set using a Perkins three cylinder diesel that I had removed from an old mobile crane when it had been scrapped. This also had a battery charging dynamo fitted to it so that every time the cooker was used the batteries were automatically charged. Later the dynamo was replaced by a twenty-four volt battery charging alternator, a similar one to that fitted to the main engine, and diodes fitted so that either engine would charge the batteries automatically. The cooling water from this diesel was used to heat the hot water system which also had a 3 kw immersion heater installed. This gave us hot water when we were on our mooring without having to run the auxiliary engine. We later fitted a small deep freeze, initially run off the two hundred and forty volt AC system, but was finally converted to run off the twenty-four volt batteries, and an air conditioning plant run off the two hundred and forty volt AC system. The deep freeze was a great boon, but the air conditioning was not very satisfactory. The modification made to the engine finally gave the range and fuel consumption I wanted; at four and a half knots our range was about six thousand miles; at nine and a half knots it was reduced to about one thousand eight hundred miles.

The final major modification was to convert the cockpit at the stern into fuel tank space and fit the fuel tank mentioned earlier. At the same time we moved our double berthed cabin as far aft as possible and built a washroom with a heads and shower next to the engine room bulkhead. This operation entailed laying a new iroko deck to the aft end. During an earlier refit at Acton Bridge we had replaced the original steel foredeck with an iroko one, which had greatly improved *Ebb Tide's* appearance.

The original steering was by chain and wire rope. This was heavy to operate and, due to the fact that the cables left the engine room through large holes in the steel trunking, it also let in the sea when severe conditions were met. They were also a danger hazard since the cables ran across the side decks and were unprotected. A simple hydraulic steering was made by using two hydraulic cylinders, one being pushed in and out by the wheel, through the medium of a rack and pinion, (from an old lathe in the works) to operate the other cylinder which was connected to the tiller. This had certain inherent faults, but it was the best that could be done at the time; cash limitations had to be taken into account, but it was a vast improvement on the original chain and wire rope system. As can be read later, we had problems with the original cylinders of this system and replaced them with a larger size which worked well until they too were replaced at a later date.

In 1964 we had fitted another make of autopilot and also had a radar installed. The problems we had had with the home built hydraulic steering were such that in 1968 I decided that a standard commercially manufactured system was the only answer and so I fitted one. This was finally modified by fitting a solenoid valve so that the autopilot could operate it directly from a hydraulic pump I had fitted to the main engine. Originally the autopilot had operated an electric motor which turned the steering wheel through a chain drive. This could not be disengaged from the wheel unless the clutch knob was kicked in, and that was not easy in rough conditions. On many occasions it gave us nasty bruises if we happened to be in the way of the spokes of the wheel when, without any warning, it would suddenly turn. The advantage of the direct acting hydraulics was that in an emergency, simply switching off the autopilot immediately made the steering gear manually operated.

Communications were initially made through a double sideband transceiver. The one installed when we bought *Ebb Tide* was an old model Pye Dolphin and it was changed for the latest one I had installed in *Dolphin,* our first boat. The new regulations which called for single sideband equipment had not been enforced for existing installations up to the time we left. I also installed a rebuilt eight channel VHF radio telephone which was extremely useful when entering port areas. Despite all theories to the contrary, we could work coastal radio stations from over sixty miles away. As a matter of interest, on one occasion when we were in Eastham lock on the Manchester Ship Canal, I tried to call up the Mersey harbour radio on the VHF so that I could give the details of our position and intentions. I could not understand why I received no response until I suddenly realized that our burgee was on an aluminium tube and had been hoisted up alongside the VHF aerial. As soon as the burgee was lowered normal communications were restored. I had completely forgotten that the aluminium tube was blocking our transmission.

Over the years several different makes of double sideband transceivers had been tried, and each one had different problems. On one occasion when we were travelling down the Bristol Channel the whip aerial decided to break internally. On another, with a different transceiver, the aerial relay was faulty. On yet another the aerial terminal blew up and a temporary one was made from a piece of polythene rod which was used until the final set was installed. Finally, for the voyage to the Solomons, we had a merchant ship type four hundred watt SSB transceiver fitted to cover both the HF and MF bands so that we could keep in touch right through the voyage. I told the manufacturers of this transceiver that all the electronic equipment I bought appeared to have a 'hoodoo' on it (this applies to the various computers as well), but they thought that I was joking. As can be seen later, this proved to be a fact!

Although *Ebb Tide* was essentially a motor yacht we had fitted twin headsails and a mizzen, but these were mainly for steadying purposes since they were insufficient to make any contribution to the propulsion unless it was blowing a force five or above. However, they played a vital part during our voyage to Solomon Islands.

During the early years we had endless trouble with the fuel filters blocking. As many will know, it is essential that diesel fuel is filtered to an extremely high standard so that the fuel pump and injectors will not be damaged by any dirt in the system.

General Motors, and some similar engines, have a circulating fuel system, ie. the fuel is pumped round, through the injectors, which have individual injection pumps built in, then back again to the fuel tank. This has two purposes, firstly to provide fuel for the engine, and secondly to cool the injector nozzles. Thus the flow is very considerably in excess of that required for propulsion. It is impossible to keep fuel tanks absolutely clean and the huge fuel flow is more than a normal filter can cope with, unless of course an enormous one is fitted. I finally solved the problem by purchasing a small government surplus heat exchanger and fitting it in the fuel line, then circulating the fuel through this, rather than through the tanks. The heat exchanger cooled the fuel and was itself cooled by using part of the raw sea water used to cool the engine.

During the time we had wintered at Stourport our two smallest boys were at a preparatory school in Tarporley where they were weekly boarders. We used to collect them on a Friday afternoon after work, take them with us and then return them to the school on the Sunday evening. The school matron used to complain bitterly about the 'Ebb Tide smell they brought back with them.

I have not logged how many hours Anne and I spent on the rebuilding, but a fair estimate would be in the region of well over fifty thousand. A lot of time was spent altering the previous winter's work as we kept getting more experience and making her into a comfortable home. Luckily I had an electric screwdriver which was a pre-war model and had no clutch. It could drive a large woodscrew into hardwood without the slightest difficulty, always providing that it was held firmly of course. We would think nothing of driving five hundred screws over a weekend.

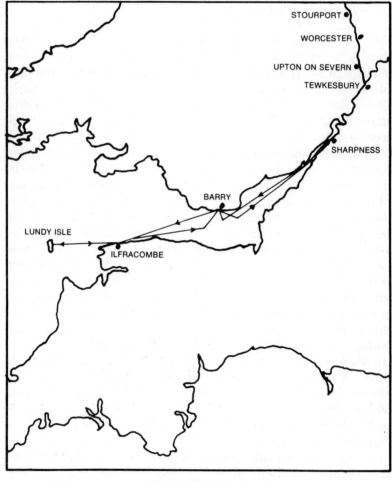

1960 – Early Voyages

3

1960

Early Voyages

We had purchased *Ebb Tide* early in the spring, so the first part of the season was spent in making her a more presentable vessel, ready for our first attempt at seagoing. We planned to make the passage down the Severn to Ilfracombe, the pretty well standard route for River Severn craft. Before we left Upton on Severn on August 1st we met the *Flying Fox,* a similar harbour launch which belonged to the RNVR at Bristol, but in its original state. During a conversation in the Swan with one of the officers, he suggested that we should follow them down the Severn and through the difficult 'Shoots', thus obviating the need to carry a pilot. The suggestion was readily accepted. When we arrived at Gloucester lock, which is on a narrow canalized part of the Severn, and through which the current runs pretty fast when the tide in the Severn estuary is low, we saw *Flying Fox* secured alongside, facing upstream against the current. I assumed that this was because she was crewed by the navy and they had exercised proper seamanship by coming alongside against the current. Nothing daunted, I tried to follow suit, but was caught by the current half way through the turn and swept downstream. We ended up with *Ebb Tide* aground and jammed across the knuckle of the lock where the side channel of the Severn ran back to the mainstream. The children were pretty shaken up by this experience and were put ashore to wait until the tide had turned so that we could be re-floated. A Gloucester inhabitant very kindly took them into her home while we waited. In the meantime a newshound heard of our predicament and at the end of that week there was a large photograph in the local paper, entitled, '*Ebb Tide* on the rocks at Gloucester'. When we met the *Flying Fox's* crew later that day, they told us that the reason that they had moored 'the right way' was because they too had done the same thing, but had not ended up as we did.

We found later, however, that this was not the first time *Ebb Tide* had been in trouble. When we arrived at Ilfracombe and looked round the lifeboat house, we saw the name *Ebb Tide* on the board on which the names of vessels 'rescued' by the Ilfracombe lifeboat were recorded. Apparently she had had engine trouble in the Bristol Channel and had been towed in by the lifeboat. It was as the result of this that the previous owner but one had removed the original heavy slow speed engine and installed the codged up Gardner.

It was on this voyage that we made our first encounter with mechanical problems at sea. We had locked into the Severn with *Flying Fox* and then followed her down as far as Avonmouth, where we parted company, since she was making for the River Avon to return to Bristol. Abeam of the *Breaksea* light vessel our engine suddenly stopped. When I went down into the engine room I found that it was impossible to turn the engine. Investigation revealed that it was gearbox trouble, both forward and reverse gears being engaged at the same time, so that the engine was effectively locked solid (as can be read later the same problems occurred in Barbados, when it was not so easily solved). I managed to free off the reverse gear by removing the gearbox cover and easing off the band which was locking it (both gears were epicyclic, so that whichever was required, forward or reverse, the appropriate band was tightened round the outside of the drum containing the gear. An automatic transmission on a car works in a similar way). We then headed for the *Breaksea* light vessel, having been told that the engineer there was most helpful, but in our case he could do nothing.

So we went into Barry where I checked the gearbox as far as was possible but could not see any major fault. We then continued our voyage to Ilfracombe and spent an enjoyable few days there, which included a trip to Lundy Island. I still have the replica of the trophy awarded by the Severn Motor Yacht Club for 'the most meritorious passage of the year'. On the return passage we took on a pilot at Portishead. A more smellier place is hard to imagine. A large chemical works is situated there. We secured in the lock entrance so that the pilot could board and then went on up to Sharpness.

On our return home I wrote to Gardners to see if the engine could be modified. They informed me that the engine, a 6LW, had originally been installed in a Glasgow bus in 1936 and said that they would fit a marine gearbox, but only if they completely overhauled and brought the engine up to date at the same time. The total cost they quoted was more than we had paid for *Ebb Tide* in the first place. I learnt later that the Gardner engine had been 'marinised' by fitting the gearbox from a 500hp Packard petrol engine removed from an American MTB. The gearbox had originally shared the engine sump oil for its lubrication. When it had been fitted to the Gardner however, no provision had been made for its lubrication, other than filling it with oil, but an oil seal had not been fitted to the input shaft so that when the gearbox was in use the oil was thrown out. During the times we had been travelling up and down the River Severn from Sharpness to Stourport and back again, the engine had not been run long enough for the gearbox problem to show up, and in any case there was so much oil around under the engine that the excess had not been seen. It was little wonder that it seized up in the Bristol Channel! I was surprised to be told by the 'boatbuilder' in Worcester who had surveyed *Ebb Tide* before we finally bought her, that this was one of two engines which had been converted in Glasgow for fitting in River Severn pleasure boats and allegedly been passed by a marine surveyor. He must have been blind; many of the nuts had a different thread from that of the bolts on to which they had been forced!

Another solution was sought and again the yachting magazines were searched for a suitable engine. I decided that a General Motors diesel was the answer since several were advertised at £500 or so, and this engine had been and still was produced in very many versions. During the war many thousands had been installed in lorries and tanks as well as in landing craft. In this latter role the six cylinder version had been built under the name of Grey Marine. The largest available injectors had been fitted to make it develop about

250HP, and a Twin-Disc gearbox added. After several fruitless visits, including one to Whitby where I found that the advertiser was working from home but the engines were in a different part of the country, a suitable engine was found at Littlehampton. I motored down to see and purchase it. The vendor also included a considerable quantity of spares which came in very useful.

Arrangements were made to bring it to Saul* where we planned to make the engine change. The original engine was sold, which eased the financial situation somewhat. During this engine change two tons of steel ballast were put in the bilges in the engine room to compensate for the estimated difference in weight between the original heavy engine and the Gardner. It is worth mentioning here that all the ballast, made from short lengths of railway line and steel billet off-cuts, was scraped and painted with red lead as part of Anne's work when she was acting as engineer's mate.

The new engine fitted, we moved back to the mooring which we had used for *Dolphin* at Upton on Severn. We carried out a trial trip down the Severn and the Bristol Channel and took Peter Oxley, a young friend from Upton, as extra crew. We set off and all went well until we were off Barry once again. This time the engine showed signs of overheating. A quick inspection revealed that the sea water pipe to the heat exchanger had blown out and, not only was the engine overheating, but the engine room was being rapidly flooded. Peter held it in by hand as well as he could while we made for Barry Dock. Here we contacted Ernie Hewett, the local General Motors agent, who could not have been more helpful. He diagnosed that the trouble was due to a blocked cooling jacket on the exhaust manifold and helped to make a suitable by-pass for the sea water. This 'repair' was used for years until the engine was changed for a smaller version. Ernie Hewett became a good friend and, as will be seen later, proved his worth several times on our voyage to Solomon Islands.

In the first season we covered just over six hundred miles at sea and up and down the Rivers Severn and Avon.

*A village on the Sharpness Ship Canal in Gloucestershire where there is a small shipyard.

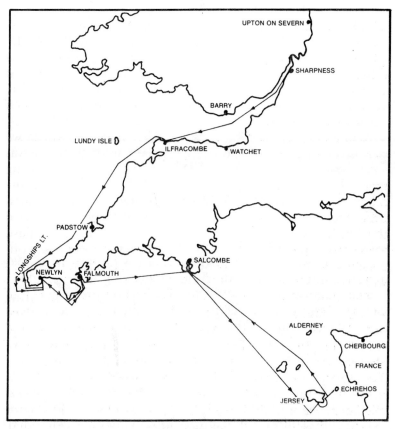

1961 – Jersey

41

4

1961

First seagoing –Jersey

After our comparatively successful voyage to Ilfracombe we became braver and decided to venture further afield. We planned to go to Jersey the following year; it was probably a case of 'ignorance is bliss'; many of our fellow members of the Severn Motor Yacht Club told us that we were mad. Nevertheless, during the winter evenings, when we were at home and could not spend time on the refit, we planned the passage. We realized that, with our youngest boy only being six, it would be advisable to take an extra hand with us. We used the Cruising Association's crew list to find someone. We made contact with Ralph Mann, a medical student, and finally arranged to collect him from Avonmouth on our way down the Bristol Channel.

We left Upton on Severn on July 31st and made our way down the Severn to Gloucester where we locked into the Gloucester-Sharpness ship canal and arrived at Sharpness late afternoon. In those days the high level railway bridge over the canal was fully manned. It was a steam-driven bridge and steam was kept up in the boiler, in spite of the fact that the line had been closed some years earlier. Later, one of the spans was demolished by a petrol barge on its way up river from Avonmouth to Sharpness. It had gone out of control and hit one of the bridge's pillars, but the opening span of the bridge was still manned. Such was the wisdom of British Rail in those days!

To digress for a moment, when the petrol barge had gone out of control, Paul Weychin, a young friend on the Severn, had decided to enter the boatbuilding fraternity. He took his speedboat out into the River Severn so that he could attach a line to the barge and thus claim salvage. Luckily for him he was unsuccessful as the barge turned turtle just as he was coming alongside. Had he been aboard there is no doubt that he would have been lost.

We had to lower our masts to clear the low level railway bridge which runs across the entrance to Sharpness basin. We refuelled and then moved into the Old Arm to secure alongside for the night. The next morning we moved into Sharpness basin, raised the masts and awaited 'locking time.' Mid-morning we entered the lock so that we could enter the tidal part of the Severn. This time we did not take a pilot since I felt confident that by now I knew the passage to Avonmouth. During the winter I had piloted a motor barge for Paul Weychin from Avonmouth to Sharpness without any difficulty, even though the engine had stopped at a critical point while we were in the Shoots – the place where the tide can run at up to ten knots. I must admit that I was a little apprehensive at the time.

As the result of going out on the first locking, we arrived off Avonmouth too early to enter the lock, so we whiled away the time slowly cruising round, just off the lock entrance. At last, in the early afternoon, we were able to enter the lock and eventually ended up in the basin. There we collected a compass adjuster who spent the rest of the afternoon swinging our compass and making out a correction card. This was the first and last time we had this done by a professional. We always did it ourselves in the years following.

For those who are not familiar with compasses, I must explain that it is essential that this navigational instrument is checked at least annually so that 'compass error' can be determined. Many people do not realize that a compass does not automatically point to magnetic north. It is influenced by local diversions such as steel plates, the engine, or even steel rigging. These influences can vary, depending on where a ship is berthed for a long period. The latitude in which it is used also has an effect. Magnetic north, as it is known, varies from place to place and alters by a small amount annually. Close to the North and South Poles the compass does all sorts of peculiar things and becomes completely unreliable.

We had previously arranged for Ralph to meet us at 6 o'clock and he joined ship on schedule. We spent the evening getting to know each other and stowing his gear. The next morning I arranged with the harbourmaster to lock out at midday. We also took the opportunity to have our 'duty frees' and other stores put on board.

Midday came and we entered the lock and nine minutes later we were back in the Severn estuary. As we had some gifts on board for the crew of the *Breaksea* light vessel we set course for her. In those days when the children were young (our eldest was only fifteen), we only planned to make short passages. The *Breaksea* being only a comparatively short distance, made a good break before Ilfracombe, our next port of call. Two hours after entering the estuary the wind rose and we met 'wind against tide' conditions for the first time. *Ebb Tide* did not like this and neither did we! One could say that all hell had broken loose below; everything, both what we had presumed was fixed, as well as what was loose, was flying about. We decided that the best course was to make for Barry where we could have a breather and repair the damage. The gas cooker had been one of the 'fixed' objects flying around and our stock of eggs had become 'scrambled eggs in coffee'! We eventually entered Barry and were able to secure to the pilot boat staging where we made good the damage and cleaned up the ship. We later moved to the Old Harbour and secured alongside another motor yacht from the 'Severn Navy'.

The next morning the weather forecast was more favourable, so mid-morning we set off down the Bristol Channel making for the *Breaksea* light vessel once again. On this short passage the engine boiled for no apparent reason and had to be topped up with fresh water. After this short break we secured alongside the *Breaksea* light vessel to pay a visit to the crew, who had by now become old friends. We left them some books and milk, then set off for Lundy Island where we would have to alter course to pass down the coast of Devon and Cornwall. All went well until midday when we were abeam of Foreland Point and once again we experienced wind against tide conditions. At that time we were very inexperienced sailors and I did not realize that if I had slowed right down, life would be made a lot easier for all concerned. I hated missing my planned estimated time of arrival, which was behind my decision to carry on.

However, one of the sliding windows in the deckhouse decided to drop. At that time they were only held up by rubber wedges of the sort normally used to keep sash windows from rattling. They were also far from being waterproof so that each time we had a 'noser' the sea poured in. Ralph stood holding a towel over the opening in a vain endeavour to keep out the sea. All the electrical instruments on the panel below were completely ruined by the combination of sea water and electricity, so we decided that the best course was to make for Ilfracombe and an hour or so later entered the outer harbour. Ilfracombe is a tidal harbour so we could not enter the inner one as on arrival the tide was falling. We secured alongside the pier where we eventually sat on the bottom as the tide went out.

It is always much easier to have hindsight and had I been more experienced I would have realized that all that would have been necessary was to have turned about; the sea would then have been behind us and the window could have been pulled up. When the tide came in we finally entered the inner harbour and secured alongside the quay where we prepared *Ebb Tide* to take the ground again when the tide went out some six hours later.

The next day the weather forecast was pretty foul so we took the opportunity to make the wheelhouse windows more secure and watertight. This was done by purchasing some strips of wood from the timber yard in the harbour, then fitting them in the gaps between the upper and lower panes and also under the upper panes, to make them more waterproof and prevent a recurrence of the dropping window episode. We spent two days there waiting for the weather to improve and finally, early afternoon on August 7th, we left and set course for Falmouth.

All went well on this passage until I called Ilfracombe Radio to pass our position and destination (our TR). During this contact the receiver portion of the transceiver decided not to work, although I could still transmit. I did not want to make the comparatively long passage down the Cornish coast to Falmouth with a young family on board, and without any means of communication, so decided to alter course for

Bideford where I knew there would be a radio engineer. As we approached Appledore we saw a regatta in progress; in order to avoid becoming entangled and because it was low water, we dropped our anchor in Appledore Pool. During the time we were there the lifeboat put out but, since it returned within an hour, we did not know whether it had been on exercise or on a false call. Had our radio been working we would have heard the radio messages being passed.

In the early hours of the next morning we were awakened by the dinghy, which had been left alongside, bumping against *Ebb Tide's* hull, so we hauled it aboard and made it secure. The wind had freshened in the night, the barometer had dropped to 29.11 inches and a full gale was blowing. We could do nothing but sit and wait for it to abate. *Ebb Tide* rode it out well, rolling and pitching like a live animal, while we watched a cork buoy in the Pool disintegrating (the owners of the buoy later tried to obtain compensation from us for the buoy, but since we had not used it, their claim was successfully rejected), however, none of us were seasick. By the afternoon the barometer had risen to 29.80 inches and the wind had dropped, so we made our way up the river to Bideford.

The channel there is somewhat tricky and moves like so many river channels, so the chart is not always accurate. We missed it and went aground for twenty minutes or so until the tide had risen enough for us to continue on our way. We finally arrived in Bideford and secured alongside the quay. We then ballasted *Ebb Tide* so that she would lean against the wall when the tide dropped. The radio was removed and I took it for repair, only to find the shop was closed. The harbour-master, in his attempt to be helpful, said that we had not secured the *Ebb Tide* in the best way for leaning, so, against our better judgment his advice was followed on the theory of 'local knowledge' always being the best. In this instance it was not. When the tide went out leaving *Ebb Tide* high and dry, the fenders slipped up and her topsides were stove in where they were against the wooden piles on the quay.

The next day we finally located the radio engineer, who had been having a half day. He was able to quickly repair and re-install the transceiver. The weather forecast was then wind SW to W force 4-5, later dropping to 2-3. There is an old adage about the weather, 'first rise after a low indicates a stronger blow.' This refers to the barometer, so we decided to wait for another day before setting off. In the meantime we visited a local art gallery and purchased a water colour of 'Little America' which is the view from above Bideford bridge. We took it to the Solomons with us and it is now on our sitting room wall at home.

On August 10th, the shipping forecast was then fairly good, so we decided to sail and left at day-break. Soon after leaving I noticed that the engine water temperature had risen to boiling point. I dived into the engine room to find that the rotor of the sea water cooling pump had disintegrated, so that no sea water was being pumped into the engine cooling system, probably as the result of being blocked by mud from the river bottom or an air lock forming in the suction pipe as the tide rose. This had not happened before so it was probably the mud, however, it was soon replaced and off we set again.

After crossing Appledore Bar we made our TR call to Ilfracombe Radio and then set course for Hartland Point. We arrived to find the race was in full swing, which made the sea pretty rough, so we moved close into the coast in order to avoid its worst effects. We then had an uneventful passage, passing outside the Longships lighthouse in brilliant sunshine. Late evening we made Falmouth, where we secured to a buoy in the harbour.

The following day, August 11th, was spent in routine maintenance work on the engine, a leak had developed in the oil cooler which had to be repaired, while the family took the opportunity to walk to Mylor. They returned with John Brockhouse, a fellow member of the Severn Motor Yacht Club, who had a cottage there and his boat *Belmura* was anchored. He recommended that we should move up river to Mylor and moor there, so we sailed up, dropped our anchor, and a peaceful night was had by all. The next morning we moved alongside the little quay to fill our water tanks, after which we took the opportunity of going up river to Truro. Unfortunately the channel was not marked too accurately so that by the time we had gingerly felt our way and had Truro Cathedral in sight, we had to turn around in order not to miss the tide, which was now falling. We also paid a visit to St Mawes, another delightful spot. On August 15th we moved back to Falmouth and lay alongside a coaster, so that when the tide went out we would be high and dry and I could then fit a 'Sum Log' through the bottom of the hull. We only had a Walker log which had come from *Dolphin*. This was driven by a rotor which was towed behind and connected to the measuring part by a long rope, rather like a clothes line. We had already lost our spare rotor, probably it had been snapped up by a fish. We also took the opportunity to paint the boot topping*, which was not exactly a straight line, having been painted from a dinghy.

In planning this cruise we had decided to make our first channel crossing to Jersey from Salcombe, it being the shortest distance, and so on August 16th we set course for Salcombe. Late afternoon we arrived there and looked round for a suitable place to anchor, but the harbour was full so we went up into the large stretch of water to the east known as the 'Bag', where we picked up a buoy. During this passage we passed a partially submerged submarine, the first time we had seen one in real life, quite an impressive sight. The weather having steadily improved, the next morning we set off for Gorey in Jersey, passing our TRs to both Niton and Jersey radio stations. After an uneventful and comparatively comfortable first channel crossing, we arrived in Gorey Harbour late evening where we cleared Customs.

We spent five days in Jersey where we met Mark Thomas and his wife Gilgi. Mark had been our doctor in our early married days when we lived in East Haddon and had emigrated to Jersey soon after the National Heath Service was formed. He and some of his friends took us around the island where we were shown the remains of the German occupation and other places of interest. We were also guided on a short passage to Les Ecrehou, the small rocky and uninhabited islets just north of Jersey and from which the French coast was clearly visible.

Time was running out and our first long cruise was coming to an end, so we left Jersey on August 23rd and headed for Salcombe. Apart from such minor problems as a leaking stern gland and a bilge pump which would not work and meant that

---

* The broad band of paint, usually a special type which is painted on the hull of a ship between the anti-fouling paint and the remainder of the out of water part of the hull.

we had to bail out two hundred gallons of sea water, bucketful by bucketful, from the bilges under our berth, the passage was uneventful. We arrived at Salcombe early evening and anchored in the fairway to clear Customs. Then on the harbourmaster's instructions, we later moved on to a buoy. I dismantled the bilge pump but no cause of its failure could be found, it then behaved perfectly and continued to do so until it was replaced some years later.

We stayed at Salcombe until August 26th while the family looked around the town, but it was so crowded that movement was nigh impossible. During this time some maintenance work was carried out. We also experienced a short spell of bad weather which made life on board somewhat uncomfortable. However, the forecast improved and so did the weather. On the morning of the 26th, when fog made visibility very poor, the harbourmaster advised us to delay our departure for Falmouth until the afternoon. As we passed St Anthony's Head, just outside Falmouth, we were met by a Customs launch which came alongside and our 'practique' was inspected before we were allowed to proceed. That was well before the days when yachts were used for drug running. We finally moored off Princes Pier in Falmouth Harbour where we spent the night.

The following day Ralph Mann had to leave us since his holiday had come to an end, so he was taken ashore to catch a train home. We then moved over to Mylor and spent three very pleasant days there, making another short visit to St Mawes. During this time, while we were at Mylor, we sighted *Belmura* entering harbour. We naturally got together for the evening pre-prandial during which we enjoyed discussing our respective adventures. As the weather was not too good, the visibility still being poor, we arranged to cruise in company with *Belmura* as far as Newlyn.

We left Mylor on August 30th and set course for Newlyn. During this short passage we kept in touch with *Belmura* by radio and arrived at Newlyn mid afternoon. It was low tide and because we had not entered this delightful port before, we anchored in Grivas Pool. Some three hours later I considered it was safe to enter the harbour and we secured to one of the many fishing vessels berthed there. We left Newlyn early the next morning and began the passage back to Ilfracombe. This time I had studied the chart more thoroughly and, after our first channel crossing, had much more confidence, so decided to take the inshore passage between the Longships lighthouse and Land's End. We had a few problems with blocked fuel filters (which necessitated dismantling them several times). Otherwise the passage was pretty uneventful and we arrived at Ilfracombe early evening, after a passage lasting eleven hours. We refuelled there in preference to doing so at Sharpness, which had previously been a problem. So it was the following day before we made for Barry. Shortly after leaving, the weather clamped right down and visibility was pretty low and, as we did not then have radar, we turned back to Ilfracombe and anchored off the pier to wait for an improvement.

In the early hours the next day our anchor started dragging and we had to re-anchor, doing the same thing again a couple of hours later. We finally left before daybreak and set course for Sharpness. As our course took us pretty close to the *Breaksea* light vessel, we took the opportunity of calling in, dropping off some fresh milk and collecting mail for posting, before finally making up the Bristol Channel for Sharpness. As usual on our arrival in the early afternoon we had to wait over an hour to enter the lock. After locking through we set off up the ship canal for Gloucester. There we found that the lock into the Severn was closed until the next morning, so the night was spent in the dock, which gave us an opportunity of looking round the port. The next day we left Gloucester and arrived at Upton on Severn, our summer mooring place, by mid morning. So ended our first long voyage.

We were thankful that when the radio failed in the early stages we decided to have it repaired at Bideford; other wise we would have been caught in a gale when we were off the rocky Cornish coast, with no means of communication had we been in trouble, other than by flares. It was good experience for us all and paved the way for more adventurous voyages in the future. We did not know then that we would eventually end up making a thirteen thousand mile voyage taking five months.

By the end of this season we had added a further one thousand three hundred and eighty six miles to our total.

5

1962

La Rochelle; Acton Bridge

Following our cruise to Jersey we decided to become a little more adventurous and extend our next summer cruise. During the winter we bought one of Adlard Cole's books on cruising the Biscay coast and saw a photograph in it of the wonderful entrance to La Rochelle. That did it! It was to be La Rochelle for the 1962 summer cruise.

We spent the winter of 1961/62 in Stourport canal basin alongside *Belmura,* where we continued the rebuilding and refitting. We left Stourport on April 24th for a working up cruise to Upton on Severn and then to Saul on the Sharpness ship canal for dry-docking. When the work had been completed we returned to Stourport. During the winter refit, when I had moved the steering wheel from its original position on the centre line of the vessel to the port side, I must have connected the wires back to front, as I had previously done with the steering cables on *Dolphin.* I was consulting an old log book while writing this and noted an entry which reads; '11.55 started engine, moved to basin lock, steering wires crossed, air in clutch hydraulics.' However, this must have soon been rectified for we arrived at Upton and moored on the Swan Hotel quay without any further comments in the log book. We then paid a brief visit to Tewkesbury and locked in to the River Avon through King John's lock. *Ebb Tide* was just able to turn out of the lock into the Avon with about two or three feet to spare but could not get under King John's bridge on account of the low headroom. Still it was a pleasant place to spend a weekend, even though we could only moor alongside the town quay.

On June 2nd we finally moved down to our summer mooring opposite the Swan at Upton. Later we decided to have a long weekend so Anne and I took *Ebb Tide* down to Ilfracombe and back. It was quite a hard passage since we did not have an automatic pilot, but we wanted to have a dummy run before attempting the long passage in the summer to La Rochelle with the family. On July 28th the second great adventure began. This time we took Mike O'Carroll with us to help with working the ship. At Sharpness we made fast to *Vindicatrix*, the Merchant Navy training ship, where we topped up our water tanks. The next morning we made our way down the now familiar Severn Estuary and Bristol Channel. On the way to the *Breaksea* we picked up an empty life raft from the sea just past the notorious 'shoots'. We made our now usual call on the *Breaksea* light vessel and then set off for Ilfracombe. During this passage the transmitter of a new transceiver I had fitted during the winter gave trouble and we had difficulty in passing our TR to Ilfracombe Radio.

We had begun this passage in company with Wing Commander Harry Nunn (who had previously advised us to buy a harbour launch) in his converted pinnace *Lelahne*. When we called on the *Breaksea* he had gone on ahead. As we approached Ilfracombe we saw *Lelahne* obviously in distress. We went over to her and Harry told us that she had engine trouble. We tried taking her in tow but she yawed about so much, rather like a kite with a short tail, that in the end we lashed her alongside and in that manner were able to take her into Ilfracombe Harbour. Her problem was a dirty fuel filter. Harry had not replaced the element during the winter.

The next day a radio engineer came aboard and diagnosed our radio trouble as being a faulty aerial relay. He promised to order a replacement but this did not arrive until two days later, so the intervening time was used to fish. The passage to Newlyn was made on August 2nd without meeting any further problems and we arrived there in the evening. We were too late in the day to make any arrangements to refuel and had to wait until August 4th for this. The weather forecasts were pretty poor so we spent a few days fishing until at just past midnight on August 8th we set off for Camaret in Brittany. The various books we had consulted advised that this was the usual port for yachts to enter France. Apart from our being almost run down by the Scillies ferry, this passage was more or less uneventful. We arrived off the Four Channel mid morning and passed through without any problems, reaching Camaret at lunch time, where we had to anchor since the harbour was full of fishing boats.

The next day, we set off for Le Palais, on Belle Ile, passing through the Raz de Seine, where the seas were quite enormous. The children at least appeared to enjoy the experience and showed no sign of nervousness. We finally arrived at Le Palais to find the harbour rather like a tin of sardines and the French most unhelpful. However, we managed to drop an anchor and lie stern-to just clear of the harbour wall with ropes to rings in the wall. We had read in Adlard Cole's *Biscay Harbours and Anchorages* about Didi's cafe in Le Palais, easily identified by its yellow painted wall. We had a meal there and found that Antony Quayle was also dining and holding an audience. Since we were not attempting to break any records, the children went off and explored the island on bicycles while we spent the next day in harbour carrying out general maintenance and rectifying a few defects which had shown up during the passage from Sharpness.

We left on August 11th and set course for La Rochelle. The passage was uneventful and the skyline of La Pallice appeared as a mirage, or so it seemed. The entrance to La Rochelle was all it appeared to be in Adlard Cole's photograph, and more. As we made the entrance a small sailing dinghy swept out with a nymph clinging to the mast, her hair streaming out in the wind. I was not sure which made the greater impression on me, the towers at the entrance, or the nymph!

We secured alongside in the outer harbour while arrangements were made to enter the inner basin. We had a minor problem in that a 'stink boat' was not really acceptable on the yacht moorings, since they appeared to be reserved for the yacht club. However, we were finally permitted to moor, bow to quay. It was quite a performance getting ashore and back on board again as our gangplank had not been designed for this method of mooring and was balanced somewhat precariously on *Ebb Tide's* stem post. We lay alongside a yacht which had been built in Hong Kong and then sailed to France some years previously. A lone paid hand was on board and we quickly made friends. Later we were invited aboard for drinks (I think that this was at the owner's expense) and still have memories of drinking dry Martinis from beautifully chased solid silver tumblers.

We spent the next four days at La Rochelle generally enjoying ourselves. The paid hand suggested that we ought to go to St Martin de Ré, which is on the Ile de Ré, just across from La Pallice. We did so, the short passage taking just over an hour. The harbour at St Martin is tidal and since we did not want to have to dry out, we made arrangements for the bridge to be swung and the basin gate to be opened when the tide and basin levels were the same, so that we could move in. We spent a day there and were so impressed with the place that we determined to return the following year. We visited St Martin again by road in 1987, to find that the ferry now runs all night and the peace which prevailed in the 60s no longer exists, a somewhat sad reflection on how tourism has affected most of the beautiful places.

We left St Martin on August 18th and headed for home with our course set for Port Joinville on the Ile D'Yeu. The passage was extremely pleasant with excellent weather. On our arrival we had to tarry awhile as Port Joinville is also tidal and we were ahead of time. We tried our hand at fishing once again, with our usual conspicuous lack of success. We finally entered late afternoon and secured to the wall where we prepared *Ebb Tide* for drying out. She finally took the ground at half past ten. This gave us the opportunity to inspect our hull and make several minor repairs to the copper sheathing.

Everything having gone pretty well so far, we decided to become more adventurous and planned a visit to St Nazaire. We left Port Joinville on August 20th with a five hour passage ahead. We did not have radar at that time so relied on our own powers of observation for piloting. We made the Loire estuary at dusk and found our way up to St Nazaire.

We secured to a tug in the lock entrance in the Avant Port and went ashore to make enquiries about entering the basin. We were told that we must use the old entrance which was further up river, and later that night we finally secured alongside in the basin. The next day was spent looking at the concrete submarine pens built during the war and now used for holding fertiliser or fishing boats. We marvelled, too, at the bomb-proof lock entrance which had been used by submarines. During a later visit in 1989 we looked at the submarine lock to see that it now has a submarine in it and is used as a tourist attraction.

We made enquiries about refuelling, and on August 22nd moved to the place in the basin where we had been told that a road tanker would arrive. Eventually we were informed that we could not refuel there and would have to go up to Nantes. That evening we locked out and set course up the Loire using a local French chart to pilot our way to Nantes, where we secured to the pleasure boat landing stage in the middle of the town. We then contacted the harbour office who were most helpful. By then it was late, so we decided to go ashore and look for a bistro, rather than eating on board. We asked a Frenchman for his recommendation and when he realized that we were English, he put his arms around us and cried out, 'Les Anglais.' He was most helpful and directed us to a little cafe where we dined for 2.20 francs each, including wine! It is a little different now.

The next afternoon we were able to refuel, having previously made arrangements with the local Esso agent in Cheshire to pay for it in England. It was some months before the bill arrived and I was horrified to find that the cost was over £50, an enormous sum in those days. In France 'gasoil' carries the same duty as petrol and I learned later that I should have ordered 'fueloil domestique' which is duty free, the same as in the UK. One lives and learns!

We returned to St Nazaire and spent the next day there while we waited for the weather to improve. On August 25th the hoped for improvement took place so we decided to move on to Loctudy. We arrived at midday, secured alongside, filled our water tank, and then anchored off. During the short, passage our sum log had stopped operating so the opportunity was taken to dive and inspect it. Some seaweed was found wrapped around the impeller, a problem with this type of log since there were no means of bringing the impeller inboard.

On August 26th we thought that it really was time to be turning homeward and so set off. During this passage the weather forecast was giving gale warnings and, since our passage was becoming somewhat uncomfortable, we made for Le Guilvenic. Course alterations were made and we had to pilot our way through the narrow rocky entrance before entering the harbour. We arrived just after lunch and secured to the fish market quay. Little did we realize then that this essentially commercial fishing harbour would play an extremely important part in our lives a few years later.

The next weather forecast was much better so we decided that we would move on. We were awakened at 3am by the fishing fleet putting out. Boats all around us were loading nets and fish boxes. The fishermen were most apologetic for waking us up. However we stayed up and took the opportunity of walking round the port. We were still feeling very adventurous and decided to set off early that day with the intention of visiting L'Abervrac'h on the north coast of Brittany. The weather was kind and we had a good passage until we arrived at the Raz de Seine where we met wind against tide conditions. The seas were mountainous, but to our surprise the children appeared to thoroughly enjoy the experience of riding a roller coaster on the sea. *Ebb Tide* also seemed to enjoy herself as well. We arrived off the Pointe de St Mathieu around midday and then piloted our way through the Chenal du Four; here again we met very heavy seas and had to reduce our speed for a while. One wave went right over the wheelhouse roof. We were certainly shipping it green!

When we arrived at the north of the Chenal du Four we altered course for L'Abervrac'h and, after a little difficulty in identifying the various buoys, entered the harbour and anchored. Since the weather forecast was still not too good, we went up the river to Paluden. One of our boys followed us rowing our Duckling dinghy. We all enjoyed this brief visit. On August 29th we missed the midnight and early morning forecasts but managed to hear the weather reports from coastal stations. Plymouth reported the wind as being NW2, with the visibility being twenty-two miles, so we set off for Newlyn. This time our second channel crossing to the north was uneventful and we arrived early evening, then cleared Customs inward. The next morning the weather forecast was still fairly good so we made for Ilfracombe where we arrived after a smooth and uneventful passage, in time for our evening pre-prandial drink. We spent the night there and left for Sharpness the following morning, where, after a passage lasting six and a half hours, we locked in.

The Stourport Motor Yacht Club was holding its annual regatta on Saturday September 1st, and since we were members at that time, we decided to join in. We stopped at Upton on Severn where our summer cruise officially ended. Our log notes that we had covered one thousand two hundred and forty miles in a hundred and forty seven hours steaming time, making an average speed of eight knots with a fuel consumption of three and a half gallons per hour. After a brief stop to visit our local, the Swan, we carried on up the Severn to Stourport and anchored for the remains of the regatta. We returned to Upton the next morning and during the rest of the season made many trips up and down the River Severn.

Having spent two winters at Stourport, during which we carried out many major modifications to *Ebb Tide,* we found that travelling to and from Tarporley at weekends was something of a trial, especially during bad weather. We had originally planned to moor a boat on the River Weaver, as mentioned in the early part of this book, so we joined the Acton Bridge Cruising Club and arranged to have a mooring there. This was only ten miles from home and gave us a far better opportunity of working, not only at weekends, but during any spare evenings which became available. We could also have a shore electricity supply for our power tools and also for keeping the batteries charged so that the Webasto heater we had fitted earlier could be left on during cold spells. We therefore planned to take *Ebb Tide* for a 'winter cruise' from Upton on Severn to the River Weaver in Cheshire, a passage of some four hundred miles.

We left Upton on Severn on October 26th, which happened to be a Friday. It is believed by some that a Friday sailing is unlucky, but this did not deter us. I had planned our departure time so that we would be able to round the south west corner of Wales in daylight. The crew for this trip was Anne and myself, George and Gill Dick from Upton Marine and Mike O'Carroll. Naturally we had been taking a very keen interest in the weather forecasts during the month, and as every perfect weekend went by we kept saying, 'This weather cannot last,' and of course it did not. When we sailed, to cheer us on our way, the weather forecast was pretty grim. Gale warnings had been given for Lundy and the Irish Sea, but the trip had been planned and I had made business appointments for the following Monday, on the assumption that we would complete the passage in under three days.

We left Upton at lunchtime and arrived at Sharpness in the early evening. I was somewhat surprised when we entered the sea lock, as darkness fell, to find that we were the only vessel to be locking out. We would normally have the company of a couple or so petrol barges as far as Avonmouth. We made Barry the first night and arrived just before midnight, then secured alongside a pilot boat. We planned to leave immediately after the 06.45 shipping forecast the next morning, so did not bother with the midnight one since we wanted to get as much sleep as we could before the long haul north to the River Mersey. The forecast was an improvement on the earlier one but still not very encouraging. We decided to have a go and push on in the knowledge that there were several ports we could enter before rounding the south west corner of Wales. All went well as far as the Scarweather light vessel, although both the wind and sea were rising, and we were able to maintain our normal cruising speed of nine knots. I called up Ilfracombe Radio to pass our TR but, as I commenced speaking, I noticed that the aerial current meter had dropped to zero, which indicated that the transmitter was not sending out any signal. I tried all that I knew to make the transmitter work, but without success.

In view of the difficult 'corner' ahead and the adverse weather, I decided to make for Pembroke Dock where I was sure there would be a radio engineer. The wind and sea were now beginning to really get up and we (and *Ebb Tide* too) were beginning to be thrown about in no uncertain manner, although we were not taking it 'green'. We were engulfed by spray, a considerable quantity of which found its way into the wheelhouse via the windows. We were all drenched and the floor was swimming in water. I had never thought that our propeller could come out of the water as the result of *Ebb Tide* rolling, but it did! I had to reduce our speed to seven knots.

The sea continued to build up and I was amazed that a small ship could take such punishment. George and Gill Dick were extremely experienced sailors and outwardly did not appear to hold the same opinion. One of the bulkheads shifted and the fuel filters were continually blocking in spite of my having fitted larger ones during the previous refit. I had fitted warning lights to the pressurised fuel system. When the yellow one lighted it indicated that the pressure had dropped and the engine would shortly be stopping. I went down into the engine room to change over the filters. All was well for a few minutes then the light came on again. I changed the filters back and cleaned the reserve one. Once again the whole procedure was repeated, but to no avail.

Having sucked mouthfuls of diesel through the pipes and taken a few mouthfuls to squirt into the filters to prime the system, I became thoroughly seasick and began to lose interest in both diesel engines and boats. By now the engine had stopped and *Ebb Tide* was lying comparatively quietly, but too close to a lee shore for safety. I have never been so seasick, either before or since. I had read that in this condition one really does want to die. I know I did, and lay on the berth in the wheelhouse while *Ebb Tide* was being pushed on to the rocks close by. I eventually realized that this must not happen, so finally made the effort to get up and have another go at the engine. I then discovered that the fuel filter was not blocked, as I had previously thought, but in my misery I had misread the fuel tank gauge, which was a circular one, so that there was little difference between the full and empty marks. Reading it while being pitched about was difficult to say the least. All the time the fuel transfer pump to bring fuel from the stern tank had been running and I had assumed that fuel was being transferred. In fact it had not been filling the tanks at all; its filter had been blocked with dirt from a brand new tank which had been fitted during the last refit. We normally had the wing fuel tanks connected in parallel in order to keep *Ebb Tide* trimmed level. When the port tank was shut off and the engine re-primed, we were soon under way again, and entered Milford Haven late afternoon.

When we were under way again, to avoid pounding into the head sea, we could only run at six knots and were then plugging the tide. It seemed that Linney Head would never move from being abeam, while we could see the entrance to Milford Haven in the distance, until the visibility clamped right down. Luckily a gap appeared for a few minutes so that we were able to check our position and make the necessary course alteration. George was sitting alongside Mike, who was on the wheel, when an unexpectedly violent roll flung him on to the bridge fire extinguisher which immediately operated and to add to our misery filled the wheelhouse with foam.

We made our way up to Pembroke Dock where we secured alongside one of the Admiralty Bar vessels, *ASV Barglow,* the crew of which could not have been more helpful. All our saturated bedding was taken into their engine room and dried out and their radio telephone was used to inform Ilfracombe Radio where we were, and later a hand came through our galley porthole with steaks for the crew. We were able to go ashore and telephone our children to tell them that we were safe. They had been listening to the weather forecasts with some apprehension. During the evening we found that the only place we could obtain beer was the local SSAFA club. We were not very popular when we were talking together as all the others were 'eyes down' playing bingo with a vengeance. There were many cries of 'Hush' so we decided that we would be more comfortable on board, and left.

During the night it blew a full gale, but we were in a very comfortable berth and able to get a good night's sleep. We were able to contact the radio manufacturer who sent an engineer to check over the radio on the Sunday, but he could not find any cause for the trouble we had experienced, although he was able to make it work again. However, the wind was still almost gale force so we decided that, discretion being the better part of valour, we would stay put for the time being.

The next morning we had to move off *Barglow* since she was going to work, so we made for the end of the quay where there was an empty berth. Just as we were coming alongside a fishing boat overtook us, cut across our bows, and pinched the berth we were making for. I eased off to come alongside her when I realized that the tide, which was running through the pier, had its grip on us and we were being carried broadside on to it. I could not go astern since *Ebb Tide* had a right handed propeller and such action would only have carried us harder on, so we waited for the bump. We hit the bridge amidships with such force that our rubbing strake was splintered and flattened in the process. The fishing boat at least had the decency to come to our assistance and pull us off the bridge.

All thoughts of going ashore again were discarded and we set off with the intention of making Liverpool our next stop.

After we had left Milford Haven and rounded St Anne's Head there was still quite a sea running and I was undecided whether to go round the corner outside Skomer and Ramsey Islands, or through Jack and Ramsey Sounds. As we made progress, the sea quietened considerably, so I decided to take the shorter passage through the two Sounds, In spite of having stripped and cleaned all the fuel filters while we were in Pembroke Dock, the fuel warning light winked on and off many times, although the engine ran perfectly. However, once again, discretion being the better part of valour, we made for Fishguard and reached it at lunchtime, when we secured to the lifeboat buoy. I called Ilfracombe Radio to advise them of our position.

During the evening the weather deteriorated and the rain came off the shore horizontally. We listened to the weather forecasts which were not encouraging, with north west gales being forecast for all round the coasts, so we decided that once again we would stay put.

We took the opportunity of looking round the town and were surprised to hear the Welsh tongue being spoken all round. We felt quite like 'foreigners.' During a visit to one of the local hostelries we were invited to look at 'the table'. It turned out that the only invasion of the British Islands since 1066 had been made by a French expeditionary force which had landed in the area. They had been subdued and a peace treaty had been signed on 'the table' which we had been invited to view.

In order to give the galley slaves a break we went ashore to the hotel by the station and booked a table for dinner but when the time came to go the wind was so strong that this was absolutely impossible. We could not leave *Ebb Tide*. The next morning, October 30th, the wind was still blowing round about gale force; our domestic arrangements had only been made for a long weekend, so we decided to send the girls home by train while the men stayed behind to bring *Ebb Tide* to our new mooring as soon as weather conditions permitted. There was no hint of any male chauvinism behind this decision. Gill had to be back at Upton to look after their business and Anne had several commitments to honour. In

61

the meantime my business appointments had to be cancelled.

As we went back on board after putting the girls on to a train, a lugubrious character on one of the Irish packet boats said, 'You will only get out of here by train, the last yacht was held for seven months.' This did not improve our spirits. We did, however, get a good reception from the Cruising Association boatman who met us ashore and gave us a different interpretation of our prospects, which took some of the sting out of the 'seven months' story.

We tarried at Fishguard until November 1st, when the midnight forecast gave further gale warnings, but the coastal station reports for the St George's Channel and Irish Sea areas stated that the wind was only force 3-4. We sailed at midnight in the hope that we would be able to reach Holyhead before the gale which had been forecast. In this we were unsuccessful! Still it was an exhilarating passage; we had the wind behind us, a clear sky for the first couple of hours, and an enormous following sea, which *Ebb Tide* thoroughly enjoyed. I went off watch and below, but had only dozed for a short while when I was awakened by the vibration coming from the propeller shaft every time *Ebb Tide* surfed ahead on the wave tops. When I went up on to the bridge I saw that the wind had increased very considerably and we had an absolutely fantastic following sea. The waves were breaking amidships and their tops were being blown off past the wheelhouse windows. The water filled our side decks, however it all drained off through the scuppers before the next wave broke. The log speed indicator went off the scale many times as we were carried along the wave tops; the maximum it could indicate was fifteen knots! It then went down to five or six knots as we climbed up the back of the next wave. Through all this, *Ebb Tide* showed no inclination whatsoever to broach; she was amazingly steady.

The engine was fitted with an overspeed governor which only limited its maximum speed (unlike most diesel engine governors, which more or less hold the set speed, irrespective of the load applied) so that each time we surged forward the engine immediately ran up to its maximum revolutions of 2,500. The noise from the propeller and shaft was such that I thought it must come adrift, but all was well. However, to be on the safe side, I reduced the engine speed by a couple of hundred revolutions and then went below and slept.

The early morning forecast gave the possibility of 'severe gale 9.' We had difficulty in seeing the Bardsey Island light an hour earlier; now the weather clamped right down with visibility being about one mile. It was impossible to obtain any sort of fix at all so I carried on plotting our position on the chart by dead reckoning. When dawn broke visibility was down to less than half a mile, and we met a large oncoming ship which passed us to port and this was the signal to hoist our radar reflector.

At this time I had fitted *Ebb Tide* with an ex RAF P6 compass, which is a grid steering one. The beauty of this was that the course could be set on the outer ring, then all the helmsman had to do was to keep the compass needle parallel to, and in between, the two grid lines, which made steering a comparatively simple process. When our DR position put us abeam of the South Stack lighthouse, I ordered a course alteration of thirty degrees to starboard to ensure that we cleared the headland. Soon afterwards when no land had been sighted, I told Mike to 'steer 090' to take us right into the coast. I was getting rough bearings from the Skerries radio beacon by using the radio direction finding loop, but I could not reconcile them with the course I thought we were steering. A further check showed that Mike had been steering with the compass needle at right angles to the grid lines! This error was quickly corrected. Incidentally this was the reason RAF grid compasses had been fitted with 'T'-shaped grid lines to overcome this particular problem. Half an hour later Holyhead island was sighted about eight miles to the south, so I gradually and very gingerly worked *Ebb Tide* round in the extremely heavy sea which was still running. I did not want her to be rolled over, and we made our way to Holyhead Harbour where we arrived at midday.

The incorrect course steered had caused us to miss the tide which we then had to stem until we reached the harbour. We went back into the new harbour, as recommended in the Cruising Association handbook, but no-one there seemed to be very helpful, so we turned and made for the old harbour. There the British Railways harbourmaster gave us berthing instructions. We secured astern of a Scottish fishing boat which had sailed from Fleetwood with a couple of green boys in her crew. The skipper told us that they had had a rough trip before seeking shelter in Holyhead and that the new boys had been 'verra frightened'; we were not surprised.

After lunch we were advised by the harbourmaster to return to the new harbour unless we wanted to stay up all night to tend our ropes; we did not, since sleep was badly needed, so we cast off and made for the new harbour where we found a spare mooring buoy (which, incidentally, was completely unmarked) and secured to it. We hardly had time to sort ourselves out before a launch, manned by an RAF corporal, came alongside. He asked if we had permission to use their buoy, and when I replied in the negative, he said that we would have to see the Commanding Officer. He took us ashore to meet the CO of the RAF Marine Unit, who readily gave us the necessary permission and also offered the facilities of the base as well. The baths and beer were most welcome! After spending a very pleasant evening ashore, the time came to return on board. We arrived at the landing stage to find that the tide had risen far more than we had anticipated and not only was our dinghy painter secured well below the water level, but the stage had eighteen inches of water covering it. However, nothing daunted, George came to the rescue, removed his shoes and socks then stretched down with a knife in his hand until his shoulder was under the water and cut the painter.

The weather forecast was still pretty grim and as we did not want to make our first passage up the channel into the River Mersey in adverse conditions, we stayed in Holyhead overnight. Then no gale warnings were given with the forecasts, which were much improved, 'variable S 3-4' being given for the Irish Sea. We sailed from Holyhead early morning, piloted our way round Anglesey, and then steered the various course to keep us reasonably close in to the shore to avoid the southerly winds. When we were off the Great Orme, I made a telephone call to Anne and I gave her our estimated time of arrival and asked her to arrange for our passage up the River Weaver. We finally entered the Rock Channel, which in those days was marked by buoys, and made our way up the Mersey to enter the Manchester Ship Canal at Eastham. I was somewhat bucked when we arrived at

Eastham lock within two minutes of the ETA I had passed some hours earlier when we were off the Great Orme. Here we were met by Anne together with five of our children who accompanied us along the Ship Canal while Anne took the car to Acton Bridge. We arrived at the lock at Weston Point as darkness was falling and, just before the entrance, went aground as the result of going the wrong side of the marker. The passage to Acton Bridge Cruising Club, our first trip up the River Weaver, was made in complete darkness. On arrival we secured to our new winter mooring. We have a cutting from the local Worcestershire newspaper headed '*Ebb Tide* goes to her winter mooring,' which gave brief details of the voyage. During this season we added more than two thousand miles to our total.

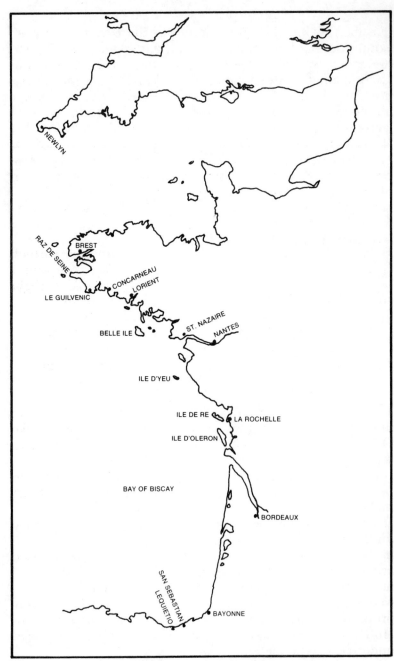

NEWLYN

RAZ DE SEINE
BREST
CONCARNEAU
LORIENT
LE GUILVENIC
BELLE ILE
ST. NAZAIRE
NANTES
ILE D'YEU
ILE DE RE
LA ROCHELLE
ILE D'OLERON
BAY OF BISCAY
BORDEAUX
SAN SEBASTIAN
LEQUIETO
BAYONNE

1962-1967 – Biscay voyages.

66

6

1963

Upton on Severn; Ile de Ré; Acton Bridge

For us the 'yachting season' began on April 19th when we took *Ebb Tode* back to her summer mooring at Upton on Severn. I noticed from the log that we seem to have had a slight contretemps at Ellesmere Port since the entry reads:

> '2045 ELLESMERE PORT – secured in barge lock, not very welcome due to misunderstanding after Anne's visit the previous day – they had moved all the barges in overtime! Not our fault.'

Since the weather forecasts were pretty bad we tarried there until April 23rd. We then called at Holyhead to collect Mike O'Carroll as an extra hand, and also another autopilot to replace one which had been fitted previously but was continually blowing up the transistors. The new one was no better, so we had to do without. This was the third one of that make!

The next morning we left Holyhead harbour and set course for Barry where we secured to the floating pier. We had to call in there. Had we continued on to Sharpness we would have arrived at the wrong time for passing through the 'Shoots'. I note from the log that we went for a trip in the pilot boat and were very bucked when the pilots told us that we were the only properly equipped yacht to call in at Barry. The passage from Holyhead to Barry was the longest non-stop one we had undertaken. The log entry reads:

'This is the longest trip we have made in one leg, the little boys (ages eight and ten) seemed to enjoy themselves so we hope to go further in the summer.'

Every time we arrived at Sharpness we had to stand off and stem the tide for up to half an hour or so. I decided that this was rather a waste of time and so planned to leave Barry a little later in the hope of timing our arrival to coincide with the lock opening. We left Barry just after dawn on April 25th. According to my log book entries:

'Thursday April 25th BARRY – AVONMOUTH – SHARPNESS: Did not bother with early forecast, now consider we are home, decided to make a later start than usual to avoid standing off at SHARPNESS for so long. 0727 cast off, went astern out from pilot boats, turned and S/C AVON-MOUTH, vis about three miles, running at 1250 rpm. 0820 ENGLISH AND WELSH L/V – spare vessel in use, made from old tanker. 0840 MIDDLE ELBOW A/C following buoys up channel, visibility not too good, about one and a half to two miles, this reduced speed is going to mean a close call for catching the tide up river.

0933 AVONMOUTH abeam, pretty certain I have missed the tide but will have a bash. 1024 AUST FERRY – as we arrived the tide turned and met us – no alternative but to put about and make for AVONMOUTH. 1100 AVONMOUTH – got here a lot faster than going up the channel, locked in with small craft.'

We spent the rest of the day in Avonmouth and tried to get the compass adjuster to swing our compass, but he was not available. The previous day a vessel *Cato* had been rammed and sunk and we secured astern of her. There were people everywhere as well as rumours about what had actually happened. I note from our log that the harbour dues had gone up from ten shillings to one pound! We locked out on the evening locking and it was pretty well jam packed full. At one time we had to move out to allow a larger vessel in, but all was well and we were back in the estuary before seven o'clock. We then made our way up river to Sharpness where, after locking in, we made our way along the ship canal to Purton Bridges and spent the night there. It was on this occasion that we purchased a bottle of sherry, drawn from a cask at the local for three shillings and sixpence. It was the most vile stuff we had ever tasted and it ended up in trifles and other food, but its taste could not be disguised. I was extremely ill after drinking it.

The next morning we made our way back to Upton on Severn where we received a wonderful welcome from friends there. We have preserved in our log book a local newspaper cutting titled, 'Return Of The Wanderer.'

During the summer we made various trips up and down the Severn and then decided to try out the automatic pilot at sea, since it had been replaced once again. During the winter, on the recommendation of the manufacturer, I had fitted larger cylinders to the hydraulic steering. They could not fault the original installation but suggested it was possible that, although the original cylinders were well within the calculated size, at unexpected peak loads, such as could be met when the rudder encountered a heavy sea, the alignment between the wheel and tiller may have been upset as the result of distortion taking place in the cylinder walls. We had some trouble with the new system and the manufacturer sent a replacement part to us at Gloucester. This seemed to rectify matters so we were able to make a short trip down to Walton Bay in the Severn estuary and secure to a buoy. During the night there was quite a thunderstorm and the tide was running out so fast that the propeller shaft spun at five knots. The rumble from this was almost as noisy as when the engine was running. The autopilot worked well for a short time on this trip, but once again packed up and was replaced by one of a different make.

For our summer cruise we left Upton on Severn on August 1st bound for Newlyn. The passage brought no problems apart from the fact that the 'new' autopilot would not work, so on our return it too was sent back to the manufacturer. In the very early hours on August 2nd, when we were south of Hartland Point, we met an unidentified motor cruiser which appeared to be in trouble, so we went alongside to offer our assistance. They told us that they were making for Poole and were lost. They had an 'un-swung' compass on board so it was not surprising that they were in trouble. They followed us for a while until we drew ahead, even though we had to make a few stops due to fuel filters blocking.

At breakfast time I discovered our eldest daughter merrily singing to pop music while she was on the wheel. To my consternation I saw that she had placed her transistor radio alongside the compass which caused a twenty degree error! The necessary corrections were made, both to our course and helmsman, and we finally made Newlyn on August 3rd. We took fuel on board and again tried to make the new autopilot work, but were unsuccessful. It steered us round and round in ever increasing circles, rather like the woozlum bird in reverse, so we gave it up as a bad job.

We left Newlyn early the next morning and set our course for the northern end of the Four Channel with Brest being our destination. An hour or so out we picked up a lifebelt with the name *Aurelia Genoa* on it and notified Land's End Radio. During early evening we entered the Four Channel and piloted our way up to Brest harbour without any difficulty. We had given up calling at Camaret as we much preferred to be able to go alongside at Brest and stock up.

On August 5th we left Brest, but because the weather forecast was not too good, set course for Le Guilvenic, this being only a short passage. However, the weather turned out to be much better than we had expected. On arrival we secured alongside the quay where we filled in a form for the Officer de Port, an unusual occurrence for us. It was not often that we experienced any form of officialdom in France.

The following morning, we were awakened by the fishing fleet leaving at 3 am. This was followed by a visit from gendarmes who enquired about the 'form'. On being told that we had filled it in the previous day they were happy and left us in peace. This time we were carrying an extra fuel supply in drums on our after deck and took the opportunity of topping up the wing tanks from them. We then set course south to find that we had the wind and sea behind us, but because we were all tired from night sailing we decided to call in at Belle Ile instead of making straight for the Ile de Ré. In the early evening we arrived at Le Palais and, after the usual messing about, managed to secure stern to wall with an anchor out ahead. The harbour was quite full. The next two days were spent there, during which I modified the fuel piping in the hope that the number of filter blockages we were still meeting would be reduced.

We left Le Palais early in the morning of August 9th with a slight following sea and arrived off St Martin to find that we had missed the lock. I had checked the tide times from the Admiralty Tide Tables and also Adlard Cole's book, *Biscay Harbours and Anchorages.* They gave different times but nothing could be done, so we had to dry out and lean against the harbour wall until the basin gate opened the next morning.

Whenever we were moored alongside where people could see into our wheelhouse, it was a favourite pastime for passers-by to peer through the windows. On one occasion at St Martin we were getting a little fed up with being gawped at so Guy stood up and scratched under his armpits as a monkey would do. To our amusement and relief, the gawpers beat a hasty retreat.

We tarried in St Martin for three days where we met old friends and generally had a holiday. We decided to take a French family we had met during a previous visit for a short trip down to Ile D'Oleron. On arrival we anchored in the Anse de Cavalier and spent a while ashore. Madame showed us how to have a *coquillage* and we were able to collect a goodly quantity of these tasty shellfish. We then walked as far as Boyardville to see if it would be a suitable place to visit in *Ebb Tide,* but were too idle to walk right up to the quay. Early evening we weighed anchor and set course back to St Martin, looking at Ile d'Aix on the way. The immense fortifications built by Cardinal Richelieu to keep out the English were most impressive, especially the huge Fort Boyard built in the middle of the passage so that its guns covered both the mainland and Ile d'Oleron.

We spent the next day at St Martin during which we decided that, since we had enjoyed the short visit to Ile d'Oleron so much, we would return. On August 15th we did so and this time took an English family with us. It was another most enjoyable day. I wrote a note in our log book:

'ILE D'OLERON, anchored off BOYARDVILLE in 20' @ HW, walked up to the town and inspected the quay, very similar to Bideford – local yachtsman advised that it could be made at HW –2.5 for a 6' draught. Will try it next year, a very pleasant beach readily accessible from the quay.'

The next three days were spent in the basin at St Martin while we all enjoyed ourselves and attended to some essential maintenance. I noticed on one occasion that when I started the engine there was a distinct 'thump'. I commented to Anne that I would have to strip it down during the coming winter's refit. Little did I realize then that the stripping down would take place on our way home. The engine governor was also giving some trouble since I had not set it correctly. Sometimes when the throttle was closed the engine would stop, instead of running at idling speed. It did this at a critical point while we were moving our berth in the basin. Dropping our anchor had no effect, the basin being lined with rock, and we hit the wall at the entrance with quite a bump, bursting one of our inflatable fenders in the process! To add to our problems the engine starter decided not to engage when I tried to re-start it. The fault was not overcome until the engine was changed. Had the starter behaved itself we would not have hit the wall.

During our visits to St Martin we had learned a little of its history. The wet basin, or dock, had been excavated and lined with rock brought from Scandinavia in exchange for salt. This was made on the island from sea water by using the heat from the sun to evaporate it in large open pans dug in the ground. There is also a large church now roofed at a much lower level than when it was built. Apparently 'Bookingham' had destroyed the original roof during our wars with the French. He had, however, been captured and his battle flags were hanging in the church. During a later visit we found that they had been removed and taken to Paris in order to preserve them, while copies were hung in the church. We were able to climb the church tower from which an entrancing view is obtained of the whole island, as well as that of the French coast, which is only twelve miles away.

In the early hours of August 19th we moved out of the basin on to the grid in the outer harbour where we cleaned *Ebb Tide's* bottom and repainted the boot topping. We then made a short excursion out to sea and spent time fishing. On our return we decided that the time had come to set off for home, weather forecast good or poor.

The next day we heard Land's End Radio calling with, 'Traffic for *Ebb Tide.*' After several attempts, which included running the engine in order to boost the batteries, the 'traffic' was relayed through the courtesy of St Nazaire Radio. It was a telegram from the automatic pilot manufacturer to say that their engineer would meet us at Newlyn when he would attempt to rectify the fault in the pilot.

We left St Martin and set course for Le Palais on Belle Ile. The passage was uneventful. We had the weather behind us most of the way so that it was reasonably comfortable although there appeared to be some excessive vibration which I could not trace. On our arrival at Le Palais, when I slowed the engine down to enter the harbour, I heard a horrible noise which I thought was a loose flywheel.

The next morning an inspection revealed that when the flywheel was moved there was a distinct lag at the front end crankshaft pulley. This only confirmed my feeling that the flywheel was loose. There was only one answer – the engine would have to be dismantled and the flywheel bolts tightened or replaced. A French mechanic came aboard and offered to assist us, promising to return the next morning with the necessary lifting tackle so that we could lift and turn the engine over to dismantle it.

The next morning came, but no mechanic, so we dismantled the engine ourselves. Luckily we still had a fair amount of timber aboard from the previous refit. This, together with the aid of a 'Spanish windlass', enabled us to lift the engine enough for it to be pushed over on its side so that the sump could be removed. My horror can be imagined when I discovered that the crankshaft was broken through one of the big end journals*. How it had managed to run in this condition for nearly fourteen hours must surely be a tribute to its manufacturer. In the evening, via the good offices of Land's End Radio, we telephoned George Dick of Upton Marine and

---

* The part of a shaft or axle in contact with or enclosed by a bearing.

73

asked him to arrange for a replacement crankshaft to be flown out. During the dismantling I found that the vibration damper at the front of the crankshaft was loose and it was probably this which had caused the crankshaft to break.

During the evening we received a message that a replacement was being flown to Paris and would arrive there on August 27th. While we were waiting for the crankshaft the time was spent in removing the pistons for checking. Two of the piston rings were found to be broken and so they were replaced; we had a goodly supply of all sorts of spares which had come with the engine. We then prepared the engine to receive the new crankshaft when it arrived.

Since we had done all we could there was nothing to do but sit and wait. One of the Dartmouth Naval College yachts *Martlett* came into the harbour. We had met her in Newlyn earlier on our way south. Our eldest son, who was hoping to go to Dartmouth after he had obtained the necessary A-levels, had met one of the officers on board when he had taken part in the entrance course at Dartmouth. He offered to introduce us to the art of being propelled by sail instead of by power. We made several short trips up and down the coast of Belle Ile. During one such trip we took our trawl and *Martlett* had the dubious achievement of a naval yacht trawling by sail.

The crankshaft finally arrived at Le Palais on the ferry. We then had a slight problem in getting the necessary Customs clearance. When this was finally received, the new crankshaft was brought aboard in the evening, balanced on one of our dinghies, which was towed by the other one propelled by oars.

During the time when the engine was lying on its side a French yacht came alongside just before midnight. When the owner popped his head through the wheelhouse door and saw the chaos he exclaimed, 'Formidable!' and immediately sent us a bottle of champagne. This was more than welcome after a hot hard day. During our stay in Le Palais we suffered one gale which made life aboard most uncomfortable, especially since the engine was lying on its side on pieces of timber and we were unable to move to a more sheltered spot. I was somewhat concerned that the buffeting we were receiving might cause the engine to slide, but all was well.

After fitting the new crankshaft, which included a complete

74

set of main and big end bearings, the next problem was to replace the engine on its bearers. We could not use the Spanish windlass this time as the lift which would be obtained by this method was less than that required to raise the engine sufficiently for it to be gently lowered into its mountings. Dismantling had been comparatively easy. We had just lifted it a few inches to clear its mountings and then given it a good hard kick, so that it fell on to its side. Replacement took a little more finesse. All the dodges we could think of were tried without any success. In the end Anne went ashore to the lifeboat house and managed to borrow a chain block. We always carried a chain block after this experience and it became an essential part of our tool kit.

The engine having been replaced and tested, we then had a further delay due to bad weather. It was during this time that a sailing yacht named *Odd Times* entered the harbour and secured alongside. We invited the owner, Peter Rose, aboard; he looked and was, visibly shaken. It turned out that he was sailing single handed and had been travelling under power when he was nearly swept overboard. We offered him both liquid and solid sustenance which were gratefully accepted. Our two young sons spent their time in cleaning his decks and generally making themselves useful. Peter became a firm friend and over the years we have kept in touch.

We had to move into the inner harbour to avoid the heavy seas which were entering as a result of the bad weather, and also to refill our water tank. On September 1st we made a trial trip to test out the engine, and apart from a few minor water leaks, all seemed well. The weather was slowly improving so we decided to sail the next morning, our holiday having been extended far longer than had been anticipated.

We finally left Le Palais at midday to find that the seas were far heavier than anticipated, so we kept as close inshore as we could. During this passage our hydraulic steering started giving trouble as the relative position of the wheel to that of the tiller kept altering. We decided to go to Le Guilvenic where I could make a close check without being thrown about by the sea in the process. We spent the night there and I checked the steering, but apart from a little air in the system, could not find any fault. This was one of the disadvantages of this particular system as, if there was the slightest amount of air in it, the alignment between the steering wheel and the tiller was thrown out of kilter.

We left Le Guilvenic on September 3rd and set course for Newlyn. This was an uneventful passage and we hit the Raz de Seine at just about the correct time so that it was completely flat. We arrived at Newlyn in the early hours of September 4th and were so dog tired that we did not hear the Customs come aboard. We were, however, woken by the fishing boats returning at 3.30 am. Our young boys did their usual stuff and reported 'mission completed' when they returned on board with a bucket of fish. Soon after this we cleared Customs and I made some more checks to the steering gear. During the passage it had not been functioning to my complete satisfaction, however once again no fault could be found. We also received a message from the autopilot manufacturer that the replacement parts would be posted, so we tarried for a day. The time was partly spent in re-rigging the aerial in order to try to improve its efficiency.

On September 6th the replacement pilot parts arrived, but they would not fit. We were most disappointed and annoyed. We took on board gas oil and left the harbour at 2 pm, piloting round the coast and taking the inside passage at Land's End. When we were off Pendeen Point we had to reduce speed since we had hit the race at the worst time possible, which made things somewhat uncomfortable. The steering was playing up again so it was obvious that there must be a fault somewhere. In the early evening, just after we had passed Trevose Head, the steering failed completely. The hand tiller was fitted, a curved tube which was attached to the tiller arm in the aft lazarette so that it could be operated from deck level, rather in the same way as a canal narrow boat. Our eldest son acted as helmsman, with instructions being passed from the bridge and relayed to him by the crew. We decided to make for Padstow and I sent out a PAN message on our radio to the effect that our steering had failed and asked Land's End Radio to arrange for a pilot to lead us in. The title, Doom Bar, on the chart did not give us much confidence to make our first entry unaided. We were most encouraged by the immediate response to our PAN by other ships in the vicinity offering to help, but luckily we did not require any.

We were finally met by a pilot boat just as we were picking

up a buoy next to the lifeboat. We had crossed Doom Bar unaided after all! We were piloted in to the harbour and secured alongside, after which we advised Land's End Radio that our PAN message was now cancelled. We ballasted *Ebb Tide* so that she could lean against the harbour wall as the tide went out, Padstow being a drying out harbour.

Once again the steering was examined and the only fault which could be found was a very slight leak at one of the pipe connections at the tiller cylinder, apparently the fault of the 'olive' used to seal the connection. We had a spare piece of pipe on which there was a used olive, so this was forcibly removed and fitted in place of the faulty one. We tested it as far as possible and it appeared to be satisfactory, so we set off for the River Severn as soon as there was sufficient water in the harbour for us to float; it was then early evening.

The passage to Sharpness was uneventful, the only event of note was as we passed Hartland Point when we were challenged by the Coastguard using an Aldis lamp. We replied in a like manner by flashing our identification letters 'GMRF' back, which seemed to satisfy them.

It is essential to arrive at Sharpness at the correct time, otherwise the outgoing tide, which can run at more than eight knots, has to be stemmed. The alternative is to have a difficult entry into the lock across the tide which is only partially broken by the piles at the entrance. To avoid this we stopped at Barry, secured to a pilot boat to await the tide, and then took the opportunity of having breakfast in relative comfort. We left Barry an hour and a half later and set course for Sharpness. When we passed one buoy the tide was running pretty fast, giving us a ground speed of over thirteen knots, so the engine speed was reduced. As we came abeam of Avonmouth it was still evident that we were carrying a lot of tide, so speed was reduced even further. We finally arrived off Sharpness just as the first vessels were locking out. We had to wait so turned to face and stem the tide until the signal was given that the lock entrance was clear. Our log showed that we were moving through the water at seven knots in order to remain more or less stationary. We finally locked in and then made our way along the Ship Canal, but because it was Sunday the lock back into the Severn at Gloucester was closed, so the night was spent in the docks there. The next morning we reached Upton on Severn mid morning – the end of an eventful summer cruise during which we had covered one thousand one hundred and seventy-one miles.

The rest of the season at Upton was spent trying to make the autopilot work. We made one more trip out from Sharpness and down the Bristol Channel to test it out, but it turned out to be completely unpredictable and was finally returned to the makers.

The time came for *Ebb Tide* to return to her winter mooring on the River Weaver. We left Upton on October 18th with George and Gill Dick and Eric Duncan as extra crew. In spite of gale warnings all round the coast, all went well until we had to reduce speed when we were off Flatholm. Later we had to reduce our speed even further. The pounding we were taking was so severe that it caused the stern fuel tank to split at one of the welds, pouring nearly two hundred gallons of diesel into the bilges! We decided to make for Barry. The afternoon forecast gave gales and storms right round the coast, so we were advised to lock into the dock rather then lie in the outer harbour. We tried several times to secure in the dock entrance to wait for the gates to open, but the scend* made this impossible so we went back into the outer harbour. We saw the *St Trillo* (a summer passenger ship making the same passage as we were) nearly go aground as she left harbour. Later, a Greek ship trying to enter the dock, was thrown against the knuckle and two ropes were snapped like string when a tug was trying to pull her off. It was early evening before we were able to lock in and secure alongside in Dock Two.

The next morning the forecast was still grim, although it was a glorious day in Barry. We were extremely frustrated at having to stay in the dock until the evening tide. Eric Duncan decided that discretion was the better part of valour so he left us and took a train back to Tewkesbury. We finally locked out late in the afternoon and set course for Milford Haven. Our speed had to be reduced right down since conditions were so bad. *Ebb Tide* was pounding badly, burying her nose at times,

---

* The scend of a sea is the vertical movement of its waves. A ship is said to scend when she rises and falls bodily on the crests and in the troughs of heavy seas; it is different from pitching, in which the bows and stern of a vessel are alternately raised and lowered.

while at others the waves went over the wheelhouse. As we passed St Anne's Head we were challenged by the Coastguard, to which we replied by flashing our call sign 'GMRF' on the Aldis lamp. We finally secured to a tug at East Angle and waited for daylight before proceeding further up Milford Haven. At first light we cast off and made our way up to Pembroke Dock where, as we had done the previous year, we secured to *Barglow*. The crew gave us a good welcome and after breakfast we went ashore to shop. On our return to Pembroke Dock, Anne, George and Gill were taken into the guard room, while I was taken before the Commanding Officer. He demanded to know who had given me permission to enter Government property. After I had explained that we had done so the previous year without meeting any problems he demanded a verbal apology. After this had been given the remainder of the crew were released from the guardroom and we went back on board.

In spite of gale warnings for the Irish Sea we left Pembroke Dock at teatime. When we were off St Anne's Head we found the sea was somewhat rough, but felt that we could make progress. However a little later the forecast was even worse so it was now our turn to realize that discretion is the better part of valour and turned round. We finally anchored in Dale Road among a French fishing fleet, where we spent a very comfortable night with the wind howling in the rigging over our heads.

The next morning, October 22nd, the forecast was much improved so we weighed anchor early and set course for the last leg of our winter cruise. The passage was uneventful and we were off Lynas Point in Anglesey by early evening. We called Anglesey Radio and made a link call to Eastham Lock to advise them of our estimated time of arrival, then entered the Mersey via the Rock Channel. At 3 am we arrived at Eastham Lock where we had to spend the rest of the night. The following morning we made our way up the Manchester Ship Canal, thence via the River Weaver to Acton Bridge.

We had logged two thousand three hundred and nine miles for the season, which was the most we had covered in any year so far.

7

1964

Upton on Severn; Ile de Ré; Acton Bridge

This was the year in which we fitted an automatic pilot which, apart from a few minor problems, really worked; we also had a Kelvin Hughes type 14 radar installed, an almost unique navigational aid for a yacht in those days. Since both these items were supplied by the same company we took their engineer out for sea trials on April 30th. All went well.

Our intention was to take our eldest son back to school at Rossall, so after the trials were completed we returned to Liverpool and spent the night in Victoria Dock. The next day we made for Fleetwood, but the weather was such that anchoring off Rossall Point and going ashore in a dinghy would have proved impossible, so the only answer was to make for Fleetwood Docks. We left Liverpool after having to wait for the tide to rise enough for the lock to operate. The passage was comparatively uneventful, other than the water tank in the cockpit came adrift as the result of the bad weather we encountered.

We arrived off Fleetwood where we had some difficulty in finding the harbour entrance, but we were finally guided in by a fishing boat. We secured in the dock to another fishing boat and managed to put our son ashore. It was not an easy task to haul his trunk up the steel ladder on the dock wall. We then spent the next three days waiting for the weather to improve.

While we were waiting we had a visit from Jim Carr, the radio engineer in response to my request to check over the radar which did not seem to be working correctly. I had not realized that it had to be re-tuned each time it was switched on, having erroneously assumed that the tuning, having been set by the engineer, would stay set. Jim soon showed me the error of my ways and then we went out for a drink in one of the grottiest pubs we have ever entered.

At last the weather improved and we were able to set off for our summer mooring at Upton on Severn. We left Fleetwood on the early morning tide on May 5th and made for the north western point of Anglesey. During the passage the weather worsened so much that, in order to be in calmer waters, we went close inshore with the intention of keeping close to the land until we were clear of Anglesey. However, that was not to be, since this time the radar did fail. I made a telephone call through Anglesey Radio to the engineer at Liverpool who promised that he would join us at Holyhead. So to Holyhead we went and arrived as dusk was falling. We first picked up a buoy at the yacht club, but on the advice of a member of the Holyhead Boat Co. dropped our anchor. That was not such a simple operation as it might seem; the passage from Fleetwood had been so rough that all the anchor chain in the locker had been tossed about, with the result that it was rather like spaghetti after boiling, so as to speak. Anne and I hauled it out, one of us in the confined space of the chain locker and the other on deck, then we fed it back in again so that it lay in the locker as it should. Since we carried sixty fathoms of half inch chain we were nearly flat out by the time the operation had been completed.

When the radio engineer appeared we moved in to McKenzie Pier and took him aboard. He soon sorted the radar out and left, but we stayed alongside. The next day we had a telephone call from him in which he suggested that he should sail with us for the remainder of the passage to ensure that all the faults had been rectified. We gladly accepted his suggestion. We also received a request from the Coastguard asking us, since we had radar, to go out and guide in a pilot boat from the school ship *Dunera* which had some sick boys on board. We left harbour at 6 pm, with the visibility being down to below a quarter mile and met the pilot boat as it was approaching the entrance. We then returned to McKenzie Pier.

The next day the weather forecast was still pretty poor but

81

we decided to sail and left just after midnight. When we had rounded Anglesey we met the full force of the wind and sea. It was so rough that when we were abeam of Bardsey Island Lighthouse we had to reduce our speed to ease the pounding that both *Ebb Tide* and we were taking.

The weather was foul! At 8.30 am the radar packed up completely and Jim decided that he would repair it. How he managed to dismantle it with *Ebb Tide* being tossed like a cork we never found out. He wedged himself on the side of the companionway and stripped out the transmitter/receiver unit and found the fault was a short circuit on one of the high voltage rectifiers and cannibalized another piece of electronic equipment we had on board to make a temporary repair.

By this time we all had had enough of being tossed about and decided to make for Fishguard where, on our arrival, we secured alongside in the Old Harbour, a very pleasant place. We spent a couple of days there waiting for the weather to improve. Part of the time was occupied in moving the automatic pilot control box to a more waterproof position and generally checking over all the electronic equipment. On Jim Carr's suggestion we also made the interior lights in the wheelhouse more suitable for night cruising by either fitting dimmers or red glasses. We carried both items in our spares kit.

On May 10th the forecast gave, 'Lundy SW 6-7 moderating 5 later,' so we telephoned the Coastguard to advise them of our intention to leave and then set course for Barry. We arrived there after a passage of some thirteen hours, and secured to one of the pilot boats. The next morning we left very early and had an uneventful passage right up to Upton on Severn, where we secured to the Swan Hotel quay before going ashore to consume a few hearty pints to mark the end of a somewhat eventful passage.

We spent the next few weekends simply 'caravanning' and carrying out the usual maintenance tasks a boat demands. On June 6th we had a short break, so the opportunity was taken to make a quick passage to Ilfracombe. We left Upton on Severn bound for Gloucester. Jim Carr had motored down from Liverpool to Gloucester to demonstrate our radar to one of the tanker companies who, at that time, were working up and down the Severn from Avonmouth to Stourport.

Jim duly demonstrated the radar in Gloucester and then motored down to Sharpness where he came aboard, leaving his car at the dock. The tanker company's representative and Jim Carr were both Yorkshiremen and a long discussion took place on the correct way of making a Yorkshire pudding. Jim was with us for the weekend and once again, soon after passing Avonmouth, the radar packed up, this time due to sea water finding its way into the rotary converter; so it was to Barry again. There Jim stripped out the converter and removed the deposit of salt which had been causing the problems. We spent the night there and then left for Sharpness and locked in.

The next morning Jim took *Ebb Tide* along the Sharpness ship canal to Saul while I drove his car there. This was the first time that I had handed over command of *Ebb Tide* to anyone other than Anne, but I had complete confidence in Jim.

We left *Ebb Tide* at Saul until June 11th, then a couple of friends, Norman and Mair Johnson, joined us for the short trip to Ilfracombe. We moved down the canal and arrived at Sharpness to await the first evening locking out into the Severn. We had an uneventful passage and arrived in the early hours of the following morning. We slept most of the morning, waking up in time to ballast *Ebb Tide* so that she would lean against the harbour wall when the tide went out and leave us high and dry.

The weather was unsettled so any plans we had to go much further were tempered by the forecasts. However, the next morning, June 13th, the forecast was much improved, so we decided to make for Bideford. Since it happened to be the Queen's birthday, we dressed overall and spent the day in the harbour. No doubt we drank the Loyal Toast several times. We left Ilfracombe and piloted round the north Devon coast with every intention of making Bideford. However, the weather deteriorated so much that we decided to make for Clovelly, the wind having gone round to the north west and blowing about a Force six. When we arrived we dropped our anchor and gave Ilfracombe Radio a call to tell them what we were doing. Shortly afterwards (we always kept a radio watch when we were on board) Ilfracombe Radio called us and enquired if we were towing anything since the Coastguard had reported having sighted a vessel towing objects. We were able to suggest that it was probably the tug towing barges which we had passed earlier, and assumed were making for Appledore. We had had a close shave at the time as the weather was so bad that the barges did not show up through the 'sea clutter' on the radar, and we were almost on top of them before we saw them visually.

We spent a somewhat uncomfortable night at anchor, a fact which our two friends did not appreciate. Mair preferred what she called 'a nightie night' – when you put on your 'nightie', go to bed and stay there for the night. It was their first introduction to small boat sailing so we made back to Ilfracombe and spent the next day there and, when the tide permitted, went out for some fishing.

The weekend having turned out to be a 'long one', we decided that the time had come to return to work, so on the Monday morning we left Ilfracombe and set course for Sharpness. There was just about enough water in the harbour and we bumped on the bottom once or twice as we manoeuvred to leave. The weather was still fairly poor so when we arrived at the *Breaksea* light vessel we were unable to secure alongside and threw rather than handed the cake Anne had made for them. We spent some time in Sharpness Lock and invited the harbourmaster to 'take gin with us'. We finally arrived at Upton on Severn after dropping Norman and Mair at Saul to collect their car, and secured to the Swan Quay before moving on to our summer mooring across the river.

During July we made one trip to Tewkesbury where we could just manage to turn as we left the lock into the River Avon. I always had a feeling of satisfaction when I managed to turn in more or less our own length, a manoeuvre which I may say, requires no little skill in ship handling.

Our main summer cruise began on July 30th. We had enrolled in a Tour de France yacht rally which ended at St Martin de Ré. We enjoyed our previous visit to this delightfully historical port so much that it was the obvious thing to join in the rally. The rules called for making a visit to as many harbours as possible in a given period and remaining there for at least four hours, in addition to travelling a long distance.

We left Upton for Gloucester where we spent the night, refuelled the next morning at the oil wharf at Monksmeadow, and then left for Sharpness. When we arrived there we began to make a final check over, but were called into the lock somewhat earlier than had been expected so we could not do very much. We locked into the Severn and piloted our way downstream. When we called Ilfracombe Radio to give our TR, they passed a telegram from Jim Carr wishing us 'bon voyage'. Since, as said earlier, the rally entailed harbour visiting, we only made comparatively short passages. We had always enjoyed our visits to Ilfracombe so we had decided to call in once again. The passage was a typical 'Bristol Channel' one with wind against tide conditions, which made life most uncomfortable. We made for Barry and secured to a pilot boat there while we waited for the tide to turn. After all, we were on holiday and with a fairly long itinerary planned, we were endeavouring to travel in as much comfort as and when possible.

On the way to Ilfracombe, we thought that it was time we took in a new harbour, so we made a rapid telephone call to the harbourmaster at Porlock. However, he advised us that there was no room there, so we continued on our way to Ilfracombe and endured a pretty rough passage in the process. We finally arrived just in time to prepare *Ebb Tide* for drying out before the tide ran out. It always amazed us to watch the tide rising and falling there, the tidal range being in the order of forty feet. It can actually be seen to be going up and down; one minute you are afloat and the next hard on the bottom. Someone must be pulling out the plug twice a day!

We left Ilfracombe at midday on August 1st with a fairly poor forecast. When we were just north of Padstow, for no apparent reason, the automatic pilot packed up. I decided that the obvious thing was to go into the harbour where I could strip down the pilot in some degree of comfort, so we altered our course and piloted up the river to Padstow Pool where we anchored until the tide had risen enough for us to enter the harbour. When there was just sufficient water we moved and secured to the pier; later we moved to the quay where we had been the previous year. I was able to strip out the pilot in comparative comfort, but could not find any fault other than possible dirty contacts on one of the relays. When I put it back together again it appeared to work satisfactorily. The next morning we had to wait for the tide to come in before we could leave so it was midday before we did. We made for Newlyn and arrived there early evening without meeting any further problems.

On the Monday, the forecast was for light winds from the north, so we left Newlyn and made for Brest. It was a completely uneventful passage, our log merely records the barometer readings every hour and details of any shipping we met. The pilot worked so well that we did not have to make any course alterations and at dawn we were abeam of the Le Four light which stands at the entrance to the Chenal du Four.

Since the channel crossing took us about twelve hours at our normal cruising speed of nine knots, I never made any allowance for the effect of the tidal stream. I worked on the theory that over a twelve hour period the tides would cancel out and they usually did. We entered the Four Channel and then it was just a matter of piloting through and round the coast to Brest, where we arrived after a passage lasting some four hours. We cleared Customs and other formalities here. I called Land's End Radio as I was a firm believer in keeping coastal radio stations informed of our intentions; it could save a lot of unnecessary work and expense if or when an emergency arose.

We left Brest and set course for Le Guilvenic. The passage was an easy one and the installation of radar made navigational life a great deal simpler. It was only a short visit and we left the following morning bound for Lorient. Again the weather was kind and we saw the Bay of Biscay at its best. When we arrived at Lorient we had to secure alongside the main quay beside some sand barges. Our log notes that I repaired the clutch lever which had broken off, but I cannot remember how and what happened on that occasion, although I seem to recall having to manoeuvre by starting and stopping the engine as required. We later moved into the fish harbour to fill our water tanks. At that time our water storage was only about a hundred gallons so with a large crew our water consumption made frequent topping up essential.

We left Lorient and made for Le Palais on Belle Ile. During this short passage we shot the small trawl we carried, but every time it was hauled in empty. We arrived at Le Palais the same evening, and secured in the usual manner, stern to wall, with an anchor out forward. It was on this occasion that another 'harbour launch' entered at an excessive speed and caught the anchor chain of one of the yachts moored in the same way. The skipper was NOT very popular!

On August 6th we stayed in harbour all day and a certain amount of sightseeing was done by the younger members of the crew. We called St Nazaire Radio for a weather forecast and after some difficulty over the name *Ebb Tide* we were finally given the local forecast in English. We left harbour in the early hours of August 7th and set course for La Rochelle. Our log has an entry which reads: 'On leaving harbour narrowly missed a racing buoy due to navigational error.'

It was dark and the buoy was right in the entrance and too small to be picked up on the radar. We then had a pleasant passage and arrived at La Rochelle and secured to the bridge at the basin entrance where we had to wait until the tide had risen enough for the basin gate to be opened. This time we did not try to moor in the yacht club area since we had only called in to refuel and also to add another harbour to our total. The next morning we took on a thousand litres of diesel and left for St Martin de Ré where the Touring Club de France rally ended. On arrival this time we were able to go straight into the wonderful basin there.

The rally had prizes for various things such as number of harbours visited etc. but we did not appear to have qualified for anything (Anglo-French jealousy?) In the evening there was a wonderful 'exercise gastronomique' held in a restaurant owned by an ex-French cavalry officer. The 'exercise' consisted of about fourteen courses with suitable wines for each, and that event is still fresh in our memories. We were introduced to 'Steak au poivre' and none we have eaten since has come up to that standard. The waiters were obviously students working for their holiday and followed French custom, so the wine glasses, including those of our brood, were kept well replenished. The inevitable result was that one by one the young ones succumbed. Guy the youngest being the first. He was taken back on board by Vivien, our eldest. Both she and Simon, our eldest boy, survived the evening to fight another day.

We spent the next three days in St Martin as we had enjoyed our previous visit so much that we wanted to make the most of the current one. We did, however, venture out to observe a regatta held in the Pertuis Breton, the stretch of water between the Ile de Ré and the French mainland. A French minesweeper which had been moored in the basin was acting as a guard vessel for the regatta and we were somewhat amused when we dipped our ensign, to see a crew member running aft and hold the ensign close to the mast. We had observed at morning 'colours' that the minesweeper crew literally 'nailed their colours to the mast' so there had been a certain amount of malicious pleasure in observing the niceties!

The previous year we had made a short visit to Boyardville on Ile d'Oleron so on August 12th we decided that we would repeat the performance. We left St Martin and slowly made our way south, shooting our trawl twice. The first one was fruitless, but the second time we were rewarded with a catch of one small skate. We spent about five hours at anchor during which we went ashore for a *coquillage* and then had to return in order to make the basin at St Martin before the tide was too low. On the return trip we trawled again and, just off St Martin, were rewarded with a catch of six crabs and one large rock.

I forgot to mention earlier that the wreck of the *SS Champlain* was then still lying off La Rochelle. I believe that it was carrying a cargo of either aero engines or tanks and was scuttled during the war to prevent them from falling into German hands. It was there in 1964 but on our last visit in 1973 it had been removed.

The next day was spent relaxing in St Martin; then on August 14th it was time to head homewards, so we set course for St Nazaire. On our arrival we had to wait outside the small lock until the tide had risen enough for it to operate. We had an almost perfect passage as once again Biscay was on its best behaviour and certainly belied its bad reputation on that occasion.

We did not spend long at St Nazaire this time, so on August 15th we moved to the lock and waited until the tide was right to re-enter the Loire. We had decided to call at Le Palais on Belle Ile, and on arrival we secured to a buoy. The harbour was pretty full, August being the French holiday season. We did not want to go through the whole rigmarole of dropping an anchor, then going astern to the harbour wall, to make our lines fast, before finally hauling out on our anchor to be clear of the wall. During the evening pre-prandial we decided rather than spend another day there, we would visit a new port, and planned to move on to Douranenez. The weather was still good and the shipping forecasts were very favourable. We left immediately and had a smooth overnight passage to Douranenez, where we arrived the next day. We first secured to a fishing vessel, then later moved to the outer harbour and dropped an anchor. During the afternoon we tried to make a phone call through Land's End Radio but reception was too poor; after all, we were well outside the normal range for working an English Coast Station (and strictly speaking it was illegal too).

Having had a look at Douranenez and, with the weather forecasts becoming less favourable, we then decided to move on to Brest. As we passed the Pointe de Toulinguet we noted that the south cones were hoisted. This indicated that a southerly gale was in the offing. The passage had not been as smooth as the earlier ones and we narrowly missed a small buoy due to it being obscured by the 'sea clutter' on our radar screen. We entered Brest and secured to the quay in our usual place. The following day, August 18th, there were gales warnings all round, so we decided that discretion was the better part of valour, and stayed put. We had a meal in one of the many dockside cafes which abound there. It was not too bad as cafe meals go, but they appeared to be having a problem with the electricity supply; the lights kept going out whenever the cooker was turned on, at least we thought this was the cause. Cockroaches ran along the top of the wooden panelling round the walls, but they were only little ones compared to the huge ones we later met in the South Pacific.

On August 19th the weather improved so we decided to call at Camaret before heading for Newlyn. We filled our water tanks from a quayside hydrant then cast off. On our arrival we had to anchor. The 1340 shipping forecast gave, 'Plymouth W 4 or 5 – moderating', so we decided to make for Newlyn and shortly afterwards weighed anchor. During this passage the forecasts kept improving, so we had hopes of a reasonably smooth trip. We heard a 'Pan' message from Land's End Radio advising shipping to keep a sharp look-out for a yacht which had left Portsmouth for Cherbourg nearly three weeks earlier. A few minutes later we were nearly run down by *MV Sabratha,* a German vessel, and had to make a pretty violent stop. We had the right of way so I sent a pretty strongly worded radio message to the master via our VHF radio. I don't suppose that he heard it, or if he did he certainly took no notice. We arrived at Newlyn early the following morning, secured to *United Boys*, a fishing boat, cleared Customs, and then settled down for a good sleep.

At this time I was the north west representative for the Cruising Association and had, in conjunction with the honorary local representative at Penzance, arranged for a 'meet' there. This took place over the weekend of August 21st/23rd. On the 21st after refuelling at Newlyn we moved to Penzance. On this short passage we tried out our trawl again, but were not really successful, and so as soon as the tide was high enough went into Penzance harbour. At that time both Anne and I were members of the RNXS and one of their vessels was in the harbour, so we secured alongside her. Later we moved to the harbour wall where we found the ladders very high and slippery. On Saturday, August 22nd, we held a cocktail party on board *Ebb Tide* for the Cruising Association members who had joined the meet. This was followed by a meal ashore at one of the Penzance hotels. We were somewhat amused when the wine was being served and the waitress passed Guy, our youngest son; he was somewhat indignant and said, 'You can serve me, I have been drunk.' As I said earlier, he had been the first of our brood to be taken back aboard at the Tour de France rally at St Martin. It was a good evening, apart from having to climb down the slippery steel ladder to get back on board *Ebb Tide,* since by then the tide had gone out. Later we took some friends from Chester, who were on holiday in Penzance, for a short cruise, but the weather rather spoilt their enjoyment. After this we moved back to Newlyn and spent a couple of days there before finally heading for home.

We left on August 26th in early afternoon, which I had calculated would put us off Hartland Point with a following tide. It was a pleasant passage and we arrived at Ilfracombe some thirteen hours later. There we spent a day to give all the crew a break and then finally made for Sharpness on August 28th. This was a smooth passage, so unlike many we had, and on arrival we waited as usual for the lock to open. This time we were able to secure to another vessel in the outer basin, thus avoiding having to stem the tide outside the harbour entrance.

The next morning we left Sharpness for our summer mooring at Upton on Severn. On arrival, we secured to the Swan Quay before taking up our mooring across the river. Our summer cruise had put another two thousand miles under our keel.

We did not move again until it was time to return to our winter mooring on the River Weaver in Cheshire. We commenced this passage on October 3rd, having left Upton mid morning and made our way to Junction Bridges, on the Sharpness ship canal. We then left *Ebb Tide* there to have repairs made to the transom and the propeller changed. Then over the weekend of October 24/25th we made a trial run to ensure that all was well before the passage to the Weaver.

We finally commenced the winter cruise on October 28th, taking Walter Leadbeater and Alan Pettigrew, a friend of his, with us. I had met Walter in the course of business when he was working for a firm of insurance brokers in Manchester. I had originally decided to appoint his firm after he had visited me at Tarporley and we were enjoying a lunchtime drink together in the Swan Hotel. He downed four pints of draught Bass without turning a hair and to me that was a good enough recommendation. He became a good friend and we only lost contact when we left for Solomon Islands some years later. His associate, Alan Pettigrew, was a polio victim but had made an excellent recovery and was able to undertake pretty well anything. He did, however, have slight problems in climbing the steel ladders fixed to harbour walls.

We arrived at Sharpness and waited for the weather forecast, which was not good. The midnight forecast was somewhat better, though confused, and we had to move into the lock while it was being read, entering the Severn later. During the passage, as we went through the tricky 'Shoots' close to Aust, the battery went flat, all the lights went out, and the radar turned itself off. At that time *Ebb Tide* had two sets of batteries. I discovered that the charging switch had been directed to the wrong bank; this was soon rectified, our power supply was restored, and we made our way to Fishguard without any further problems. On our arrival, there was just sufficient water for us to enter the old harbour and secure alongside.

On October 30th the forecast was not too bad so we moved to the main harbour and secured to a buoy before setting course to Dun Laoghaire. We had a good passage and on arrival cleared Customs, then secured to a fishing vessel in the coal harbour so that we could get ashore without having to use our dinghy. We had called at Dun Laoghaire before and taken the opportunity of dining at the Gresham Hotel in Dublin. We repeated the visit and enjoyed an excellent meal.

The weather forecast was varied so we decided that we must get on home before any real break in the weather came. We left Dun Laoghaire, piloting out of the harbour by radar. The weather was 'thick', with visibility down to less than a quarter of a mile; we were glad to have radar on board, a small sailing dinghy showed up on the screen as we made our way down the Liffey; it was closer than was comfortable. At one o'clock in the morning, Anglesey Radio broadcast a PAN message to the effect that a yacht was overdue and asked all shipping to keep a good look-out. During the passage we made a telephone call to Eastham Lock on the Manchester Ship Canal and gave them our estimated time of arrival. We also advised Anglesey Radio that visibility was extremely poor. In fact, it was so poor that we could not see the light on the Great Orme even though we were fairly close to it.

At half past six the radar packed up completely and, in spite of all the checks I made, I could not trace the fault. We then had to keep a sharp look-out for buoys in order to check our position; in this we were lucky and we were able, by picking our way from buoy to buoy, to enter the River Mersey through the now closed Rock Channel. We arrived off New Brighton after navigating the last part of the passage by the New Brighton sewer outfalls! We secured to a buoy and then, after finding out if any ferries were expected, moved to the end of the pier. We made a telephone call to the radar manufacturer's Liverpool office and an engineer came on board. Unfortunately he was only used to 'big ships' and was sea sick while we were moored at the pierhead. He was unable to repair the radar and suggested that it should be sent back to the factory for a complete check and re-build during the winter.

We finally left New Brighton and made for Eastham where, before we could lock into the Manchester Ship Canal, we had to secure to the piles at the entrance. This was quite a hair-raising operation since the tide did its best to push us into the Mersey, but *Ebb Tide* was match enough, and when the traffic had eased we were able to lock in.

We spent the night in the sluice entrance since we could not travel along the Weaver in darkness, all the locks being closed during the night. For some reason or other I was suffering from a sickness so, while I was lying prone below, Anne took *Ebb Tide* up the ship canal and into the Weaver, then on to our winter mooring without any trouble.

We arrived at Acton Bridge at midday, having covered two thousand four hundred and sixty-four miles during the season. Soon after we arrived home we received the following from Walter Leadbeater:

Leadbeater's Log

We pitch and roll and 'ship it green'
But never the crew shall quake,
For they are anchored to the deck
By the ballast of Anne's fruit cake.

Make fast forward – make fast aft,
The warps through fairleads run,
But what! Are we drifting from the quay?
Yes! Walter's knots undone.

Pettigrew – steadfast at the stern –
a humorous dog of the sea,
Is peering into the depths below
Can he a fender see?

Now the skipper he would breakfast make,
But really he should have learnt
Like Alfred, if you go 'off watch'
The blasted cakes are burnt.

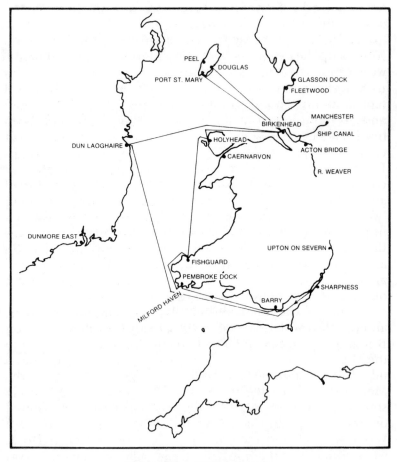

1962-1966 – Winter Cruises

94

8

1965

Upton on Severn; Lequietio; Isle of Man

After a fairly extensive refit and modification during the winter months, *Ebb Tide* was ready at the beginning of May for us to return to our summer mooring on the River Severn. I had undertaken extensive alterations to the propeller shaft and its couplings. A new intermediate shaft had been obtained and taken to the shipyard at Northwich to have a half coupling fitted. When I tried to align the engine with the shafts I found that this was impossible. A check revealed that the half coupling fitted by the shipyard was running over an eighth of an inch out of true. I took it back and complained, to be told, 'well we thought that it was only for a yacht, so that it was not important.' When that yard made propeller shafts for the tugs they built, they spent days reaming out the coupling bolt holes and checking that everything was true to a thousandth part of an inch. It is little wonder that, like so many others, they went out of business shortly afterwards.

We took our accountant, Norman Johnson, his wife Mair, and Jim Carr with us for this 1965 spring cruise and left Acton Bridge at lunchtime on May 11th. This enabled us to lock into the Mersey, then into the Liverpool Dock system on the same tide; Jim was joining ship in Liverpool. As we went down the Mersey we checked our compass for error, a comparatively simple matter since all the compass points were then painted on the river walls. We entered Liverpool Docks through Waterloo Lock and then went through into Trafalgar Dock, where Jim joined us and we spent the night. At that time I was wearing a pair of red sailing slacks and was congratulated by one of the dock workers for being 'a Liverpool supporter'. Since I am not a football fan, I did not know what the docker was referring to! Eventually the penny dropped.

The next morning the dock system came to life as the tide rose and so we locked out. We had planned to pay a visit to Dun Laoghaire, which by now, had become part of the spring/winter cruise ritual. The wind was calm, and the sea smooth, so we had an extremely pleasant passage and arrived at Dun Laoghaire at half past ten the same evening. We secured in the coal harbour to one of the dredgers named *Sysiphus,* a very apt name for a dredger. On our arrival we thought we ought to go up to Dublin and early next morning did so and secured to the wall opposite the Guinness brewery. If this heavy black stout is made from water from the Liffey, as some say, then it is hardly surprising that it is black. The Liffey STANK; large lumps of what could only have been decomposing sewerage kept rising, accompanied by a retinue of bubbles. In addition we were plagued by a host of small boys demanding money; when their requests were denied we were verbally assaulted in the most basic Anglo-Saxon. We went ashore to have a look around, leaving Jim on board, and on our return had to borrow a ladder from a barge in order to get back on board. The tidal range there is fairly large and it had gone out during our walk around. We also found *Ebb Tide's* wheelhouse plastered with stickers of the Irish flag. We decided that Dublin harbour was no place for us and soon returned to Dun Laoghaire.

We found the coal harbour full of MFVs, so we went back to the main harbour where we secured alongside the German motor yacht *Hamburg.* During a discussion with her skipper, we were told that her hull was made of Muntz metal, a highly expensive copper/zinc alloy, and that she was in fact a scale model of the battleship *Scharnhorst.* She had been built in Germany before the war when they were not allowed, under the Versailles Treaty, to build any capital ships. Interestingly, just before we sailed for Solomon Islands, we saw she was advertised for sale in *Motor Boat and Yachting.* I was extremely disappointed that I could not buy her for scrap. The asking price was only £3,000!

On Friday May 14th we left Dun Laoghaire with the intention of entering Wexford harbour. The visibility was under a quarter of a mile so all the navigation was radar assisted. We were off Wexford entrance just after 'the sun had gone below the yard-arm', but could not see any way into the estuary as the sea was breaking right across. We anchored and hoisted our 'G' signal flag, which means that a pilot is required, but there was no response. We then called Anglesey Radio and asked for a telephone call to the Wexford pilots, but they were unable to connect us. While we were doing this, Norman had been studying our *Reeds Nautical Almanac*, a *vade mecum* for all yachtsmen, and it stated that Wexford harbour was closed, so we had to make for Fishguard.

Just on midnight the autopilot packed up once again so we had to revert to hand steering until we arrived at Fishguard some three hours later. It was low water which meant that we had to anchor off, there being insufficient depth to enter the Old Harbour. When we awoke at daylight we saw that the whole of the harbour wall was covered in scaffolding so our plan to secure alongside was frustrated. It was a good thing that the tide had been out when we arrived, otherwise I might have tried to enter, which would have had disastrous consequences. We went ashore by dinghy to purchase some stores and then weighed anchor and went for a fishing trip. As per usual we returned empty handed.

The next morning, Sunday, we set off for Ilfracombe, the autopilot having been repaired by Jim. As there was hardly any wind, it was a comfortable passage and we arrived early evening, secured in our usual place, and ballasted so that we were leaning, ready for when the tide went out. Norman had said earlier that he and Mair wanted to take us out for dinner, so we looked around for a suitable hotel. It was a Sunday and, the 'season' not having begun, most of the restaurants were closed. The only hotel which was open was fully booked.

Monday morning we left Ilfracombe with the intention of boarding the *Breaksea* light vessel to give Norman and Mair the opportunity of seeing round one. When we arrived, in spite of there being almost no wind, the swell was far too large for us to go alongside with safety. We had to throw the magazines we had brought to the crew and naturally Norman and Mair were very disappointed. We continued on our way to Sharpness, where as usual, we had to stand off until the tide was right for the lock to operate. After entering we made our way up the

Ship Canal to Purton Bridges and spent the night there as all the bridges over the canal closed at 8 pm. The next morning we continued our way along to Saul, where we left the *Ebb Tide* to have a few odd jobs done, and so our 1965 spring cruise ended.

A fortnight later we moved *Ebb Tide* to our summer mooring at Upton on Severn and, apart from one or two short trips up and down the river, did not move again until we set out on our summer cruise.

This year we were more ambitious and planned to visit the north coast of Spain, with Santander as our destination. As well as our children, we took a couple of extra 'hands' with us. John Gozzard, and his girlfriend Judy Pemberton. John was a naval officer at Manadon and Judy was at that time attending the same secretarial college in Manchester as our eldest daughter. During one bumpy passage in the cruise, Judy was thrown against one of the berths, bruising her thigh. We have a photograph of this which makes the bruise look rather like a glorious sunset!

We left Upton on Severn mid morning of July 26th, which enabled us to arrive at Sharpness when the lock into the Severn estuary would be working, and so avoid our having to wait there. We had sufficient fuel on board to take us to Newlyn, where we had found that it was much easier to refuel. As we passed down the Cornish coast we realized that, in the rush, the bread had been forgotten. We altered course for Padstow but on arrival it was low water, so we anchored in the River Camel, lowered the dinghy and the women went ashore to shop. Later, when the tide had risen sufficiently, we moved up to the Pool and collected the shoppers. Some four hours later we continued our passage to Newlyn where we arrived late evening and secured to one of the fishing boats lying against the harbour wall.

We stayed there for a couple of days while we re-fuelled and then moved to the head of the harbour in order to dry out. There was an accumulation of weed round our log impeller, which was removed and our propeller was checked for signs of any damage. We then moved back down the harbour where we could remain afloat at all states of the tide. The weather forecasts were not too good so we tarried until they improved, and then one evening set off for Brest. On our arrival there the following morning, after completing the usual formalities, we took on board the essential 'liquid stores' and made for Camaret, to spend the night. We set course for St Martin de Ré the next morning. During this passage we heard gale warnings being given for the Biscay area, so decided to head for Le Palais on Belle Ile. We arrived there early evening the same day and, after the usual manoeuvring, which included dropping our anchor and then going astern, we secured with our stern to the harbour wall.

We spent the following day at Le Palais and listened to the traffic list broadcast by Land's End Radio. We heard there was 'traffic' for *Ebb Tide* and so tried to make contact, after all we were well beyond the range for coastal radio stations. We were unsuccessful so we enlisted help from St Nazaire Radio. However, we did not manage to get through and gave up the attempt.

The gales forecast for Biscay not having materialized, we left Le Palais on August 23rd for St Martin de Ré. Contrary to popular belief about the Bay of Biscay, the sea was absolutely flat. The whole passage was made under these conditions. Where the gale which had been forecast went we did not find out. We heard a 'Mayday' message from a German ship, but Land's End Radio was in contact and, in any case, we were much too far off to be able to make any attempt to go to her assistance. The next three days were spent at St Martin, part of the time we went on to the grid in the outer harbour to attend to our stern tube, and also to file out some marks in our propeller blades caused by striking underwater objects. I had a thing about propellers and always tried to keep ours in perfect condition in order to obtain the maximum efficiency.

The weather being perfect, we left for Bayonne at midday on August 8th. During this passage we checked our compass at night against the moon and found that there was a five degree error. The necessary course alteration was made and we arrived at Bayonne the following midday, after another completely calm passage. We only stayed there overnight and the next morning we left for San Sebastian after breakfast. On our arrival at lunchtime we entered the extremely small harbour and tried to find a place where we could secure against the wall, but it was jam packed solid with fishing boats. I managed to back out without hitting anything, no small problem, since going astern in a single engined vessel is not as simple as it may sound. We had heard of problems being met by both yachts and motorists visiting Spain, so this operation was accompanied with a little breath-holding by all on board. Eventually we anchored in the outer harbour where the harbourmaster and other officials visited us. They advised us to move on to the yacht club moorings in preference to where we had anchored. The following day, August 11th, we checked our compass against the sun this time and confirmed the error we had obtained from the previous check against the moon.

We all enjoyed the stay in San Sebastian, sun and sea bathing being the order of the day. Anne and I flew to Madrid in an effort to open an avenue for our company to export. It was rather like taking coals to Newcastle, since Spain has a large enough steel industry. It was, however, a bit of a conscience-clearer to take an extra week on this holiday.

We had selected an hotel listed in our Diners' Club handbook and were somewhat shattered when the hotel refused our credit card; luckily we had sufficient cash with us to settle the bill. The buildings in Madrid made a great impression and made us realize that the civilizations of other countries were far older than that of the British Isles.

While we were at San Sebastian we enjoyed a fantastic firework display given in honour of some saint or other, and had a grandstand view from where we were anchored. However, the weather changed and we had to take shelter in the lee of Ile St Clair. It was so rough that we had to lay a kedge anchor as well. Our original plan had been to visit Santander, but time was running out and we felt that we had at least made the north coast of Spain, which was quite an achievement in itself. Another yachtsman suggested that we ought to visit Lequietio, which is about thirty miles along the coast. So, after lunch on Friday August 13th (once again an unlucky sailing day), we moved on and arrived late afternoon. There we were able to secure to the harbour wall and cleared Customs but we then had to move to make space for a fishing boat to come alongside. During the course of the day we met Mr Nicholson, the British consul in Bilbao, who lived in Lequietio and always made contact with British yachtsmen whenever he could. He recommended that we moored in the middle of the harbour, since it was the busy fishing season and the boat traffic had to be seen to be believed. One of the days we were there was a saint's day, and instead of the more conventional bunting, all the fishing boats were dressed overall with strings of pots and pans and other kitchen equipment.

Mr Nicholson invited us to visit his home and meet his wife, who was Spanish. We were made extremely welcome and had our first taste of squid which had been cooked in their own ink. They were delicious. It is impossible to cook them this way in England since all the ink is removed before they are shipped. Mr Nicholson had a small boat, crewed by a local fisherman, and he took us out fishing. He said that the fishermen could 'smell' their way back to the harbour, and told us about the time when he himself had been about thirty miles out and a fog had come down, blotting out everything, but under the guidance of his boatman they made the harbour safely. The little boats did not even have compasses, let alone corrected ones!

Lequietio is an absolutely delightful place. We climbed the hill overlooking the harbour, pausing at each of the Stations of the Cross which wind their way up the hill, to take photographs of the town and surrounding area. The young members of our crew thoroughly enjoyed themselves, swimming in the daytime and dancing in the square in the shadow of the cathedral in the evening. They met a little officialdom when Judy unwittingly offended local custom by returning from bathing in her swimming costume. John lent her his shirt, so honour was satisfied and there were no more problems.

We spent the next three days there, determined to return the following year. When we were preparing to leave, we found that our kedge anchor had become entangled with the heavy chain forming the 'trot' to which the small boats were attached. We had to use our winch to bring the whole trot up to water level, and then hold it up while we disentangled our kedge anchor. That was quite an operation, but not as difficult as when Anne and I had had to sort out our own anchor chain in Holyhead some years earlier.

The passage to Belle Ile was almost perfect, the weather being ideal for a motor yacht, although the sailing ones would not appreciate it so much. We were able to use our sail at times, though only for steadying purposes. We checked our compass as often as possible, since it had not been 'swung' at the beginning of the season. The errors discovered were only in the order of a degree or so. We did, however, on one occasion, suddenly realize that the compass error had been applied the 'wrong' way, and accordingly had to make a four degree course alteration. We arrived at Belle Ile early evening to find the harbour full, so we had quite a problem in finding a place to anchor.

We left Le Palais the next morning, bound for Brest. During this passage we heard another 'Mayday' from St Nazaire Radio, but once again we were too far off to make any attempt to give assistance. The coastal areas of Biscay are busy fishing grounds so many times we had to make course alterations to avoid fishing nets which, in accordance with the local practice, were simply buoyed and left to be collected later. The passage was uneventful, and the weather was kind with only a Force Two wind, which left the sea more or less flat calm. After our arrival at Brest, the weather suddenly deteriorated in the evening so we spent a day there waiting for an improvement. The next morning the forecast was pretty poor but we decided to have a try. When we were off the Pointe St Mathieu the rain was horizontal, the visibility was too poor and the sea too rough to attempt the Chenal du Four, so we turned round and went back to Brest.

We left Brest after lunch on Monday August 23rd, bound for Newlyn. The weather had improved very considerably from the day before. The sea was still lumpy and we had to reduce speed in order to make the passage more comfortable. As we neared the English coast we sighted an enormous dry dock being towed by two tugs; the whole extended over a mile and was lit up like a football ground is today. When we were close enough we found out that it was Russian and advised Land's End Radio accordingly. The adverse weather we met on this passage meant that it took over sixteen hours instead of the usual thirteen, so we did not arrive at Newlyn until late the next morning. John and Judy had to leave us here since we were much later than had been planned and they both had to return to work.

On our return to Upton I noted in our log that we had covered more than one thousand five hundred miles this summer cruise, an improvement on the previous year's total. We were somewhat amused when we were in the Swan later and discussing our cruise with Peter, the landlord, to be told that another customer had been in the habit of enthusing about the little Spanish town where he spent his holidays, but would not tell anyone its name. He happened to be present and was somewhat surprised to overhear where we had been. His secret was no longer!

We only made one more trip on the Severn and that was to check the propeller vibration which I felt was more than it should be, but could do nothing about it. On Friday October 13th we set off on our winter cruise back to the River Weaver. We took George and Gill Dick, who had sailed with us before, and two other friends, Walter Leadbeater and Allan Pettigrew, both of whom also had made several passages before. We left Upton after lunch and arrived at Sharpness just after the evening pre-prandial refreshment. There I had to dismantle the engine's fuel pump since its pressure relief valve had been giving some trouble. We locked into the Severn a couple of hours later and had an almost flat calm passage to Fishguard. On our arrival we tried to enter the old harbour, but we were too early and there was insufficient water, so we anchored off Saddle Rock. We overnighted there and after breakfast the next morning, set off for Dun Laoghaire. Once again it was a flat calm passage and Dun Laoghaire was made early evening where we secured to an MFV in the coal harbour, our usual spot.

Established ritual was followed and we went to the Gresham in Dublin for dinner. It was over this meal that Walter began enthusing about the Isle of Man. The decision was made there and then that we would make a diversion to call in on our way, it being only slightly further than going direct from Dun Laoghaire to Liverpool. We rushed back to the coal harbour and set off just after half past ten. Once again the sea was flat calm and the weather balmy. I stood on the foredeck without a shirt and was warm. We made the island just before daylight and, because Walter had a friend with a cottage in Castletown, we made for Castletown Bay.

On arrival it was too early on the tide to enter the little harbour, which dries out, so we dropped our anchor in the bay and waited until the tide had risen enough for us to enter.

When we weighed our anchor it was covered with kelp and one of the flukes was bent in the process. After we had entered, we secured to the quay and hoisted our 'Q' flag to inform the Customs that we had 'come from foreign.' We waited and waited, but nothing happened, so we went ashore to look for a waterguard. We were unsuccessful so Walter went to telephone his friend to ask if we could use his cottage and Mini-Minor utility. While Walter was away the Customs officer appeared and came aboard. Our explanation for the absence of one of our crew was not received very gracefully and, as skipper, I received a verbal dressing down. While all this was happening, Walter returned and George tried to keep him out of sight until we had got rid of the officer. However, he was unsuccessful and Walter came aboard, full of the joys of spring, to be greeted by the Customs officer with the words, 'We have been very naughty, have we not, sir!' And Walter was taken away to the Customs office for a formal dressing down.

After all this we went to the cottage, had a good wash and then Walter took us in the Mini-Minor for a tour of the island. We were taken over Fairy Bridge where he informed us that local custom insisted that all who passed over the bridge must wish the fairies, 'Good morning,' or whatever time of the day it happened to be. We complied with some very sleepy, 'Good morning fairies.' I can add here that while we lived on the Isle of Man, on our return from Solomon Islands, we met this superstition many times. One driver who was in court for causing an accident complained bitterly afterwards that he had passed over Fairy Bridge that day and 'wished the fairies good day.'

While Walter was driving us around he gave a lively running commentary and potted history of the various places we passed. Unfortunately, since we had been up all night, we were all more than half asleep, so the commentary fell on some very deaf ears.

We left Castletown the next morning, bound for Acton Bridge. Again the sea was still almost a flat calm, but the visibility was pretty poor, after all it was mid October, with an area of high pressure over the British Isles, so that we were glad of our radar. We arrived at our winter mooring in time for lunch, which was taken in a nearby restaurant by six very scruffy persons.

We had so enjoyed our very brief visit to the Isle of Man that we decided we could make a cruise there over Christmas. We left Acton Bridge on Christmas Eve, arrived in Douglas early evening and secured to the Victoria Pier. We were then directed to the inner harbour, which dries out, where we secured to the quay outside St Matthew's Church. Anne had put a Christmas tree at the top of the foremast and also set out all the Christmas presents in the wheelhouse around a smaller tree which had been decorated with fairy lights. We then attended the midnight Eucharist and returned on board. *Ebb Tide* had been ballasted so that she would lean against the quay wall when the tide went out. Anne expressed the view that I had set her too upright, but I overruled her. In the early hours we were awakened by being thrown off our berth in an almighty crash. *Ebb Tide* had fallen over. Anne had been correct. I had set her too upright. There was absolute chaos on board, with all the Christmas presents scattered around the wheelhouse and the smell of fuel was almost overpowering. I found that it was running out of some of the tanks, but I was able to get into the engine room and close the valves. We had to sleep on the ribs of the hull and that was not very comfortable. However, we were grateful that the tide had returned before the early worshippers visited St Matthew's and we were afloat again. The only outwardly visible sign of our overnight problem being the Christmas tree on the mast which had fallen to a horizontal position.

It was not the best of Christmases. We did not realize at that time that the island closed down immediately after the short holiday season ended in October. All the hotels were shut for the winter so that it was our first 'dry' Christmas for many years. On Boxing Day we were advised to move down to Port St Mary where there is plenty of water at all states of the tide, so we went there and found a berth against the harbour wall. It being Sunday, we attended Evensong and were amused when a choirman and a diminutive choirgirl sang Good King Wenceslas and at the words 'come hither page' the choirman placed his hand on the girl's shoulder. He had to stoop so far that we had difficulty in controlling ourselves.

Christmas over, we made our way back to Eastham where we spent the night secured to a dredger in the sluice, and then the next morning went back to Acton Bridge. A Christmas cruise of some two hundred miles.

This season we added a further two thousand six hundred miles to our total.

9

1966

Upton on Severn; Lequietio again; Acton Bridge

After a fairly extensive winter's refit, the time came to take *Ebb Tide* back to our summer mooring on the River Severn. We took Norman and Mair Johnson with us and left Acton Bridge after lunch on Wednesday May 11th. Due to the fact that we were too early on the tide to lock out, we had to overnight at Eastham lock. Early the next morning we set off for Dun Laoghaire. Other than bumping on the bottom we made our way out of the Mersey via the Rock Channel, the passage was calm and uneventful. We arrived at Dun Laoghaire some fifteen hours later and secured in our usual place in the coal harbour. The winter's work paid off since we did not meet any problems on this short passage. However, the autopilot decided to go on strike and nothing that I could do would induce it to call off its industrial action. After the ritual dinner at the Gresham Hotel, the next morning we called the autopilot manufacturer's agent in Dublin and he spent the following two days trying to repair it.

At this time there was a threat of a shipping strike. As Norman had business appointments on the Monday following and the engineer could not give us any firm promise of repairing the pilot, both he and Mair decided to leave us on the Saturday and return to Holyhead by the ferry. We were thus left on our own. Sunday was spent in the coal harbour at Dun Laoghaire, while the engineer struggled to make the autopilot work. Eventually he had to admit that he could not trace the cause of the fault so we decided to move on. We left early afternoon of the next day and since we had a long passage ahead of us, decided that the best way of tackling this was to work the watches three hours 'on' and three hours 'off', and to make direct for Upton on Severn without the usual visit to Fishguard. Luckily the weather was kind, which made watch keeping considerably easier. Had it been bad, we would have had no alternative but to call in at Fishguard, and possibly Ilfracombe too. Steering a motor yacht is very different from steering a sailing one as there is no 'lashing the tiller' to hold an approximate course. Every time a course deviation occurs, corrections have to be made through the steering wheel, and this takes no little effort. There is also the problem of keeping awake; three hours on the wheel followed by three hours for sleeping and feeding are extremely tiring, especially for the cook. However, we arrived at Sharpness soon after 7 pm the following evening, after a passage of twenty eight hours, and were able to lock in without any problems. We secured to the quay and then slept the sleep of the just.

The next morning we were visited by the Customs waterguard who had seen that we were flying the 'Q' flag. When we told him that we had come from Ireland and that we had no idea of what dutiable goods were on board, he said that he would have to get an officer and went ashore. In due course the officer arrived and asked the usual questions. He was told the same thing, that on this trip our guests had provisioned the ship but had left us at Dun Laoghaire. I was still extremely tired and so told him to look in the spirits cupboard himself. To our surprise he found it almost empty. We had obviously depleted Norman's contribution while we were in Dun Laoghaire! He then casually picked up a bottle of Red Label whisky and said, 'Where did you get this from, sir?' Luckily I said that we had bought it in France the previous year (how it had lasted through the winter I don't know). Honesty is always the best policy in life, and certainly with Customs officials. We discovered afterwards that in very small print across the Red Label bottle label were the words, 'For export only'. I often wonder what would have happened if I had given another answer. We then left Sharpness and arrived back at our summer mooring in time for a visit to the Swan before it closed after lunch.

Other than sundry trips up and down the river for the odd

trial run to check the accuracy of the new log I had fitted during the refit, we did not move again until July 1st, when we decided that we would make another foray down the Bristol Channel. This time Lynton was our objective and since we had a young friend, Ted Reé who worked at the Permali factory in Gloucester, with us, we did not have sufficient time to make Ilfracombe and back so that he could return to work on the Monday morning; in any case we wanted to try another harbour. After collecting Ted from his factory on the banks of the Gloucester/Sharpness Ship Canal, we arrived at Sharpness late evening and spent the night there. Early next morning we locked out and made for the *Breaksea* light vessel where we went aboard for a social call. We then set course for Lynton, but on arrival we could not see any room in the harbour, so we made for Watchet instead. It was then half tide, so Anne and Ted went ashore in the little launch we carried and arranged with the harbourmaster for a berth in the harbour.

Some three hours later the tide had risen sufficiently for us to enter, so we weighed anchor and moved into the harbour. there we secured to the large wooden wharf which is designed for cargo ships, not yachts; Watchet being a commercial harbour serving the paper factory in the town. Although we could not see it at the time, the ship which berthed before us had left a large depression in the mud forming the bottom. We thought that we had secured safely so that *Ebb Tide* would lean against the wharf, but were soon proved wrong. In the evening, as the tide went out we toppled over; it turned out that our keel had been halfway up the outside of the depression in the mud and *Ebb Tide* had slipped down it towards the wharf, thus our mooring ropes were ineffective in holding us upright. There was mud everywhere! It sploshed up the scuppers so that the deck on one side was literally a sea of mud. We had a most uncomfortable night sleeping on the ribs of the hull, as we had done before in Douglas on the Christmas visit. It was only the second time we had fallen over, apart from 'being on the rocks at Gloucester', and I had some doubts whether or not *Ebb Tide* would be able to overcome the suction from the mud when she had water round her again. I need not have worried however. As the tide rose, so did *Ebb Tide*. On Sunday morning we headed back and made Sharpness in time for the first locking, then we went up the ship canal to Purton Bridges where we spent the night. We were awakened at 5.30 am the next morning by the bridge keeper, who opened the bridge for us, and we continued up the canal, dropping Ted off at Gloucester before we returned to Upton on Severn.

Our summer cruise began at midday on August 6th as well as five of our own children, we took with us our eldest son's study mate, Philip Walker, and his sister Jane. Philip's initials are PK so that at school he was always known as 'Chewey' and is still Chewey to us to this day. We made Sharpness early evening but the forecast gave gales for Lundy so we decided to stay put until the next morning. Before locking out into the Bristol Channel I took the opportunity to check our barometer for the first time with the standard one in the harbour office, a check not always easy to make. In spite of having every intention of making Newlyn our next stop, we had only been under way for some three hours or so when we met the usual Bristol Channel 'wind against tide' conditions which made for a very bumpy passage. At least we did not suffer to the extent we had on our first major cruise; this time we stayed close inshore and reduced our speed. We were off Porlock Weir when the radar packed up. I immediately altered course for Ilfracombe so that I could have a steady base to work, rather than trying to work on it under the bumpy conditions we were experiencing. On our arrival, about two hours later, there was sufficient depth of water for us to secure to the outer harbour wall.

The radar problem turned out to be a failed crystal in the radio frequency head (that is where the magnetron and klystron are) and, as we had a good supply of first line spares, this did not cause any problem; it only took a few minutes to change it, so we were soon under way again. All the time the weather had been improving and the wind falling; this put us well ahead of our planned time of arrival at Newlyn. When we were almost at the end of the passage and off Penberth Cove, we tried fishing under sail; needless to say, as usual, we caught nothing. We arrived in Newlyn Harbour at midday and made arrangements for stores and fuel, both of which arrived the following morning. This made us too late for crossing the Channel in order to arrive off the Four light with a favourable tide, so we went out fishing again. The only thing of note was that one of the engine's cooling pump pipes came adrift. This resulted in the rubber impeller of the pump disintegrating and necessitated my fitting a new one. Luckily we had several spares on board. It also broke Jane in to small boats!

We left Newlyn early on Friday August 12th and had an excellent passage across the channel, with a large school of porpoises playing around our bows. Towards midnight fog began to build up and visibility was reduced to less than half a mile. We were too far from the French shore to get a radar fix, but there was a very faint trace on the screen from which I interpreted that we were too far west, so the necessary course alteration was made. Shortly afterwards we spotted a tug steaming across our course and, in the murk some distance to the west, a blue light seemed to be following it. Luckily I realized in good time that this was a tug towing a 'dracone', which is a flexible oil barge, hardly visible above the water. It would have been somewhat disastrous if we had tried to go between them! Finally the weather cleared up and we were able to obtain a good fix from the Four light. After piloting through the Chenal du Four we arrived in Brest mid morning.

We spent the night at Brest and left twenty-four hours later. The Bay of Biscay was at its best and we arrived at St Martin de Ré after a passage of some twelve hours. We had to anchor off until the tide had risen sufficiently for the gates of the wet basin to open. We then secured in our usual place right in the centre of the town. Only a day was spent there during which we all walked over to the beach on the west coast, a comparatively short distance, the island being pretty narrow. We were somewhat intrigued to see an ox drawn plough and greatly amused to hear the ox being urged on by its driver, an old woman, calling out, 'Allez Lulu, allez Lulu.' After this brief break we left on the evening tide bound for Lequietio. It was at around midnight on this passage when we received news, via Land's End and St Nazaire radio stations that the A-level exam results which had been anxiously awaited by both Simon and Chewey, had been received and passed on by Rossall, their school. Both had passed with good results, Chewey in particular. We tried to contact his parents by radio telephone to obtain their agreement for him to go to Oxford, as recommended by his school. Our log keeping was

111

somewhat disrupted by all this so that all which was recorded is a note:

> '23 miles off coast, no position logged at 2300 due to working St Nazaire radio to obtain message from Land's End.'

After a calm passage of some twenty hours we arrived at Lequietio just after lunch on Saturday August 20th. A couple of days were spent there, during which time we returned to Mrs Nicholson, the consul's wife, the dish which had contained a parting gift of cooked squid the year before. The young members of the crew were able to swim and dance in the town square in the evening.

On our way north we had intended to call at Le Palais on Belle Ile, but on arrival we put our nose in and found the harbour crowded, so decided to make for Lorient instead, where we arrived after a passage lasting thirty-one hours. There we filled our water tanks which had become depleted through having ten persons on board! The weather was not so kind on this passage, but it was good enough.

After lunch the next day we set off for Le Guilvenic, a passage taking five hours. A day was spent there and we left early morning of August 27th for Brest. No problems were met on this short passage of six hours. We spent one night there before we made for Newlyn. I had overcome the problems we had experienced with fuel filters blocking in previous years.

During this stay in Newlyn a lifeboat exercise with a helicopter was carried out, so we went to see what it was all about. We returned to harbour before setting off late evening for Ilfracombe. Again we did not meet any problems on this passage and arrived mid morning the next day, before setting course up the Bristol Channel for Sharpness. We paid our now usual call on the *Breaksea* light vessel, so that Chewey and Jane could go aboard, and also to drop off some milk and papers. We had to spend a little time in Barry until the tide was right for going on up the Bristol Channel. We had some difficulty in finding a berth in the little harbour, so had to secure to the harbour wall at the entrance to the commercial docks.

Since *Ebb Tide* was registered at Bristol, we decided that she ought to pay a visit to her 'home port' as we were sure that she had not done so before. We left Barry early in the morning, made our way up the Bristol Channel, and then the River Avon through the most impressive Clifton Gorge before we arrived in Bristol docks some five hours later. During the manoeuvring to moor in the Cumberland Basin I endeavoured to execute a 'short turn' and in the process sheared off one of the flexible couplings on the propeller shaft. I had obviously been going ahead and astern too enthusiastically. We carried a spare, so it was a comparatively simple task to fit the replacement. Mooring up was the greater problem since we were way out when this happened. However, we managed to throw a line to one of the dock workers and he made it fast so that we could haul ourselves alongside. We spent the night there and the next morning locked out on the early tide, made our way to Sharpness back to our mooring at Upton on Severn, where we arrived mid afternoon.

On our summer cruise this year we had logged one thousand five hundred miles which is no mean achievement for an amateur crew.

We did not move again until the time came to return to our winter mooring at Acton Bridge. This winter cruise commenced on October 21st and, unlike the first time, we had a completely trouble free passage, calling at Dun Laoghaire for the ritual meal at the Gresham. Unfortunately we found that the Gresham had been 'modernized' and had lost its old world charm, so this was our last 'ritual dinner' there.

We then called at Port St Mary for a brief visit, before securing to our winter mooring at Acton Bridge a week later. The only point of note was that, while in the Bristol Channel, we picked up an empty plywood pram dinghy which was floating around. We reported it to Ilfracombe Radio and on our return, to the Customs officer at Connah's Quay in Flintshire. The problems we had with officialdom almost made us resolve not to collect any more floating objects at sea! I was threatened with having to pay the estimated value of the 'salvage' into some fund or other, but this was not put into effect.

So ended another yachting season during which we had covered two thousand four hundred miles, a few less than the previous year. It was also a season during which we did not meet very many mechanical problems, but this was probably due to the fact that by now we were not quite as 'green as some of the seas we had shipped in our yachting career so far.

10

1967

Bordeaux etc.

At the end of the 1966 yachting season we decided to keep *Ebb Tide* at Acton Bridge for the summer as well as winter mooring. We felt that we could make more use of her at sea. In those days it was a comparatively simple matter to slip down the River Weaver into the Manchester Ship Canal, then into the River Mersey through Eastham lock, when the world would be at our bows. Much as we loved our mooring at Upton on Severn, getting out to sea at weekends was becoming difficult as British Waterways imposed more and more restrictions on the hours for opening the bridges. Outside the 'working hours' they decreed that bridges could be opened on the payment of £1 per bridge. There are twelve bridges on that sixteen mile length of canal! By staying at Acton Bridge we could get over to the Isle of Man for a weekend and still be back at work on a Monday morning, albeit a little late, but considerably earlier than if we had stayed on the River Severn, and of course we would not have had to drive over ninety miles each way.

It had been a hard winter's work refitting. Amongst other major alterations we had rebuilt the wheelhouse. This of course meant that we were considerably later than we had hoped to be in getting ready for the season. It was therefore May 26th before we were able to make our first cruise, which was to Port St Mary in the Isle of Man. During this passage the only excitement was a message from Anglesey Radio that two men had been washed overboard from a submarine in the area. On arrival we found the harbour full of fishing boats and so for the first time had to lie alongside in the inner harbour, which meant drying out. We had some of the family with us and they were in a rebellious mood but of an age to appreciate pop music. In those days Radio Caroline was anchored off the Isle of Man so we took the opportunity of going alongside and then aboard. Our rebellious crew had never moved so fast before. We were secured alongside almost before we could say Jack Robinson. The children thoroughly enjoyed the experience, hearing greetings broadcast to them after we left. We then went north to make our first visit to Ramsey where the tide happened to be in, so we were able to enter the harbour on arrival. After a brief stop we went round the north of the island to Peel, but only stayed there for an hour or so, and then tried Port Erin, but did not enter. It looked so uninviting that we only poked our nose in. We returned to Port St Mary to overnight. The next day we swung the compass, then once again tried our hands at fishing, this time off the Calf of Man, but with the usual conspicuous lack of success, so we returned to our mooring at Acton Bridge.

Our next trip was to Holyhead, then to Bangor in the Menai Straits; we had some difficulty here because *Ebb Tide* appeared to want to have an affair with the buoy to which we were moored. It was only when the tide turned that she realized that buoys are not boys!

We made several visits to the Isle of Man and during one we tried to enter every harbour on the chart. Apart from minor problems, such as fuses in the autopilot blowing for no apparent reason, and the log impeller being broken off, all these trips were trouble free.

During the winter we had decided to make a change from St Martin de Ré and Lequietio and our summer cruise would be to Bordeaux. We knew that the vineyards there would accept visitors and I arranged for introductions through a couple of wine merchants who were members of my club in Chester. We set off on August 5th with most of our children and made Holyhead our first port of call, arriving there just before midnight. The next morning we set course for Newlyn but, on hearing gale warnings being given for sea area Lundy, decided to call in at Fishguard. All the time we were in St George's Channel the wind and sea were getting up so that eventually we were nosing into it. Our lifebelts were washed off their holders by the waves breaking over the bow so, much to my annoyance, I had to reduce our speed.

We spent the night in Fishguard and the next morning when the forecast was much improved, we continued on our way to Newlyn. In spite of little wind, the sea was still quite rough so that our progress was slowed, but at least I did not have to reduce the engine revolutions. We went through a thunderstorm during which the lightning damaged our radio receiver. We had made a good friend in Mike Webster, the radio engineer for the fishing fleet at Newlyn and he came to our assistance. We had to spend the day there while the repair was carried out and then finally left mid morning on Friday August 11th for Brest. The channel crossing was reasonably comfortable, although the wind and sea were pretty well on our nose. We hoisted our small foresail to steady us, which it did very effectively. We arrived off the Four light much too early and consequently had to plug the tide during the first part of the passage through the Chenal du Four.

We spent the day in Brest, buying vital stores, and then set off for Le Guilvenic. Stocking up with 'duty frees' in France was so much easier than in England. Unlike the UK, there appeared to be no restrictions placed on visiting yachts consuming duty frees purchased in France, while they were in French waters. During this six hour passage we stopped alongside a fishing boat and bought some fish; even though we carried a small beam trawl, we always seemed to be unlucky with our fishing attempts. Our youngest children were still quite small at this time, so we did not attempt long passages, hence the many ports of call. After Le Guilvenic we made for Le Palais on Belle Ile. It was on this passage that Marion, our middle daughter, received her A-level results through Land's End Radio. They were not as good as she had hoped, so she was somewhat subdued for a while.

When we arrived at Le Palais, the harbour was full. To our disgust we had to secure to the wall of the inner harbour and dry out when the tide went out. Later we moved to the deep water inside the entrance and anchored until we set off for St Martin the next afternoon.

The next leg was uneventful, apart from the autopilot playing up after a long trouble free run. However, I soon found the fault and made a temporary repair. After a thirteen hour passage, we arrived at St Martin to find the basin gates open so were able to enter and secure in our usual position. At that time St Martin had not been 'discovered' by yachtsmen; not so today. We always enjoyed our visits there and were greeted by the gate keepers with, 'Ah, encore les enfants.' We spent three days before setting off in the early hours for Bordeaux.

We left just before breakfast on August 22nd, bound for the Gironde estuary and then up river to Bordeaux. It was only a twelve hour passage and no problems were met on the way. It was an interesting trip up the river and much simpler than I had imagined from reading the various pilot books. On arrival, we had to secure to a tug which was lying alongside the quay in the river. We were both waiting for the dock gates to open when the tide had risen to the level of the water in the basin. It was only a short wait, then we moved alongside a barge in the entrance and entered some fifty minutes later. Bordeaux was the dirtiest port we had ever been in, a complete change from all the other French ones. Oil and rubbish were everywhere so that our hull and ropes were soon covered. It took a long time to remove all the filth.

Armed with my introductions, I made my first call on a wine exporter. He had a somewhat unpretentious office in the middle of the city and greeted us warmly. During the course of our conversation he invited me to lunch. I had to explain that I had my family with me and that eight of us would be too much. He readily agreed and then asked if I would like to look round his cellars. I accepted and waited for him to make a move towards the entrance door, but no, he went to another door in the wall. This opened onto a flight of steps which led down into the cellars. I was amazed when he told me that there were seven miles of cellars right in the middle of Bordeaux. I saw bottles of wine which went back some hundreds of years and were obviously priceless. How he had managed to preserve them from the Germans during the war I do not know.

On my return to *Ebb Tide*, Anne telephoned M. Ginistet, the owner of Chateau Margeaux, who was also a keen yachtsman. He immediately offered to send his niece to collect us from the docks. She duly arrived in an old Citroen and we all piled in. As we went round the large roundabout in Bordeaux with a monument in its centre, the engine stopped and so we had to push the car out of the traffic, no easy task since it was somewhat busy.

On our arrival at the chateau, M. Ginistet took us round the vineyard himself. To our great surprise he then invited us into the chateau and we ascended the wonderful entrance staircase which figures so prominently on the Chateau Margeaux bottle labels. We were then introduced to Madame who offered us refreshment in the form of grenadine, a sweet drink made from gooseberries. When the time came to leave, M. Ginistet asked if there was anything he could do for us. I asked him for the name of a reputable ship chandler so that we could buy some wine to take back to England. There was a hurried aside conversation with the niece, after which we were driven back to *Ebb Tide* in the docks. There we were handed a parcel from the boot of the car which turned out to be a gift of six bottles of Chateau Margeaux. We managed to keep this at home, finally drinking the last bottle on the last night in our home at Tarporley before we embarked for our voyage to Solomon Islands in 1973. In exchange we gave them a bottle of whisky.

During the time we were in Bordeaux we also visited Chateau Haut Brion and the Mission Haut Brion, both of which were extremely interesting. I took a photograph of the water pump in the yard of the Chateau. It was an almost perfect setting under its own little open-roofed shed. This is one which made quite an impression on me. We still have many photo slides of these visits, unfortunately, most were spoilt by the tropical climate during our time in the Solomons.

The time soon came to head homewards, so in the morning of August 26th we left the dock and made our way down the Gironde to arrive at St Martin de Ré late the same evening. We only spent a couple of days there and then followed our usual route home – Brest – Newlyn – Holyhead – Acton Bridge. The weather was pretty well perfect for the homeward voyage and apart from a few minor problems, such as a radar failure and an engine overheat, all went well. We finally arrived back at our mooring at Acton Bridge mid morning on September 9th. We had tarried on the way and tried our hand at fishing in Rhyl Bay with the little trawl we carried, this time with a modicum of success, though unfortunately a rock tore the net.

While we had been anchored in Holyhead Harbour we saw a speedboat with only one occupant, towing a water skier. The skier fell off and the driver turned his head to see what had happened, then he fell out of the speedboat which went careering round the harbour, luckily without hitting any of the boats moored there. It crashed into the harbour wall and did not, as we expected, break up but careered off in another direction to finally run ashore on the beach at the far side of the harbour entrance. It confirmed the wisdom of the regulation made later, that all speed boats towing water skiers must have two occupants.

We made several more trips out before the end of the year. One was to the *Bar Light* vessel, but it had to be aborted before we left Queen's Channel due to adverse weather, so we spent some time in the Liverpool dock system. Another time, in November, we went up the River Weaver. I decided to re-set the engine governor to see if it could be made more responsive. We stopped at Saltersford Lock for lunch when I spent time in the engine room until Anne called out that lunch was up. After we had eaten, I started the engine and was horrified when it ran away with itself. The revolutions were well above those for safety so I dropped into the engine room and tried to stop the engine, not knowing what the trouble was at that time. In the end I had to hold cushions over the air intakes to starve it of air so that it could not run. This was successful and then I found that I had set the governor to move the injector racks to the 'full fuel' position! The correction was made and we continued our trip which had been originally to check the automatic pilot.

Another trip was made in mid-December, when we took a couple of friends with us with the intention of visiting the *Bar Light* vessel. It snowed hard and the sea was so rough that once again we had to turn back. We spent the night in the Birkenhead dock system and tried again the next day. This time we were successful and were able to reach our objective.

Reading our log books whilst writing this I think that we must have been mad! Once we had moved to the River Weaver we sailed right up to the end of each year, and 1967 was no exception. After Christmas was over we thought that we would try another harbour and decided to set out for Glasson Dock on the River Lune. This lies at the seaward end of the Lancaster Canal which opens out here into a large canal basin, connected to the dock by a lock. Glasson used to be quite a busy port, but in 1967 it was mainly used by yachts, although a few small coasters loaded and unloaded there.

We left Acton Bridge after work on Wednesday, December 27th and arrived at Glasson just after 2 am the following morning. This was the first time we had visited it by sea, and I underestimated the strength of the tidal stream as we made our way up the Lune Estuary. Being the middle of the night and dark, the many unlit buoys marking the channel were naturally difficult to see. Their sudden appearance on the radar screen was the only indication of their presence. We were being carried up the estuary pretty rapidly by the tide and on one occasion bumped one of the buoys before we could take any avoiding action. Luckily no damage was done either to the buoy or *Ebb Tide*, but we continued upstream at greatly reduced revolutions until we arrived at the dock entrance and waited for the lock gate to open. We only spent one night in the dock before returning to Acton Bridge the following day. We had made many visits to Glasson before, but by road when our sons were at Rossall School. It was a delightful place in those days but now it is a fairly busy little port used by coastal shipping.

At the end of the season the passages added nearly two thousand miles to our overall total.

1968 Pavillon d'Or – at Ardrishaig

1969 Pavillon d'Or flying proudly

1968 – Pavillon d'Or – Ramsgate

11

1968

First Pavillon d'Or – Ramsgate

It had been another hard winter's work refitting. Amongst other things, we had rebuilt the whole of the after end of *Ebb Tide*, making a comfortable cabin for ourselves in the process. During this work we found that the lower part of the transom was rotten. It was supposed to have been replaced at the small shipyard in Gloucestershire before we moved our winter berth to Cheshire, but their 'replacement' had been to put a piece of plywood in front of the rotten part and then paint the whole lot. This of course meant that we were very much later than we hoped in getting ready for the season. We had to take out the whole of the transom, which was four inch thick elm, and replace it with one in oak. We managed to get the lower part of the transom out of the water by ballasting the forward end of *Ebb Tide* with weights of various kinds. We dry docked at Northwich over the weekend of June 21st/22nd to make a propeller change and then had a trial run to Holyhead over July 7/9th to test everything.

When we had moored on the River Severn and been members of the Severn Motor Yacht Club we had seen, hanging on the clubhouse wall, a frame containing a gold burgee and a sketch map of the route followed by a member when he had taken part in, and won, a Pavillon d'Or some years earlier. He owned a converted twin screw torpedo recovery vessel and had taken professional crew with him. In those days this international motor yachting event was held every two years in a different country, the premier motor yacht club of which, acted as host.

We had read in *Motor Boat and Yachting* that the 1968 Pavillon d'Or was to be held in Ramsgate, with the Yacht and Motor Boat Association acting as host and, as I was a member, I decided that we would have a go. It had been won at least three times by a Swede in a fast twin screw vessel which was in fact a works sponsored entry, although according to the rules, the skipper had to be an amateur. The motor yachting fraternity had come to believe that he was invincible, so we thought that we could give him a run for his money. We very nearly did too!

The rules were that the start could be made anywhere on the specified starting date; the average speed over twenty-four hours must not exceed nine knots; the log had to be signed at every port visited; the specified finishing date, place and time had to be rigidly observed. If I remember correctly, twenty days was the time specified for the cruise. The winner was determined by points given on the basis of the square root of the distance travelled, plus up to ten points for the quality of the log keeping.

The maximum possible points which could be scored, assuming that it would be possible for a vessel to carry sufficient fuel to run non stop for twenty days, was seventy five. Obviously this could not be achieved. There was also an award for the competitor whose average speed was closest to the one stated at the time of entry, and another for the longest non-stop sea passage.

After our entry had been made, we received all the necessary forms, details, official log book etc. and then began planning our route. As usual it was bottoms up on the sitting room floor, with charts and books strewn around. Having read the accounts of previous events, I was of the opinion that if we could cover about one thousand two hundred miles we would stand a good chance of being in the first few. We then planned our route – north up the Irish Sea, through Scotland, south down the North Sea, into Holland, possibly Belgium and thence to Ramsgate.

We left our mooring at Acton Bridge in the early morning of Friday July 19th with our youngest boys, Neil and Guy, and moved to the small wharf below the road bridge where we filled our water tanks, so that we would be ready to leave as soon as the river opened the next morning at 6,30 am. In the evening, Walter Leadbeater, who had sailed with us many times before, joined ship. After casting off we followed one of the ICI boats down river and entered the Manchester Ship Canal, then made towards Ellesmere Port. We had to secure in the entrance to the barge lock there to wait for a large tanker on passage to Stanlow, to clear the narrow part of the canal. After this short delay we made for Eastham Lock and entered the River Mersey. It was just past 11 am before we were able to secure to Princes Pier at Liverpool where Jim Carr joined ship. One of the Liverpool pilots also hitched a lift to the *Bar Pilot* boat which was stationed at the entrance to Queen's Channel.

The weather was kind to us on this part of the voyage and we made the Crinan lock basin at Ardrishaig, the southern entrance to the Crinan Canal, in time for breakfast on July 21st. Since it was a Sunday the canal was not working so we had to moor alongside in the lock entrance. The next morning, after collecting some special local bread recommended by the lock keeper, we entered the canal as soon as it opened at 6.30 am and made our way through. We had been somewhat amused by the lock keeper at Ardrishaig when he referred to the people who lived on the other side of the estuary as 'lowlanders'.

We were impressed by the scenery. It certainly is a beautiful part of the world. We arrived at the Crinan sea lock after three and a half hours, which was quite an achievement since we had passed through fourteen locks on the way. The canal is only eight miles or so and I was horrified at the charge of £8 for passing through it.

We were certainly blessed with good weather, the wind had not been above a Force Three and it had been almost a flat calm most of the way. We decided to go through the Caledonian Canal, which includes Loch Ness, rather than attempt to go round the north of Scotland, in case the weather got too bad and we became stormbound, which might have caused us to miss the finishing date.

We arrived at the northern end of the Crinan Canal just after ten o'clock the same morning and then made the short passage to Corpach, which took us past the Island of Luing. We didn't realize at the time that we would be visiting that island a few years later on our way to the Faroe Islands. Mid afternoon we arrived at Corpach, the entrance port at the southern end of the Caledonian Canal, and locked in and up through the first flight of locks, to make Gairlochy at the southern end of Loch Lochy. Early evening we locked up into the loch and then secured to a barge just outside the lock entrance to await the morning. It had not been a fast run. I note from our log that we had only averaged 5.15 knots for the passage from Ardrishaig, but this did include the time taken in passing through all the locks, so it was nothing to be ashamed of.

We had a very peaceful night, apart from being attacked by myriads of midges. Jim and Walter kept our crew amused while Anne prepared our evening meal. Guy and Walter spent part of the time fishing for eels and generally fooling about. The fishermen were moderately successful in their efforts and caught a few eels, but they were far too small to make any addition to our diet, so were thrown back. The next morning we left just after half past six and made our way up the loch to the flight of locks at Laggan, where we locked up back into the canal and eventually into Loch Oich. It was then a simple run to the north end of the loch where there is another flight of locks back into the canal. At Fort Augustus we locked into Loch Ness. There is a magnificent abbey just past the lock entrance and we were able to take some photographs, one of the few times we were able to do this on the voyage. After leaving one lock I was reminded of Magnetic Hill, in Canada, where the water in a stream appears to be flowing uphill; looking out ahead it appeared that the canal was running downhill.

After passing through Loch Ness (no monster seen) we arrived at Clackanharry lock. Here there was a very dour lock keeper whom Walter tried to rag by using his imitation Scottish accent, but without any response or change of expression appearing on the lock keeper's face (no doubt he was used to Sassenachs). We then continued through the canal until we arrived at Inverness where we had to go down through all the locks to return to sea level. The whole passage through the Caledonian Canal had only taken just under nine hours, during which we passed one fishing boat travelling in the opposite direction as we went through Loch Ness. The Caledonian Canal had been a thriving waterway not so many years earlier; now it was almost unused.

We decided to make Fraserburgh our next port of call. The Missions to Seamen representative there had previously been at Newlyn so we knew him fairly well. It was nearly midnight when we arrived so we just secured to the harbour wall and slept. The next morning we paid our respects to the mission and then, soon after mid morning, departed with Aberdeen being our next port of call. It was only a short passage and we arrived some four hours later. As we entered the harbour I was impressed by the view of the 'granite city'. It looked very bleak and grey with the slate roofs glinting in the afternoon sun. The whole of the passage so far had been made in almost perfect weather conditions with a flat calm sea. The wind had not risen beyond a Force Three at any time. We refuelled in Aberdeen and Jim extended us an invitation to dine with him. We eventually found a cafe which was open and, after placing our orders, were somewhat disgusted to discover that it was 'dry.' I imagine that Aberdeen is somewhat different today!

Morning called for an early start as we had a passage of nearly two hundred and fifty miles ahead of us, the next port of call being Grimsby. Apart from a heavy following swell from the north east, which imparted a corkscrew motion to *Ebb Tide,* and hearing various navigational warnings from the coast radio stations which were in range, the whole of this passage was uneventful. However, I had not quite solved the problem of blocked fuel filters, so during the early hours I had to slip down into the engine room and make a filter change. On our arrival at Grimsby we secured to a fishing vessel in the dock entrance to wait for the gates to open. After we were secured in the dock, Jim and Walter left, since they both had business commitments to honour, which left only Anne and myself, plus our two young sons, Neil and Guy, to continue the voyage. We took on stores and generally spent a quiet day. I was not amused when we returned home later to receive a bill from British Waterways for 1/9d 'for passing Grimsby harbour.' I spent far more than this on postage stamps disputing the charge and eventually received a credit note because it had been discovered that we had entered the port to 'victual'; at least that was the reason given.

We left Grimsby in the early hours of July 27th and set

course for Great Yarmouth. The only event of note was that a bucket was dropped overboard so we had to make a smart turnabout in order to recover it. When we were off the buoy at Scroby Elbow I realized that we had time in hand, so decided to carry on to Lowestoft where we arrived mid afternoon and moored in the yacht club area. We still had time in hand since our next planned port of call was Amsterdam. The weather continued to be kind so if we stuck to our original planning we would be arriving at Ramsgate far too early. We therefore spent the next day in Lowestoft and left after our evening meal in order to make a night passage across the North Sea and arrive at IJmuiden after breakfast. The passage across was uneventful, although we had to reduce our speed for nearly five hours since a heavy swell from the north east made life somewhat uncomfortable.

On arrival at IJmuiden we met the Dutch Customs for the first time. Amongst other things we had to declare the amount of marmalade on board, which amused us somewhat. This did not cause much of a delay and mid morning we left for Amsterdam and arrived after a passage along the canal of one and a half hours. We moored in the yacht basin in the centre of the city and spent the rest of the day looking around. We decided to travel through the canals to Rotterdam and left the following morning. To comply with the Dutch waterway regulations we had to carry a canal handbook, but since it was in Dutch it was not much of a help and somewhat difficult to decipher. The passage through the canals was interesting and we only had one slight problem at the junction with the Utrecht Canal. We tried to go through the commercial lock and were directed to the old lock; no doubt if we had been able to read the regulations we would have realized this. We arrived at Rotterdam late afternoon and secured to a barge to lower our masts. This was necessary so that we could pass under the bridges before finally entering the yacht club moorings.

The next day we filled our water tanks and left Rotterdam, setting course down the river. We had to secure alongside in the tug basin at the Hook to clear Customs outwards, an operation which only took half an hour, and then made for Ostend. The weather was still almost perfect, apart from the visibility which was down to under a mile at times. We heard a

PAN message from one of the coast radio stations asking shipping to keep a look out for an Australian yacht. After an eight hour passage we arrived at Ostend early evening and moved into one of the basins for the night. Anne went ashore and bought a large bucket of rollmop herrings, which provided us with an excellent feast to round off the day.

As a result of the weather having been almost perfect, we were well ahead of where I anticipated we would be after eleven days, so we decided to have a real go at finishing at the top of the leader board instead of just on it. We left Ostend mid morning on August 1st, bound for Cherbourg, which was as far as I thought we might get before we would have to turn round and make for the finishing line at Ramsgate. Once again the weather was perfect; the wind did not rise above a Force Four and it was behind us all the way. We arrived at Cherbourg after a passage lasting twenty-seven hours. We had had such a smooth passage that I realized we could go even still further before making for Ramsgate, so the next evening we left harbour and set course for Braye in Alderney, where we arrived about three hours later, and anchored.

During the night we experienced the only bad weather we met and as I recall we dragged our anchor so that we almost went aground. We left the following afternoon bound for the finishing line at Ramsgate. Once again it was almost a flat calm and surprisingly we heard a PAN message to the effect that a catamaran was in difficulties and the Yarmouth lifeboat was searching the area. A couple of hours later we heard the lifeboat had found the cat and taken her in tow. We finally arrived at Ramsgate at a quarter to nine in the evening of August 8th, the specified finishing date, after a passage of two hundred and twelve miles, taking twenty-nine and a half hours.

On our arrival, after first clearing Customs, we were allotted a berth in the Royal Thames Yacht Club moorings where I handed in our 'official log'. Anne had dutifully filled it in every day and had it stamped by the authorities at every port of call. Our eldest son, Simon, was able to join us here, having obtained leave from Dartmouth.

The next day the results were announced and we were all delighted when we were told that we had won four prizes –one for coming second, one for making the longest non-stop sea passage, one for keeping closest the speed I had declared on our entry form, and one for the best kept log. Several of the other competitors came to see me afterwards and recommended that I should lodge a protest at not winning, on the grounds that the Swede who had won again was a professional, whereas we were a true amateur crew, but I declined to do this.

So ended our first attempt at the Pavillon d'Or. There was an official dinner and prizegiving held in the municipal restaurant at Herne Bay which was a bit of an anti-climax. The staff did not appear to know what to do, or how to serve, so that the gin and tonic I had ordered as a pre-prandial did not arrive until the main course. This resulted in my having a dry glass for the loyal toast, which had been drunk before the meal so that the 'foreigners' would be able to smoke during it.

The official functions over, the next event organized by the YMBA was a revival of the 'London-Cowes' motor boat race. This was on our way home, so we entered and had an enjoyable passage to Cowes, during which we were passed by the leaders in the Round Britain Power Boat Race, accompanied by the navy's *Brave Borderer*. We had a good time at Cowes and as it was our first visit we made the most of it. Unfortunately, Simon had to leave us here, but we enjoyed his company for the short time he had been able to spend with us. His place was taken by our youngest daughter Gillian, and a friend, Alison.

Since one of Anne's relations lived at Bosham, at the top end of Chichester Harbour, we decided to pay a call on her. The short passage took only three hours and I was somewhat surprised to find the harbour full to overflowing. However, we managed to find a space in which to anchor and luckily very close to the house, so we did not have very far to walk through the mud. We spent a day there and then returned to Cowes. As was to be expected, the harbour was packed, but we were able to find a mooring space. We went up the River Medina as far as we could, then made Yarmouth our next port of call. A regatta was in progress there. Gillian and Alison left ship here and our middle daughter, Marion, who had been on a holiday job, joined us for the remainder of the voyage.

After spending a couple of days at Yarmouth, we set course early in the morning of the third, bound for Dartmouth, where we arrived late in the evening. I had a little difficulty in mooring to one of the buoys, damaging one in the process. The log entry reads: 'Amazing cross current at mooring point.'

I arranged with a local skin diver to make the necessary repairs to the damaged buoy. We spent a couple of days here during which time Simon was able to visit us from Dartmouth.

Our next planned port of call was Newlyn. We left the River Dart on the evening tide and arrived at Newlyn early the following morning. The passage, apart from fog bringing the visibility down to ten yards, and not lifting until we were abeam of Eddystone lighthouse, was without incident. During the whole of this summer cruise the weather was pretty well perfect. We spent five days at Newlyn just relaxing and enjoying that part of the world. The Dolphin had become our 'local' there, so some time was spent in partaking of the local brew. When it was my turn to visit the fish and chip shop to buy our supper I was somewhat amused, when I asked what the fish was, to be told, 'A local fish.' It was, of course, rock salmon which in those days was not regarded as a respectable fish. It is a little different now. When we used to visit the Isle of Man the fishermen who caught coley fed it to their cats. When we lived there some ten years later it was in the fishmongers' shops at over £2 a pound!

But I am digressing. We left Newlyn early in the morning bound for the Scilly Isles and arrived after an easy passage of some four and a half hours. We dropped our anchor in Hughtown, the harbour of St Mary's, then later moved to Tresco, anchored, and spent the next day walking over the island.

The following morning we weighed anchor just after seven o'clock and set course for the Smalls. The visibility was under a mile so once again our radar proved to be a great asset. During this leg of the passage we had to reduce our speed due to the fact that both the wind and sea had risen enough to make life uncomfortable. One of the lessons I had learned during my experience with the RNXS was that it is only necessary to make a slight reduction in engine revolutions to make life easier. In this case I only reduced by 150 rpm and that made all the difference. We arrived off the Smalls just under thirteen hours after leaving Tresco and continued our passage to Port St Mary. As we passed Holyhead Island and our radio was tuned to Anglesey Radio, we heard a message that there was a link call for us. On making contact this turned out to be a phone call from Walter Leadbeater who was on holiday in the Isle of Man, asking us to join him on our arrival. We arrived at Port St Mary from Tresco after a passage of thirty three and a half hours.

The next morning we moved to Peel, passing through the Calf Sound in the process. On our arrival we contacted a friend from the RNXS branch and invited him for a fishing trip. Our decks were soon covered with friends of friends and we made for a point off Jurby, on the west coast of the island. We were more successful this time and our total catch was one hundred and thirty four mackerel, twenty six cod and three plaice. After the fishermen had taken what they wanted, we were still left with an enormous quantity of fish. These were later distributed among the various lock keepers on the way home. When we were living in the Isle of Man some years later the local greengrocer, a keen fisherman, was a little surprised when Anne told him where to find fish!

We left Peel the next day and made our way back to Port St Mary to collect Walter Leadbeater, who had asked to return to Acton Bridge with us. It was another straightforward passage and we arrived at Eastham lock soon after seven o'clock in the evening and spent the night moored in the sluices which are alongside the lock. The next morning we returned to our mooring at Acton Bridge at the end of a pretty crowded and eventful yachting season. I note from our log that we had covered two thousand three hundred miles, making the total for the season three thousand eight hundred and ten, which was no mean achievement for an amateur crew.

1969 Pavillon d'Or – being boarded by Dutch TV

1971 Pavillon d'Or – alongside coaster in Ilfracombe

1969 – Pavillon d'Or – Kampen

12

1969

Second Pavillon d'Or – Kampen – Holland

At the closing dinner of the Ramsgate Pavillon d'Or it was announced that one would be held the following year in Holland, with the host club being the Koninklijke Nederlandsche Motorboot Club. The finishing point was later announced as Kampen on the River IJssel, which runs from the Zuider Zee to the Rhine.

Since we had been so close to winning in 1968 we decided to make a serious effort to win this time. The route we selected was:

Leg one:	Ellesmere Port to St Martin de Ré
leg two:	St Martin de Ré to Brest;
leg three:	Brest to Newlyn;
leg four:	Newlyn to Ramsgate;
leg five:	Ramsgate to Great Yarmouth (to refuel);
leg six:	Great Yarmouth to Esbjerg;
leg seven:	Esbjerg to Grimsby;
leg eight:	Grimsby to IJmuiden;
final leg:	IJmuiden to Kampen.

Before we could participate, there was the small matter of a winter refit to be undertaken. Every year the refit seemed to involve more and more work and the 1968/69 one was no different. I completely rebuilt the diesel generating set, giving its engine a major overhaul in the process. Anne and I lined the whole of the engine room with 4lb/sq. ft. lead sheeting to act as a sound barrier. This was glued to all the bulkheads and under the deckhead with two inches of fibreglass sheet in between. A new propeller, made to the specification I had finally concluded was the most suitable, was fitted and distillation plant was installed to produce fresh water from sea water by using the heat from the main engine. The wheelhouse furniture was completely rebuilt and the main engine was given a minor overhaul. At one stage I had bought some ex-submarine batteries which I hoped would have been satisfactory, but they would not charge properly and took up an enormous amount of space in the engine room, so I decided to install proper marine batteries and fitted a twenty four volt bank of Exide marine batteries with a capacity of four hundred and ninety amp. hr. which would provide an adequate supply of power for all purposes during the 'silent hours'. They were kept fully charged by a mains operated constant voltage ex-telephone exchange battery charger when we were alongside. This battery bank in fact lasted right the way through to Solomon Islands and for several years there. The whole refit was quite an operation, and only made possible by the fact that our mooring was only just over fifteen minutes from home.

In the meantime Anne had undergone an operation and was supposed to be taking things quietly, obviously not permitted to take part in any strenuous work. This, together with the major refit, resulted in it being May 23rd before we were able to make our spring 'shakedown' cruise to Peel, on the Isle of Man. We met one or two problems on the way, but nothing serious. Apart from the 'shakedown', another purpose was to take a friend and his crew from Acton Bridge to collect a motor vessel he had bought in Peel, and then escort him back to Acton Bridge. A fellow club member, Ron Pritchard, a retired Liverpool pilot, was also with us to assist me on the return passage.

On our arrival at Peel early the next morning, our 'passengers', all three of them, took over *Katrina*, their new possession, and we left the harbour at lunchtime the following day. All went well as they followed us round to Port St Mary and we arrived safely a couple of hours later. In view of their subsequent performance I should not have taken them the short way through the Chicken Sound, between the Isle of Man and the Calf.

In the afternoon we took some of the locals out to fish off Wart Bank but, as was more or less usual, nothing was caught. We arrived back in harbour some four hours later after travelling through a heavy rainstorm on the way. We then had a discussion about the return trip, planned for the next day. We agreed that *Katrina* would lead and we would follow at a discreet distance in *Ebb Tide,* so as to be able to give any help they might need.

At about 3 am the following morning we suddenly realized that *Ebb Tide* was adrift in the harbour. The fishing fleet had left and, contrary to their usual practice, had simply untied our ropes and let us go. The efforts Ron and I made to re-moor proved too much for him and he collapsed, apparently from a mild heart attack. Anne, operation or no operation, had to assist in re-mooring, with the added burden of looking after Ron as well.

We left after a late breakfast, with the weather forecast giving the wind as SE Force Five. As soon as we left harbour we found that the weather forecast was a fact and we rolled badly, so much so that a battery we were carrying in the wheelhouse as a spare for *Katrina,* fell over and spilt acid all over our new wheelhouse carpet, leaving a large hole in it, which was not popular. In the meantime *Katrina* was going round and round in circles ahead of us. We decided to return to the harbour. During the later discussion it turned out that *Katrina's* helmsman, who professed to be able to handle a boat, had been chasing the compass, a fatal error! Ron then asserted that he had fully recovered and insisted on taking *Katrina* out to see if the crew were capable of taking her home.

On his return, a council of war was held, the outcome being that Ron would travel aboard *Katrina* to help them, and he was fit enough for the purpose. His short trial run had only confirmed his suspicion that the helmsman was incapable of steering a vessel by compass; he had only had river experience in spite of his claim to be a 'sea' man. We finally left Port St Mary just after the evening pre-prandial and with a reasonable weather forecast. The sea did not believe what the forecasters had said and so we had to travel at reduced revolutions. In order to avoid the worst of the sea then running, Ron decided to head pretty well due south for Anglesey and then along the north Welsh coast. This worked admirably and when we met up with *Katrina* at Eastham lock the next morning, we learnt to our horror that Ron had had to steer her the whole of the way, a passage of thirteen hours, and this was in spite of the heart attack he had suffered earlier! We finally made the mooring at Acton Bridge at just after 10 am.

All the surgeon's advice to Anne had been disregarded; she not only coped with a heart attack at sea but also worked ship as well. She did not seem to suffer any ill effects as a result. I was somewhat peeved, however, to find on our return that another club member had taken over our mooring and I hit an underwater obstruction as I backed *Ebb Tide* into the small space he had left for her berth and damaged the brand new propeller which had been fitted just before we left.

When we commenced the Pavillon d'Or, we left Ellesmere Port on July 10th at 6.30 am. Walter Leadbeater had joined our crew, which at the beginning was Anne, Walter and I. Guy, our youngest, joined later at Newlyn, after he had broken up from Rossall. Walter had previously asked if we would take two of his business associates with us as far as the Ile de Ré. They were hitch hiking around Europe and joined ship with him. Soon after we had entered the River Mersey and were just off Cammell Laird's shipyard, we came on a dead body floating alongside. Luckily the pilot boat *Puffin* was not far away so I gave her a call on the radio and asked her to take over, since her crew were quite used to dealing with this sort of thing. All went well on this first part of our passage, apart from the fact that the log was under-reading. During the refit, after the problems with the sum log becoming entangled with seaweed, I had fitted one with a retractable impeller, so it was an easy matter to withdraw it and remove any seaweed entangled round it.

Just before Midnight we sighted red flares at about five degrees on our port bow but, despite determined efforts on our part, we could not contact either Anglesey or Ilfracombe radio stations. We eventually made contact with the coast-guard at St David's Head and passed on the sighting. We then saw flares again and altered course to head for them. Shortly afterwards we heard on our radio that a lifeboat had been launched to go to the assistance of the German vessel *Metric*. We could not be of any assistance so altered our course back to the original one for South Bishop light.

All this time the wind was westerly Force Three, which meant that it was on our beam. We had to make a temporary course alteration to ease the rolling so that Anne could cook breakfast. After 'the inner men' had been satisfied, we altered course to head for the Longships lighthouse, and after travelling through some fog, passed it at 2 pm. The wind dropped and visibility was less than a mile so our radar was invaluable as we passed outside Ushant for the first time (we had previously always taken the inside passage through the Chenal du Four). Unfortunately the radar decided that it wanted a holiday and packed up soon afterwards, but only a minor repair was necessary and some twenty minutes later it was serviceable again.

We were not impressed by our 'passengers' who spent almost the whole of the daylight hours sitting on the bridge reading, while we passed whales and other interesting sea creatures. However, we later learned that they managed to hitch hike through Europe and ended up in Norway as they had planned. When we arrived at St Martin de Ré at 3.30 am, after a passage of just over six hundred miles, we secured alongside and then landed our 'guests' after giving them a quick meal. As soon as a port official appeared we had our log book signed and turned round and set course for Brest at 4.40 am.

The passage to Brest was completely uneventful, the sea almost a flat calm so we were able to cruise at nine knots. We poked our nose into Le Palais on Belle Ile, but the harbour was full, so we continued on our way and arrived at Brest almost exactly twenty four hours after leaving St Martin. We had to make the usual diversions to avoid the many fishing floats attached to nets which were left for collection by their owners at a later time.

After having our log book signed, we left for Newlyn at 9.40 pm. We had previously arranged for Guy, our youngest (then aged fourteen), to join us after he had broken up for the school summer holidays. We had a little trouble with the fuel filters blocking, but this only caused slight delays. We also heard a PAN message from Land's End Radio asking shipping to keep a sharp look-out for a Mirror dinghy which was missing after last being sighted off the Runnelstone buoy. We arrived at Newlyn just after midday and waited for Guy, who joined us at

7.30 pm, having travelled by train from Blackpool.

Early the following morning we left Newlyn, bound for Ramsgate. Again the weather was kind and a light wind was behind us, so we were able to keep our speed up to nine knots. We passed a submarine periscope a cable to starboard. A helicopter was hovering in attendance so there was no doubt we would have had some warning if we had been too close. Again our perennial problems with fuel filters caused a couple of unscheduled stops. We finally arrived at Ramsgate at 1.30 pm and secured to the wall in the outer harbour. Walter left ship here to return to work and we had our log book signed.

After spending just over twelve hours at Ramsgate, we set off for Great Yarmouth where I had previously arranged to refuel. This was a comparatively short passage taking only eight hours. On our arrival we took on gas oil, had our log book signed, and then mid afternoon left for Esbjerg. On the passage we saw oil and gas rigs for the first time, a most impressive sight. Once again the weather was kind so we had a calm passage with no fuel stoppages this time.

I was pleased with both my navigation and the autopilot, since we did not have to make any course alterations during the passage and, after a run of two hundred and fifty miles landed up at the 'YYL' light vessel within three miles of our planned position. I must admit that it was with a certain amount of trepidation that I went across what was described on the chart as 'danger minefield', but I felt fairly certain that, if there were any mines left, *Ebb Tide* being a wooden vessel, would not activate any. In the event there was no problem. As we approached Esbjerg we met a heavy swell at the bar which required full applications of the wheel in order to maintain our course. At 1.20 am, after a passage lasting approximately thirty three hours, we entered the harbour and secured to a tug. We slept until mid morning and then looked around for someone to sign our log. We did not meet any problems with Customs or Immigration officials. I think that they thought us a little mad just to come into the harbour for such a short time.

Leg seven was from Esbjerg to Grimsby. We left on July 21st at 6.45 pm and had a pretty smooth passage until the evening of the following day when we had to reduce our speed as we passed through some particularly heavy swell. Shortly afterwards we came up to an oil rig which was not marked on our chart. The tug 'East Shore was standing by so I gave her a call on our radio and asked them to give us its position so that I could mark the rig on our chart. Shortly afterwards the old bogey of blocked fuel filters reared its ugly head and we had to heave to for a few minutes while I fitted new filter elements. We heard a PAN message sent out by Humber Radio that red flares had been sighted about three miles east of Scarborough and that the lifeboat had been launched. It turned out that a man had gone overboard in Scarborough Bay but he was soon picked up and the message was cancelled fifteen minutes later. We arrived at Grimsby at 8.45 am on July 23rd after a passage of thirty eight hours and secured to a tug in the dock entrance until we could lock into the dock itself.

Leg eight, the last seagoing one, was from Grimsby to IJmuiden at the entrance to the ship canal to Rotterdam. I was not completely satisfied with the radar since we had extreme difficulty in picking up the Humber light vessel at a close range. A radar engineer came aboard and told me that there were two ways of tuning the receiver and showed me another way which overcame the problem.

The distillation plant had not been functioning correctly. Since the makers were in Hull, I contacted them and arranged for a different sea water pump to be supplied. I fitted this and it cured the trouble. Once again the weather was kind so we were able to make a good and fairly comfortable passage. We crossed the North Sea to Smith's Knoll Light vessel, where we arrived at 3 am. We then altered course for IJmuiden and soon came upon yet another oil rig which also was not shown on our chart. I called up its accompanying tug *Signal Service* to obtain the position so that it too could be marked on our chart.

As I said earlier, our intention had been to enter Holland via IJmuiden and then make for Kampen through the canal system, but I realized that we still had some time in hand and so turned and headed north instead of turning in to the long mole at the entrance to IJmuiden. We then made our way round the coast to Zeegat van Terschelling, where we could enter the Zuider Zee through the lock at Harlingen in the north.

142

In spite of comparatively calm conditions we had to reduce our speed to avoid some heavy pounding, but this only lasted for about half an hour. We made Harlingen at 10.30 pm, nearly hitting a moored dredger which, in the dark, I had taken for the end of the polder. We secured for the night at the bridge entrance. The next morning saw another early start when we entered the IJsselmeer through the Klorenz sluice and set course for Enkhuizen. On arrival we followed the buoyed channel round until we were off the buoy at Pampus and then altered our course by nearly one hundred and sixty degrees to finally make our way under the new road bridge at Kamper Hoak. We arrived at Kampen on Saturday July 26th at 1445, two and a quarter hours before the deadline. After mooring up and handing in our log book we were fairly confident that we had done pretty well. We had covered two thousand three hundred and six miles in nine days and maintained an average speed of 8.76 knots. Our declared speed had been 8.75 knots! We were somewhat disconcerted, however, when a German entry manned by three large Germans wearing wellington boots and in a high speed twin screw vessel, secured alongside. They looked as if they had won on distance, and they probably would have done if they had bothered to keep a log. They obviously had overlooked the fact that good log keeping was just as important as a distance run. So we had won after all! We were told it was a popular win since we were the first truly family amateur crewed boat ever to win this international event.

In the evening the Burgemeester held a reception in the Stadsherberg for all the contestants. We were naturally highly delighted not only to have won the coveted Pavillon d'Or, but also the prizes for the best kept log, the closest average speed to that declared on entry, and the longest non-stop passage at sea. The Pavillon d'Or was presented and we proudly flew it at our mast-head as soon as the reception was over. The following afternoon we were all taken by a 'waterbus' through canals to Kalengerg and Stapshorst. It was an extremely pleasant outing and we were able to see some of the Dutch countryside without having to worry about navigation.

On Monday July 28th we proceeded in convoy to Medemblik with the commodore leading in his motor yacht *Eros*. As winners we followed him, and the remainder of the contestants – ninety-four of them – followed three abreast in line astern. Our route was: IJssel, Keteldiep, Ketelmeer, IJsselmeer, Aankomst then Medemblik, a total distance of thirty two sea miles, taking four and a half hours. During the passage we were boarded from a speedboat by a Dutch television crew and then interviewed. On arrival we all secured in the small harbour and were royally entertained by the Burgemeester, then later by a fashion show in the historic Kasteel Radboud.

The following day we again travelled in convoy to Hoorn, calling at Enkhuizen on the way. This was only a two hour passage and on arrival, amongst other gifts, we were presented with Dutch cheeses. I forgot to say that every day each boat was given a gift of some sort. In the evening there was yet another reception which was enjoyed by all.

The next day, Wednesday, was a day off and we stayed at Hoorn with various entertainments being laid on. A navigational exercise was held in which competitors had to declare the time it would take to complete a course without altering the throttle settings or using an automatic pilot or radar. Boy Scouts were stationed on each boat to act as invigilators. Ours did not appreciate the fact that I had to shut down quickly when a sailing boat cut across our bows. We did not win anything for this event and assumed that we had been disqualified.

Thursday, we left after lunch for Monnickendam and travelled line astern in three columns. It was a somewhat chaotic passage since the commodore hoisted signal flags to tell the convoy to travel either: line astern, two abreast, or three abreast, as the occasion demanded. Some of the boats seemed to be completely unable to keep station. However, we finally arrived about an hour and a half later and filled the small harbour to overflowing. Again, presents were distributed all round. If my memory serves me correctly, this time it was a bottle of Bols Genever, a well appreciated gift.

Friday, August 1st, the flotilla set off for Amsterdam, the final port of call. As we passed through one of the waterside towns we saw our eldest son, Simon, standing on the quayside with a friend, David Agley. Anne tried to get me to stop for him but that was impossible as there was enough chaos behind as it was. We told them to meet us at Amsterdam.

144

When we arrived there we found that a small harbour had been especially opened for us all. After mooring behind the commodore's boat we were entertained by the police band playing 'Puppet on a String'. A lot of photography took place here, both personal and for publication in the various yachting magazines. It is unfortunate that so many of ours were spoilt in Solomon Islands, but a few are still fairly clear. During our stay we were taken along the canals by water buses and various places of interest were pointed out. One which remains in my memory was the house in which Anne Franke lived until her capture by the Germans during the occupation of Holland.

The Pavillon d'Or closed on Saturday, August 2nd, with a dinner in the Amsterdam Hilton Hotel, the prizes being presented between courses. I duly collected several trophies which included a Sailor receiver and direction finding loop. The loop was left in Solomon Islands, it having been 'tropicalized'. Unfortunately I was taken ill at the dinner and had to leave early, so I missed a lot of the 'eating' part. I suspect that it was the result of drinking champagne and eating shellfish, since I had suffered in this way before.

We left Amsterdam just before midnight on August 4th and made our way to the road bridge which ran across the harbour. There we had to wait a couple of hours for the bridge to open before we could enter the canal to IJmuiden. On our arrival we had of course to clear Customs 'outward' before we could enter the lock, which we did just before 4 am, nineteen minutes later we were on our way to Ramsgate.

The weather was still kind and the log book entries for 'wind' are 'light airs'. We made Ramsgate just before 9 pm and secured in the outer harbour entrance where we cleared 'inwards'. We only stayed there until 4 am the following morning and then set course for Newlyn. When we were off Beachy Head we hove to for about half an hour to let the 'hands bathe' (the log book entry made by David), after which we continued on our way. We paid a call at Dartmouth to put Simon and David ashore, arriving at 5.45 am and only stayed until 10.10 am, then set off for Newlyn. This leg of the passage only took about ten hours and on arrival we secured to one of the fishing vessels.

We spent a couple of days in Newlyn and left at midday on

August 11th bound for Upton on Severn. We were naturally very bucked with our successes in the Pavillon d'Or and wanted to show them off to friends at our old mooring. Apart from the necessary stop at Sharpness, the whole passage only took twenty hours. A couple of days were spent there and then we headed for Gloucester where we collected Simon and David again, and then made for Dun Laoghaire, a passage taking some thirty four hours. We spent a day in coal harbour there, then made for Peel in the Isle of Man, where we arrived at 4 am the following morning.

From Peel we made a fishing trip with about six Manx and other men and went up to the bombing range targets which are moored off Jurby Head. We were pleased with our catch, which was fifty cod, two whiting and innumerable mackerel. The problem with fishing there was to get the lines through the shoals of mackerel before any other fish could be hooked. The next day we moved to Port St Mary, spent a day there an then took a Manx RNXS friend aboard to give him a passage to Liverpool. We left at 4.40 am and, after dropping off our passenger at the Princes Stage in Liverpool, made our way back to our mooring at Acton Bridge where we arrived at 5.40 pm.

The total distance we covered during 1969 summer cruise was 3,535 miles and 4,008 miles for the season!

A report of our success was published in a Dutch yachting magazine *Waterkampioen* and our daughter Gillian, who lives in Holland, sent us a copy while this was being written. She translated the accompanying article into English and I reproduce her translation below:

'The winner, an Englishman, Mr LePine-Williams, was very popular with the other contestants. This 50 year old constructional engineer came with a very old, converted by himself, 16 metres fishing boat in a very good condition. The boat was crewed by himself, his wife and 14 years old son. They all had 4 hour watches. Workwise Mr LePine-Williams had no connections in boating, but he knew what he was doing as he and his wife had done evening courses at the Liverpool Maritime School. In other words, a real amateur who takes his hobby seriously. Mr LePine-Williams began his trip from Ellesmere Port by Liverpool and sailed to St Martin de Ré in the Gulf of Biscay, a distance of more than 500 sea miles. From there back to the French port of Brest and via the English harbours of Ramsgate and Great Yarmouth to Esbjerg in Denmark. Then across the North Sea to Grimsby in order to sail to Kampen via Harlingen. His 2,305 sea miles took him a total of 263 hours – meaning that he sailed approximately 17 hours per day. His answer to the question – "whether this was too much?" was "why? everyone took his/her turn on watch with an eight hour rest in between, and with a speed of 8-9 knots in nice weather it is a very good rest, and certainly in a boat that is seaworthy and comfortable, such as *Ebb Tide*." '

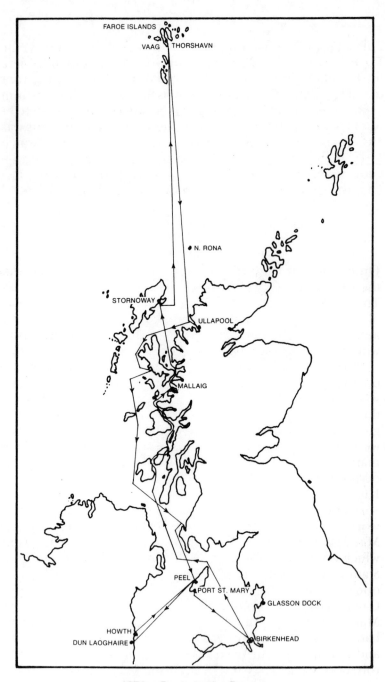

1970 – Route to the Faroes

148

13

1970

The Faroe Islands

On our return from the Pavillon d'Or in 1969 I found that
there were many problems waiting for me in our business.
The first priority was of course to set about solving them. Part
of this process included designing and building a semi-
automated plant for fabricating steelwork. Thus the usual
winter refit was somewhat curtailed.

Over the winter, whenever possible, we entertained friends
on board. During one of the Sunday lunchtime sessions,
when Ron Pritchard was with us, we discussed our plans for
the summer cruise for 1970. After consuming a fair amount of
gin we finally settled on Iceland as our destination and in this
we were ably abetted by Ron. However, in the cold light of
many mornings later we altered our destination slightly and
decided to make for the Faroe Islands – half way to
Iceland.

During the winter we had not undertaken a great deal of
work, other than the normal essential maintenance. It was
May 20th before we could make our first cruise of the season,
which was to Port St Mary, Isle of Man. We left Acton Bridge at
8 am which was the normal time for the bridges and locks to
open. Following the now usual route via the Manchester Ship
Canal, River Mersey and the Irish Sea, we arrived at Port St
Mary just after 10 pm the same day. The weather was not too
bad. We did not encounter any wind in excess of a Force Five
and that was on our beam which of course made it a rather
roly-poly passage. We were, however, able to cruise at our
usual engine speed of 1500 rpm.

We spent a day there and then decided to have a look at the Menai Straits where a fellow Cruising Association member, Roy Smylie, kept his boat *Deo Volente*. Since we had not been through the Straits before and Roy lived at the southern end, we decided to make our entry via the south. We left Port St Mary just before midnight on May 22nd so that we would arrive at the entrance to the Straits when the tide would be favourable for crossing the bar. However, we made a greater speed than anticipated and arrived off Caernarvon bar at 6.30 am. In order to be sure that there was sufficient water for us to cross, we anchored for a couple of hours. After we had weighed anchor we made for Caernarvon and secured to the quay in the shadow of the famous castle. Roy Smylie happened to be in the harbour and suggested that we should join him at his mooring in Tal-y-Foel pool, across the Strait. He had come over in *Deo Volente* and offered to guide us across. We followed him and anchored there soon after the evening pre-prandial time.

After a very pleasant day gathering a large bucketful of mussels, Roy offered to show us the way north through the Menai Straits. We had no difficulty in following him through the difficult passage just south of Menai Bridge and once we were safely through, he waved us farewell. We decided to return to the Isle of Man and so set course for Peel where we arrived some ten hours after leaving Tal-y-Foel.

On the passage one of the engine cooling pipes fractured so we had to stop for a short time while I made a temporary repair. Once in harbour, as well as making a permanent repair to the cooling pipes, I took the opportunity to fit new thermostats in the engine cooling system since the engine had been running at too low a temperature. This cured the trouble and, after spending the remainder of the day at Peel, we moved to Port St Mary to wait until the correct time to leave the island to arrive at Eastham Lock on the tide. We finally arrived back at Acton Bridge late afternoon after a cruise lasting a week.

Before setting out on our summer cruise we made one more weekend trip to the Isle of Man when we took a few Sea Scouts from the Chester Unit as passengers. I don't think that they had been to sea before and quite a few were seasick. One of the reasons we had moved our summer mooring from the

River Severn to Acton Bridge was so that we could get out to sea over a weekend without the hassle of the Sharpness Ship Canal and this was a prime example.

Our summer cruise began after lunch on August 7th. The crew was myself, Anne, Gillian, our youngest daughter, and Guy, our youngest son. We stopped on the way at Ellesmere Port on the Manchester Ship Canal to fill up our fuel tanks and also take on the vital duty free stores. The Customs office did not have a 'blue book' (this is an official record of all the duty free stores taken on board) for yachts so the waterguard simply entered the stores we had taken on a piece of paper and gave us strict instructions not to lose it.

It was half past seven in the evening before we finally entered the River Mersey and after passing the Bar light vessel, we set course for the Mull of Kintyre. During the night hours we passed the Isle of Man, little knowing then that we would be living there twelve years later. We had to slow down once or twice in order to ease the pounding; we were heading into a north westerly wind of Force Four or so. We did not have to alter course until our radar showed the Isle of Islay to be some six miles off. We finally made Port Askaig soon after eight o'clock in the evening and secured to the wall in the little harbour there.

The next day being a Sunday, in anticipation of some good Scottish cooking, we decided to lunch at the local hotel. We were a little disappointed when all we could obtain was frozen food probably warmed in a microwave, green peas, carrots and some beef! After lunch we set off on the next leg up to Ardnamurchan Point. We had been under way for less than a couple of hours when we heard Roy Smylie aboard *Deo Volente* calling us on the radio. He had heard us giving our TR to Portpatrick Radio. We immediately made contact and were surprised to hear that he was in Ardinamar Bay which was not far off, so we turned round and set course to join him.

Here we had two alternatives available to us, either go a long way round south of the island of Luing, or take a short cut through the Gulf of Corryvreckin, a place with a notorious whirlpool dreaded by many mariners. We chose the latter course and passed through the whirlpool without any problems, but it was quite a sight to see the water whirling around, rather like a washbasin emptying, but on a much larger scale. Unfortunately Anne had left the porthole over the berth in our cabin open, so that the water which was sloshing about on our side deck came through. Her side of the berth was damp for the remainder of the holiday. We then made for Ardinamar and dropped our anchor just outside the pool where Roy was anchored and which was guarded by a rocky entrance. Shortly afterwards we were guided into the pool by Miss McLoughlin who was well known for her assistance and hospitality to yachtsmen. We almost scraped on the rocks, but Miss McLoughlin had a pretty lusty voice and we were able to hear her directions to make the necessary course alterations so we entered unscathed. Later we visited her home and made our entry in her visitors book.

The next morning we had to say farewell and get on our way on the next leg, our destination being the port of Mallaig, We left after lunch, returned through the Gulf of Corryvreckin and at eight o'clock in the evening passed Ardnamurchan Point, the most westerly part of the British Isles, which entitled us to wear a sprig of heather at our masthead. We made Mallaig soon after ten o'clock the same night and secured to a fishing boat in the harbour. It was chock-a-block with fishing vessels of all sizes and types.

The next morning, Tuesday, we set course for Stornoway, our next port of call. This passage only took ten hours and was problem free. The weather was kind, there was no wind for most of the way, although at times it was a Force Four from the west. We heard a PAN message from Stornoway Coastguards that a boat was missing off Lewis. When we arrived in Stornoway harbour we secured to the quay. The next day, Wednesday, was spent in looking round Stornoway, and hearing tales about the ill-fated attempt Lord Leverhulme had made to industrialize the island. We also walked round the grounds of his former mansion which is now a public park, and I think the house is used for local government offices. Some of the fishermen told us the government was giving grants to anyone who was prepared to invest in a fishing boat. I was very tempted I had had enough of manufacturing for the building industry, but luckily the temptation was overcome. While we were there, we took the opportunity of scrubbing *Ebb Tide's* bottom when the tide went out. We made a short trip to make a final check to our compass before setting out on what was going to be our longest open sea passage so far.

We set course early morning on Friday, August 14th, bound for Torshavn, which is almost due north of Stornoway. We were able to check our position from time to time, using the Consol radio beacons in Northern Ireland, Iceland and Scotland. After a passage of twenty three hours, our first landfall was made at 5.20 am when Akraberg light was abeam, some six miles off. We then continued on our way north until we reached Torshavn at 10 am and secured in the harbour to await the usual visits by Customs and Immigration.

To our great surprise our duty frees were sealed in the stores locker. It was the first time we had experienced this, having only been 'foreign' in France and Holland before. When we had visited Esbjerg the previous year the Customs had not even bothered to ask the usual questions, but that could have been because we were setting off as soon as we had cleared. Later we learnt that the Faroe Islands are 'dry' and that anyone wanting to import alcoholic beverages from Denmark can only do so after they have produced a certificate from the taxman to certify that the applicant has paid his/her income tax. However, the Customs officer visited us each day we were at Torshavn to ask if we wanted to bring out any more from our sealed locker.

One day we decided to go ashore for an evening meal and repaired to a nearby restaurant. We were presented with a menu, written in Faroese. The waitress could not understand English so could not help us in our choice. In order to pass the time while we tried to sort out what to order, we thought that we had asked for four beers. We waited and waited, until finally four plates of lamb cutlets garnished with prunes were placed before us. We did not realize then that beer could not be bought in public!

After we had a good look round the town and surrounding district we met a Faroese woman who could speak good English. She was a great help and took us home where she entertained us remarkably well. She told us about the annual whaling custom when the whales are driven on to the beach by men in boats and then slaughtered. There is a 'whaling song' to accompany this which has an extremely powerful beat and stomp. She later confirmed that most women in her age group could speak English since Britain had occupied the islands during the war, but very few would admit to their husbands that they had 'fraternized.' We were surprised to see so many of the roofs of the houses covered with turf. This we were told was to act as an insulator against the cold in winter. Being so far north, the daylight hours were much longer than we had been used to, living as we did in latitude 53 degrees, so it was only dark for about a couple of hours.

We decided to have a look at some of the other islands and made a day trip to Langesand. This only took about five hours. On our arrival we had a look round the little harbour and then walked inland for a while before returning to Torshavn late the same evening. After this we went to Midvaag, a passage taking just over a couple of hours. We spent the night there and having had a good look around the harbour area, left the next morning, Wednesday, August 9th, for Sandsvaag. We arrived mid afternoon and looked around by simply going up the fjord and back to the entrance. We then made for Transvaag, where we arrived at half past ten the same evening. The scenery was glorious. In most cases the harbours lay in fjords so that the entrances were most impressive. There was no need to worry about navigation since all the fjords are 'steep to', giving a great depth of water close in to the sides.

While we were alongside at Transvaag a young couple with their children approached *Ebb Tide*. As they did so, Gillian said they were English. We laughed at her, but it turned out he was the local doctor who had been recruited from Edinburgh unseen, having been the only applicant for the post. The family seemed to be enjoying life there but were looking forward to returning to Scotland when their contract was completed.

The next day we left for Vaag, our final destination and also the closest port to Scotland. We left Transvaag just before 6 pm, cruised around the Fjord for a while, then set course and and 9.30 pm arrived at Vaag, where we secured to the quay for the night.

We left the Faroe Islands just after lunch on Friday, August 21st after clearing Customs and we set course for the Summer Isles in the north of Scotland. During the passage we were again able to check our position by Consol, a useful navigational aid in those days, no 'satnav' for yachts then!

When we were abeam of Rona we made a course alteration of ten degrees to head for Cape Wrath. Luckily I noticed that the oil temperature had risen above its normal level and when I checked the engine I found that one of the main oil pipe joints was leaking. I had to put two gallons of oil into the engine and repair the leak, but the whole operation only took a quarter of an hour.

We decided to make our landfall at Ullapool where we could clear Customs 'inward'. After making the necessary course alterations, we arrived just after 5 pm and secured to the quay. We then flew our 'Q' flag to indicate that we had 'come from foreign'. We waited and waited but nothing happened; the waterguard was out sailing in his dinghy, it was a Saturday! The next morning he paid us a visit and after perusing the makeshift 'bluebook', went ashore. He returned later to tell us that he could not give us our clearance inward since a Customs officer was necessary. I suggested that we should move on to Oban, but he said that the officer was on his way by car from Inverness! This we took as a bad omen. Soon after 5 pm the Customs officer came aboard and greeted us with the words, 'What's all this about your having fifty two gallons of spirits aboard?' We were absolutely staggered and when he showed us the piece of paper used as our 'bluebook', which had been taken ashore by the waterguard, it turned out that the officer at Ellesmere Port had written '3 l.g gin' and '2 l.g whisky'. The waterguard had read the entry incorrectly and thus thought that the total was the thirty-one and twenty-one gallons instead of three liquid and two liquid gallons!

We explained we wanted to bring in as much spirits as we were allowed and were then going to call at the Isle of Man, where we hoped to do the same and thus bring in the remains of our 'duty frees' duty free. He said, 'Empty out your locker,' which we did; he then put a couple of bottles back in, sealed the door and gave us our practique. After this was over the waterguard said, 'By jove sir, he has treated you far more favourably than I would have done.'

During the night Anne woke up and said, 'I'm sure there is someone in the wheelhouse.' I got up, and sure enough, she was correct. It turned out to be a drunken Scottish fisherman. I presumed he had heard about the Customs estimate of the quantity of spirits aboard and had come to see what he could find. Anyway he was no problem and left quietly enough, after which I locked the wheelhouse doors, a thing we had never done before when we were aboard.

We left Ullapool mid-morning on Monday August 24th and made for Loch Dunvegan. Before we had left Acton Bridge, Ron Pritchard's wife had extolled the beauty of Dunvegan Castle and said we ought to try to see it on our way home. We entered the loch just after a quarter past six in the evening and then stopped to fish (another abortive attempt!) We finally secured to the little quay there where we spent the evening and walked to the castle.

The next morning we left just after 6 am headed for Peel on the Isle of Man. As we made our way, the visibility worsened the further south we went. At just after two o'clock in the morning the steering failed so I called Portpatrick Radio to advise them of our problem. It was, however, soon solved and we were under way again within a quarter of an hour. When I made a further call to Portpatrick to tell them that all was well, they asked us to keep a lookout for a boat which had been reported missing. We immediately altered course to head in the direction in which the boat had last been seen and advised that we would keep in touch with the Portpatrick lifeboat by radio. A couple of hours later Portpatrick Radio sent out a PAN message advising that a blue and white pleasure boat with two occupants had been fishing off Corsewell Point in Lock Ryan but had failed to return to Stranraer the previous evening as expected. We made contact by radio with the lifeboat and then kept in touch. By now the visibility had dropped to less than ten yards, so when a 'blip' appeared on our radar we immediately made towards it. When we arrived, we discovered that it was a fishing boat going about its lawful business. We informed the lifeboat to this effect and told them that we were going to commence a square search of the area.

After searching for about three hours we received a message from the lifeboat that they were going into Stranraer. We did the same, navigating the whole way by radar since by that time we could hardly see our bow. When we were finally in the harbour we secured to the lifeboat and Anne cooked a breakfast for us all. The lifeboat crew did not have any water or food on board so had not been able to make a drink of any kind during the whole time they had been out. Whilst we were breakfasting we could see the Stranraer/Larne ferry gliding past, not many yards away in the fog. After breakfast the lifeboat cox said they were going to continue the search. We accompanied them, searching in the area they had allocated to us in Loch Ryan. After a half hour or so the lifeboat called us on the radio to advise that they had picked up the lost dinghy. We then continued our interrupted cruise. When we were abeam of Portpatrick we altered course for Peel. At half past two we received a radio message from Portpatrick Radio thanking us for our efforts and assistance with the search. As we made our way south along the west coast of the Isle of Man, the steering packed up once again. The repair took about half an hour so we did not reach Peel until a quarter to six in the evening.

We spent the next afternoon taking a few RNXS members for a fishing trip off Jurby Head but the combined efforts were not very successful so we returned to Peel, dropped off the passengers and then decided to pay a visit to Dun Laoghaire in order to return a few Beamish stout bottles which had been acquired on a previous visit and had been rattling about in our bilges for over a year. We set course and arrived in Dun Laoghaire coal harbour just after five o'clock the following morning. When the pub opened we took the bottles back, to find that they had stopped selling Beamishes, so we reluctantly threw the bottles into a waste bin.

We then thought we would have a look at Howth since we still had a short time of our holiday left. We left the coal harbour late afternoon and arrived just before seven o'clock when we secured to a MFV and looked around. It appeared to be a pleasant enough spot and we decided to pay a return visit some time in the future. After two hours we left for Peel and arrived just after half past seven the next morning. The following morning, Sunday, we went to the cathedral for the 8 am Eucharist before setting off for Port St Mary at midday. Little did I realize then that before twelve years had passed I would not only be living on the Isle of Man, but I would also be a Reader in the Church of England and secretary of the Readers' Board in the Diocese of Sodor and Man.

We left Port St Mary after lunch the next day, bound for Eastham, and arrived there just before midnight. The Weaver locks and bridges being closed until morning, we had to spend the night in the sluices alongside the locks. The next morning we set off for Acton Bridge where we arrived just after ten o'clock and secured in our usual spot. Our 1970 summer cruise had put another 1,564 miles under our keel.

In September I dismantled the main engine and found that one of the valves had been blowing. The engine was an early version of a General Motors type 71 and the valve seats were ground at a different angle from the later models. I decided to replace all the valves and seats with the latest type and at the same time fit new valve guides. Having done all this, I heard about the ex-Shell engine and purchased it. I took off its cylinder head, which was a four valve version, and fitted it to our existing engine with the intention of replacing the whole engine during the coming winter. This occupied me for the whole of September and, since I wanted to make a check of our fuel consumption, we made a weekend visit to Peel, Isle of Man, during which the fuel consumption showed a great improvement on that obtained previously.

Over the last weekend of October we made another trip, this time taking some friends and ten members of the RNXS to the north Wales coast, where off Rhyl we tried our hands at trawling again. The result was the same as usual – nothing. We returned to the Mersey and dropped off some of our passengers at the Woodside landing stage and then made arrangements to spend the night in Alfred Dock. The next day we disembarked our remaining passengers and made for Acton Bridge. On the return trip we overtook a tug in the Manchester Ship Canal and in doing so I caught our propeller on an underwater obstruction. We only made the lock into the River Weaver just before it closed for the night and, by the time we had locked through, all the river bridges were closed. We moved up river and moored at Rocksavage Bridge until it opened the following morning. The last part of this short foray was completed soon after nine o'clock and we returned to home and work. We had covered a total of 2,400 miles for this season.

1971 Pavillon d'Or – being chased up the Rhine

1971 Pavillon d'Or – sailing from the Hook to Ramsgate

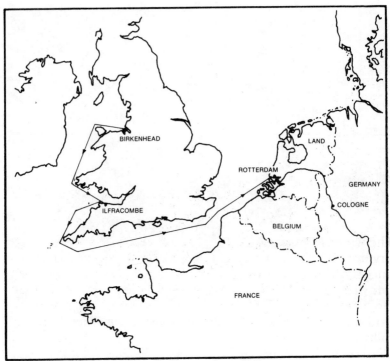

1971 – Pavillon d'Or – Cologne

14

Third Pavillon d'Or – Cologne, Germany

The winter refit, amongst other things, included a visit to the dry dock at Northwich to change the propeller, and so it was once again almost the end of May before we were able to make our first cruise. We decided to make a return visit to Glasson Dock on the River Lune. We left Acton Bridge after work on Friday, May 14th, and arrived at Glasson just after 2 am the following morning. This was the second time we had visited Glasson by sea. When our sons were at Rossall School we had made many visits there by road. It was a delightful place in those days but in 1971 it was busy with coastal shipping.

The next day we left after lunch and, apart from a somewhat rough trip, made our way without any difficulty to Morpeth Dock in the Birkenhead Dock system. We decided to make our summer mooring here in preference to Acton Bridge since it was becoming more and more difficult to get out from Acton at weekends, rather in the same way that it had been on the River Severn. As it turned out, Morpeth Dock became our permanent mooring until we left in 1973. We arrived at the Woodside landing stage in the River Mersey, just before 10 pm the same evening and moored alongside until it was time for the Alfred Lock, at the entrance to the Birkenhead Dock system to open. We left Woodside at half past one in the morning and were securely moored in our new berth an hour later.

For our next cruise Anne and I took *Ebb Tide* on our own to Brest for a spring cruise and left Birkenhead on May 21st, again a Friday. Apart from stopping to pick up a large hose

pipe we found floating about when we were off Bardsey
Island, and again just after we had passed Longships
lighthouse to repair a bearing in the engine, the passage was
completely uneventful. The weather was kind to us the whole
way and we arrived at Brest late on Sunday., May 23rd, where
we secured in our usual place. This was the first long passage
Anne and I had undertaken on our own. We did not know
then that we would end up in Solomon Islands just over
eighteen months later after a somewhat longer voyage and
with a larger crew.

We left Brest after a day's stay and headed back for Newlyn.
The passage took fourteen hours without any problems. We
had to make several course alterations to avoid shipping as we
crossed the channel, but that was all. We stayed in Newlyn for
three days and then set course for Howth in the Republic of
Ireland, which we had visited for the first time the year before.
Again the weather was kind, the sea calm, and we entered
Howth just after lunch on Saturday, May 29th, the passage
taking just under twenty-four hours. We secured to a fishing
boat and had a walk ashore. We were not very amused on our
return to find *Ebb Tide's* jackstaff had been broken off,
apparently by one of the many fishing boats in the harbour.
The Northern Ireland problems were building up about then
and the general attitude was far from friendly. We decided to
curtail our visit and left the next day for Port St Mary, Isle of
Man, our initial good impression of Howth having been
severely dented.

We spent half a day in Port St Mary, then returned to
Morpeth Dock on May 31st and were back in our berth in the
very early hours of June 1st.

We made another visit to Port St Mary for the weekend a
fortnight later and on our return moored *Ebb Tide* on the
RNXS berth behind the XSV *Loyal Governor,* permission having
been obtained from the officer in charge of the 'afloat' section.
We made another day trip out to the *Bar* light vessel carrying a
few RNXS members with us during which we tried fishing
once again, but the result was nil.

Since the officer in charge of the afloat section of the
Birkenhead RNXS unit was also a member of Blundellsands
Sailing Club, he asked us to act as the stake boat for their
regatta, which was to be held over the following weekend. We

took some of the unit members with us on this trip and collected the Blundellsands officers and officials from the Princes Pier at Liverpool before going to the regatta area at the end of the Queen's Channel. When the regatta was over we returned back to our berth in the Birkenhead Docks.

We began our attempt for the Pavillon d'Or on Friday July 23rd, the crew being Anne and myself, Gillian our youngest daughter, Neil our middle son, with Anne, his current girlfriend, and Guy, our youngest son, The finishing point was Cologne on the River Rhine, and the date August 2nd, giving us eleven days to complete the passage. We left Morpeth Dock at 8 pm and set course down the Mersey with the intention of making a non-stop passage to IJmuiden in Holland. *Loyal Governor,* the RNXS vessel, was also out that weekend. When we were off the South Stack lighthouse we received a radio message from her to say that she had broken down twelve miles south of the South Stack lighthouse. We immediately replied that we would go to her assistance and altered course to do so. We saw her on our radar and half an hour later received another message to say that she was under way again. However, we intercepted her and offered our help, but the offer was declined, and she headed back to Birkenhead under her own power. We resumed our original course for Longships lighthouse, our turning point for going up the English Channel.

The wind was more or less on our starboard bow which made the motion somewhat uncomfortable. We had to reduce our speed so that Anne could prepare lunch in a measure of comfort. After the inner man had been satisfied, we increased our speed, but a couple of hours later had to reduce again in order to make the passage more comfortable. Late that night the weather forecast was pretty grim and, since this was young Anne's first passage in a small boat, I decided to make for Ilfracombe. We arrived in the early hours of the Sunday and anchored in the outer harbour to wait for the tide to rise before we could enter the inner harbour to go alongside. As soon as there was sufficient water we weighed anchor and entered the inner harbour and saw that *Ebb Tide's* usual berth was occupied by a coaster. We moored to her and then ballasted *Ebb Tide* so that she would lean against the coaster's hull as the tide went out.

As we entered the harbour we saw *Lelahne,* Harry Nunn's boat, moored in the middle. He was able to take the ground because *Lelahne* was fitted with 'legs' (these are made from heavy timber and bolted to the sides of a boat to hold it upright when it takes the ground). As soon as *Ebb Tide* was secure we decided to pay her a visit for our mid morning pre-prandial. Anne, Gillian and I went over in our dinghy and took gin with Harry and his wife. One of the unfortunate side effects of taking gin in the middle of the morning is that 'one' tends to become three or four and the time passes equally fast. I looked out at *Ebb Tide* as the tide was going out to see if she had been moored correctly and realized that she had been ballasted to lie too far off the upright position. I quickly left *Lelahne* and made my way to *Ebb Tide*. As I have said earlier, the tide in Ilfracombe goes out rather as if a plug has been pulled out. I was too late! By the time I boarded she had taken the ground very firmly and was leaning in against the coaster at far too acute an angle. Shortly afterwards, as the tide went out further, the wheelhouse roof was jammed hard up against the side of the coaster and one of the navigation light boxes was damaged in the process. I know that it served me right, but we had not seen Harry since we had left the River Severn in 1967, so we had a lot to talk about.

The weather having improved during the day, we decided to set off late that night as soon as there was sufficient water in the harbour for *Ebb Tide* to float. I decided that any thoughts of visiting Newlyn would have to be cancelled, since we did not have a lot of time at our disposal, and that we would make direct for IJmuiden in Holland as originally intended, a passage of just over five hundred miles.

The passage took fifty-seven hours, during which we encountered varying weather conditions so that we had to reduce our speed at times for Anne to cook our meals. We passed one of the RNXS inshore minesweepers, *XSV Portisham* and tried unsuccessfully to make radio contact. In spite of keeping a radio watch we missed any announcement about distress working, otherwise we would not have transmitted. Niton Radio pointed out the error of our ways and told us that 'distress working' was in progress, so we should not be transmitting on 2182 khz.

On arrival in Holland we cleared Customs and Immigration inward, but before doing so we met a slight problem. When I presented our passports to the immigration officer he pointed out that Gillian's had expired! We had a few moments of consternation, but the officer was extremely helpful and gave Gillian a temporary entry certificate for the period we expected to be on the continent. We then set off up the Nordzee Canal to Amsterdam and secured in the yacht basin near the Amsterdam railway station, so that Neil and young Anne could have a quick look around. On their return we left for Princess Beatrix Lock and arrived just after half past ten the same night, so we had to moor up there for the night. As soon as the lock began operating the next morning, we set off after breakfast for Emmerich on the River Rhine, our next port of call. We had to negotiate a couple of locks and since our course took us through Arnhem of 'A bridge too far' fame, we secured to a barge there for a short while. While we were alongside we picked up a good helping of fresh black tar from its side. We arrived at Emmerich at half past eight in the evening and secured to the police pontoon where we cleared inwards to Germany.

From the pilot books I had calculated that it would take us a couple of days to get up the Rhine as far as Cologne, but the previous winter had been so dry that the Rhine was almost the lowest it had been since depths were recorded. Instead of having to stem a current of seven or eight knots, it was only four or five in places, and generally considerably less. This made our progress a lot quicker which gave us some time in hand. We decided to overnight in the yacht mooring at the Dusseldorf Yacht Club so that the younger crew members could have a look round. We moored alongside a German motor cruiser. Later we heard voices from it raised in a vociferous argument. We made friends and Anne, who had spent some time in Germany immediately before the war, was able to make conversation. We were amused when the wife told us vehemently that 'humour' was absolutely necessary in life. I must say that we both agreed with her then and still do now.

The passage to Cologne was only a six hour one, so we left early on Sunday, August 1st, and arrived at the finishing point just after lunch. We were allotted a mooring spot on the long pontoon in the harbour there and to which a large number of other participants were already moored. Many of Pavillon d'Or entrants went only for the pleasure of joining in, rather than making any real effort to win awards, so they arrived well before the official finishing time. I handed in our log book for assessment and awaited the results. We had not tried to win this time, but were hopeful of winning the trophy for the longest sea passage, the best kept log and the closest speed to that declared on entry. Our passage had only been nine hundred and eighty four miles, a little different from the total achieved for the Pavillon d'Or in 1969.

We had to wait until the official finishing time had passed before the results were announced. We were disappointed that after our efforts we had not been declared the winner of the longest non-stop sea passage. I decided that this time, unlike the 1968 Pavillon, I would lodge a protest since I was certain that none of the other entrants had covered a greater non-stop distance at sea. My protest was duly lodged and investigated, with the result that we were declared the winners of this prize. The committee had not understood our log book in spite of awarding us the prize for the best kept log, or else had assumed that we had stopped somewhere at night! We also won the prize for keeping our speed closest to that I had declared on the entry form. We were happy enough with what had been achieved. Many of the other contestants expressed their disappointment that we had not been the winners of the Pavillon d'Or itself. They could not understand why I had not tried this time, but I had remembered words of wisdom imparted by a poultry breeder in East Haddon, the village in Northampton where we lived in 1945. He had won the prize for the best cockerel at the international poultry show held in London and had said to me, 'It is difficult enough to get to the top, but it is much more difficult to keep there.' In retrospect, had we realized that this would be the last Pavillon d'Or to be held, we might have made the effort.

We had a wonderful time in Cologne, with outings arranged to different places each day. In Bonn we went to another wonderful country house where I was able to take photographs in spite of a ban on cameras, and to a lunch party during which we were entertained by a German band. At this last outing I felt that I could really let myself go and danced with great abandon with everyone I could. The wine flowed without ceasing and that no doubt added to my enjoyment.

We were all impressed by Cologne Cathedral and amazed that it did not appear to have suffered any great damage during the war in spite of buildings all around being flattened. We also saw a most moving memorial in the remains of a bombed church.

The last day of the event a parade of all the competitors took place in front of the mayor. We all had to have pilots on board since the Rhine authorities were pretty strict on this, which is hardly surprising with all the commercial traffic on the Rhine. One of the English entrants on his way to Cologne had stood on his rights and assumed that the enormous barge following would give way when it overtook him. He was most indignant when the barge hit his boat and dented his stern! There was almost an international incident over this, but all was eventually smoothed out.

The parade included demonstrations by fire fighting boats and we all had to run the gauntlet of the fire hoses. After it was over, we returned to the dock where the event had been held, dropped off our pilot, and then made our way downstream to Dusseldorf where we spent the night. The river was by now so low that I had difficulty in making the entrance to the yacht club mooring and hit bottom in the process. The following day, Monday, August 9th, we went to Dordrecht, a passage taking over thirteen hours. We arrived in the late evening and secured in the yacht harbour entrance to spend the night there.

It was at Cologne that our youngest daughter, Gillian, met her husband, Hanns, who was then crewing on the motor yacht which had been moored close to us. It was owned by a Roman Catholic priest who used it to take young men to give them some experience. As can be read later, we took Ebb Tide to Amsterdam in 1973 so that she could be married from our 'home'.

We left Dordrecht the next morning and made for Rotterdam, a passage taking a couple of hours. On arrival we filled our fuel tanks and then proceeded to the yacht harbour where we found a berth alongside another Cruising Association yacht. Here we were plied with 'genever', the Dutch gin which we drank neat. I had previously tried English gin neat, but could not stomach it and had not tried the Dutch variety in this way before. Genever is, however, very different and very enjoyable. The weather forecast was not at all favourable and we decided to stop over in Rotterdam until a better one was given. However, in the shelter of the yacht harbour under an encouraging sky, and with liberal draughts of genever adding further encouragement, we decided we would set off for Ramsgate without further delay.

We left at ten o'clock that night, made our way to the Hook of Holland, where we cleared Customs and then set off for Ramsgate. It was completely still with practically no wind or sea running. When we arrived at the end of the long mole at the entrance to the Hook, it was a very different story; the forecast was not far wrong. Shortly after half past one in the morning we had to reduce our speed in order to ease *Ebb Tide's* motion. The wind had now well and truly risen and was on our starboard bow with a sea to accompany it. At one stage it was a Force Seven and we actually overtook a small coaster which was also making heavy weather of the passage. The launch we carried on our aft deck was securely clamped down with rigging screws, but it came adrift and was bouncing about on the after deck, so I went out to re-secure it. This was the first and only time I have been close to going overboard. Providentially I had fitted fairly high rails with stanchions securely bolted to the deck. I was thrown against them with some considerable force, but sustained no injury. If I had gone overboard I doubt if Anne would have been aware of the fact until later. There is a moral here: don't drink Dutch, or any other gin, before sailing.

It took us nineteen and a half hours to reach Ramsgate, and we were glad when eventually we were in the shelter of the harbour wall. Clearing Customs was no problem. We spent three days there during which I did some work which had been posted to me from the factory. When this was completed we set off for Newlyn early on August 16th. On our way we called in at Plymouth to visit the RNXS headquarters and were able to secure in the naval harbour to the RFA *Regent* (Neil was in the RFA at that time), and later to the RNXS *MFV 1257* in which I had crewed for a NATO exercise some years earlier (that is another story). After making our number at the RNXS HQ we set off again for Newlyn where we arrived late evening. At least I was not arrested as I had been at Pembroke Dock on our winter cruise in 1963.

The remaining passage from Newlyn to Birkenhead was accomplished without any problems and we were back on our berth in Morpeth Dock at half past nine in the morning of August 18th, having covered 1,865 miles for the summer cruise.

Moving *Ebb Tide* to Birkenhead certainly gave us more flexibility for getting out to sea. A fortnight after we returned from the Pavillon d'Or we made a visit to Tal-y-Foel in the Menai Straits. On this occasion we had our first experience of being blown ashore. We anchored in the pool at Tal-y-Foel after a fairly rough passage from Birkenhead, the wind having been Force Six to Seven. In the very early hours of the following morning I discovered that our anchor was dragging. The wind was SW 7 at the time so I decided to weigh and re-anchor, but in doing so *Ebb Tide* was caught by the incoming tide and we ended up on a shingle bank at the north of the pool. Via Anglesey radio I telephoned Roy Smylie, who lived a few hundred yards away, and asked him if he could assist with laying a kedge anchor so that we could pull ourselves off when the tide had eased. He promptly came to the rescue, but the wind was far too strong for him to launch his dinghy, so we had to wait until the tide turned at high water and were then able to get off under our own power and re-anchor. We returned to Morpeth Dock in Birkenhead the following morning. During this trip we tried fishing with our small beam trawl, but as usual were unsuccessful. By the evening we were back in Morpeth Dock and moored on the RNXS berth behind XSV *Puttenham*. the official vessel of the unit there, *Loyal Governor* having been returned to Plymouth.

We made only two more weekend trips, one in September to Hilbre Island at the mouth of the River Dee and the other in December to the *Bar* light vessel. We thoroughly enjoyed our visit to Hilbre and asked ourselves why we had not been there before instead of always making comparatively long passages for weekend trips. Hilbre is an absolutely delightful place and, apart from a bird warden, is uninhabited.

So ended our cruising for 1971, during which we had added another 2,265 miles to our total.

15

1972

Last Visit to St Martin

During the winter in Morpeth Dock we were able to undertake a considerable amount of refitting and modifications. The lower part of the front of the wheelhouse was completely rebuilt so that it sloped outwards to balance the upper part carrying the windows, which we had rebuilt previously, and this considerably improved her appearance. The object of sloping the windows forward was to reduce reflection and it certainly worked well. Most of the wheelhouse furniture was also completely rebuilt to make it more suitable for a long voyage. All this meant that we were not ready to make any cruises before June 1st, the latest we had ever been.

Our first 'shakedown cruise' was to Brest with Anne and I on our own as crew. We left Birkenhead on the first locking at 9.30 am and had a pleasant run to Newlyn, our first port of call. The only problem encountered was that the engine revolution counter decided to cease working, but it only took me twenty minutes to make the necessary repairs and we did not have to stop during the process.

The weather was reasonable and, although all the shipping forecasts were giving gale warnings, we did not meet anything stronger than a Force Five which, being on our starboard bow, made the passage somewhat bumpy. We arrived in Newlyn after a passage lasting thirty two hours, averaging a speed of 8.75 knots. We spent a full day there and then left for Brest at 5 am on June 4th. We had a slight problem after we had slipped our mooring ropes, due to a fishing net fouling our rudder, but this did not cause much of a delay. After a comfortable passage we arrived in Brest just before 8 pm the same evening; the gales decided not to pay us a visit as had been forecast. We spent a day there to stock up with 'vital' stores and bid farewell to M. Fournier, the ship chandler, before we left in the early hours of the following morning, June 6th, bound for Port St Mary, Isle of Man.

At this time I had agreed to sell our business, but the formalities had not been completed, nor were they until July 14th, Bastille Day. As can be read in the next chapter, Anne and I had offered ourselves to several Church of England related organizations so that we knew we would have to undertake a long cruise the next year, but had no idea to where it would be. We had deliberately made longer and longer cruises on our own in order to obtain as much experience as possible. This was the reasoning behind choosing the passage from Brest direct to the Isle of Man. It took forty two hours and was the longest non-stop trip Anne and I had made by ourselves, longer that that made from Dun Laoghaire a few years earlier, but this time the automatic pilot worked perfectly.

On this passage the weather was not too bad, the wind being on our nose the whole way, but it did not rise to more than a Force Five. Several times we had to reduce our speed slightly for a few hours. It always amazed us that by reducing the engine speed by even a hundred revolutions a minute, life on board was made considerably more comfortable.

We spent a couple of days in Port St Mary and then headed back to our base in Morpeth Dock. The whole voyage had added eight hundred and fifty miles to our total. Later we made a couple of trips out to the *Bar* light vessel, one in June and another in the early part of July. In between these two trips the final formalities for the sale of our business were completed and I was told by the new owner to go off on holiday.

Guy, our youngest son, had gone to America to work for the new owner of our business during the school holiday. It was an excellent experience for him and also quite profitable. So on July 29th Anne and I set off on our own for a nostalgic last visit to the Ile de Ré, with Newlyn being our first scheduled port of call. We locked out of Alfred Lock just after 10 am and had a wonderful passage, the sea being almost flat calm most of the way. However, the barometer had dropped five millibars by the time we had arrived, some thirty two hours later, but this did not affect the excellent weather. We spent the next day in harbour checking over equipment and generally being idle. We had taken our duty free stores on board in Birkenhead so there was no need to call in at Brest for this purpose. We therefore headed for Le Guilvenic, little realizing that this busy fishing port was going to play an important part in our lives the following year. This passage took just over seventeen and a half hours and conditions were almost perfect, with the Bay of Biscay on its best behaviour.

We set off for the Ile de Ré and planned to make Le Palais, on Belle Ile, our next port of call, but on arrival saw that the harbour was chock-a-block. As it was always a difficult place in which to moor at the best of times, we headed for La Trinité instead. Before we had left England we had visited Michael Rylands, our Rural Dean who was then Rector of Malpas, where we now live. He told us that he and his family were going to France for their summer holiday and would be in the area of La Trinité round about the beginning of August. Since it was now August 3rd we decided to call in on the off chance of meeting them. We eventually found a space to moor on one of the pontoons which filled this popular yachting harbour, when, to our great surprise and delight, we were met by Michael and his family who had also looked in on the off chance of meeting us.

It was well past the evening pre-prandial time so we invited them to join us and we had a very pleasant hour or so together. We offered to take them out for a short cruise the next day, which was accepted with alacrity. They joined ship the next morning and, after having a quick look at Souris on the way, we went on to the little island of Houat. There is a delightful little bay there in which we anchored so that a swimming party could be held. This was followed by a picnic lunch before our return to La Trinité. The Rylands invited us to join them for an evening meal in one of the little cafés which abound round the harbour. That meal firmly sticks in our memories since we had 'chicken and pommes frites,' the frites were the greasiest we had ever had, even worse than those in Fleetwood! (I cannot understand why England is renowned for 'chips with everything' since they figure prominently on all French café

172

menus and in America of course they are referred to as 'French fries').

The next morning we left for the last stage of our cruise to St Martin and arrived there after a thirteen and a half hour passage, at just past 1 am. We had to wait for the basin gate to open, so we moored to a fishing boat until we were able to enter. We spent nearly a week there and were somewhat disappointed with the changes brought to this small island by tourism. The ferry to La Pallice, on the mainland, which during our earlier visits had stopped at 9 pm, now ran twenty-four hours a day. The noise of visitors and discotheques was unbelievable to us, but then we had not been there for three years, since when it had been 'discovered'. It was a great disappointment since we had spent so many happy holidays with our family there in the past. We were told that during the 'season' over a quarter of a million people visited this small island.

We left early in the morning of August 12th, having decided to visit some other places on the Atlantic coast of France. We were in no hurry. I had been told to take as long as I wanted for the holiday, so there was no pressure to return. In fact, rather the opposite since I was glad to have disposed of a business in which I had previously thought I would have to work until unable to do so. I had no plans for retirement, although it was something I occasionally thought about. For the self-employed in those days, things like pension schemes which today form an important part of being self-employed were one of the last things one thought about. There were always far more pressing matters to be dealt with, finance usually being the most important.

With time to spare, we decided to have another look in the Morbihan, the great inland sea on the Atlantic coast. Pornic is one of the yachting centres there, so we decided to pay a visit. The passage from St Martin was only a short one of nine and a half hours, so just after 4.30 pm we secured to a pontoon in the marina.

We were walking round when Anne suddenly spotted a yacht named *Odd Times II*. She said, 'That can only be Peter Rose, let's go and have a look.' We did, and sure enough it was Peter, with Monique, his French wife, together with her sister and a priest. During the course of our conversation he told us

173

that the original *Odd Times* had been sunk off the coast of Greenland when he had once again been sailing single handed; that he had married; had given up being a schoolmaster, and was in the process of being ordained as a curate in the Church of England. It was a completely unexpected reunion and we had a delightful time chatting about life in general. Peter was obviously intrigued about our plans for the future, but they had not become firm at that time. We spent the next day in Pornic and then headed back home with Le Guilvenic our next port of call. It was only a twelve hour passage, and since we had left at a reasonable hour that morning, it was past 7 pm before we were secure in the harbour. We thoroughly enjoyed loitering on this holiday. It was really the first time we had been able to do so. Earlier holidays always had deadlines of some sort or another or, as has already been said, major breakdowns to cope with. Nevertheless we only stayed in Le Guilvenic for a few hours then left for Brest in the early hours of the next morning and arrived just after morning coffee time.

We thought it was time to head back for England and have a look in at some of the ports we had visited in the past. We left Brest after lunch the next day. During the evening we heard a distress message relayed by Land's End Radio that a yacht was in trouble off the Lizard. We increased our speed to the maximum but about two and a half hours later heard that the Lizard lifeboat had gone alongside, so we resumed our normal cruising speed. We arrived in Newlyn just after 4 am the following morning and were able to secure to a fishing boat, which made life easier since we did not have to stay awake to tend our ropes as the tide went up and down.

We left late the following night bound for Fishguard. For some reason or other I chickened out of taking the shorter inshore passage round Land's End and went round the Longships Lighthouse. I cannot think why I was chicken, unless I was wanting to extend our cruise by a few miles. We had made the inshore passage many times and in all sorts of weather. As navigator I had taken one of the RNXS inshore minesweepers through, much to the consternation of the skipper who kept his eyes glued to the echo sounder for the whole time.

We still enjoyed almost perfect weather. The wind never

rose above Force Two and the sea was flat calm most of the time. A small snag arose when the engine oil pressure suddenly went low. I had fitted warning lights with an audible warning system to monitor all the important engine temperatures and pressures and it was this which gave the warning. A quick investigation showed that there was a leak at the main oil filter, but this was soon dealt with and the lost oil replaced. We were in Fishguard main harbour by early evening, where we secured to a buoy, there being no room in the old harbour. After spending a day there we left late the next evening bound for Tal-y-Foel in the Menai Straits. The time of leaving had been calculated so that we would arrive off the Caernarvon bar when the tide was right for crossing it. We duly arrived just after 6 am the following morning and were anchored in Tal-y-Foel pool before breakfast.

After spending the weekend there, we set off up through the Menai Straits bound for Birkenhead and arrived in time for the afternoon locking so that, just after lunch, we were back on our mooring in Morpeth Dock. Anne and I had covered one thousand two hundred and ninety miles on our 'farewell cruise' to places we had always enjoyed, plus of course visiting two new harbours and the pleasure of meeting old friends.

The following weekend we made another trip to Tal-y-Foel pool in the Menai Straits where I had arranged a 'meet' of the north west section of the Cruising Association. We left Morpeth Dock in the early hours and on arrival in the Straits secured to a buoy at Menai Bridge to wait for the tide to turn so that we did not have to stem a four knot current as we passed through the tricky part. An hour later.we continued and arrived at Tal-y-Foel in time for morning coffee. We had arranged for the 'meet' to be held in Aber Menai pool, just round the corner from the southern entrance to the Menai Straits so the next morning we moved down and spent the night there. It was an excellent meet and we were presented quite unexpectedly with two engraved pewter goblets as a farewell gift from the north west members. We left on the Monday morning together with several buckets of mussels we had collected. The tides being what they are, we had to time our departure to pass through the narrow parts of the Straits with the tidal stream behind us. This, of course, did not coincide with the time we had to leave the Straits in order to arrive in the Mersey when the locks would be working. So on our arrival at Bangor Pool, we secured to one of the barges for three hours before finally leaving for home.

Our penultimate trip of the season was the first weekend in September when we visited Hilbre Island in the River Dee estuary. Following our visit during September the previous year we had so enjoyed this delightful spot so close to home that we decided to make more visits, but it was not to be. Our circumstances changed so rapidly during the following year that there was no time for very many weekend trips. We had to pull out all our stops preparing for the trip of our life, something which had not been anticipated.

Our last trip was to try our hands at fishing again. This time we went as far as the Horse buoy off the north Welsh coast where we drifted with the tide for a couple of hours, but no fish were tempted by our trawl. We set off for Morpeth and as we did so heard another Mersey fishing boat on our radio telephone. We made contact and the skipper offered to lead us through the Rock Channel. For economic reasons all the buoys had been withdrawn the previous year and the passage is continually changing. We arrived back on our mooring during the evening having had a pleasant if unprofitable day out.

During the 1972 season we had added another 2,516 miles to our travels, mostly with just Anne and myself as crew.

During the winter we took out the main engine, stripped it down and had the crankshaft 'crack tested'. I did not want to have another broken crankshaft on the voyage we would be making the following year.

16

How we came to go to Solomon Islands

Anne and I had a dream that some day we would be able to take six months sabbatical and sail *Ebb Tide* across the Atlantic, up the river/canal system in the States, to the Great Lakes, then down the St Lawrence and home again across the North Atlantic. This was the reason we had fitted the large capacity fuel tanks and experimented so much with engines and propellers in order to determine whether or not this would be possible. Like many dreams this one was fulfilled, but in a completely different way from that anticipated.

Quite out of the blue in mid June, 1972, an opportunity to sell our business arose, and after a little hesitation, we agreed. This made it possible to fulfil another ambition, which was to work for the church, some ten years earlier than we had planned. We were then in our middle fifties. We had both been keen church workers for many years. Anne was highly involved with the Mothers' Union and was in fact the deanery enrolling member for the Malpas Rural Deanery in the Diocese of Chester. For my part I had been a member of the Tarporley Parochial Church Council for many years (at the time we left in 1973 I was lay chairman). I was also treasurer of the Malpas Rural Deanery, a member of the Chester Diocesan Board of Finance and also of the Finance and General Purposes Committee. I was also chairman of a committee to supervise the Suffragan Bishops' houses.

How and why we came to be sailing to Solomon Islands is quite a story and an essential part of this saga.

While negotiations were proceeding for the sale of our business, I enquired of a bishop friend if there would be any opportunity for a middle aged couple with a boat to work for the Anglican Church anywhere in the world. His immediate response was 'Yes.' We could, for instance, work in the Bahamas, ferrying priests between the islands. It was on this basis that we went ahead with the sale of our business.

When the sale had been completed, and all the necessary agreements signed, I went back to the bishop and told him that we would be free in a year to go to the Bahamas. He made enquiries and came back with the answer that since we were not Bahamians, now that they had become independent, we would not be welcome. In fact the European bishop had been forced out. This was a serious blow. We had literally burnt our boats. We had not only sold our business but our house also went with it so we would be homeless in another eighteen months.

We sat down and wrote to three Church Organizations the bishop had told us could well be interested in our offer. Time went by without any positive results, and we were naturally getting somewhat concerned, so we decided to travel to London and see the organizations we had previously approached 'eyeball to eyeball'. One organization told us that it could not use us since its work was only in the field of publishing. The secretary of another one, closely connected with the sea, was very helpful and suggested that there might be an opening in Singapore, Kobe or Yokohama, but said that his organization could not make a definite commitment for a year ahead. He was, however, very helpful and telephoned the organization which had not responded to our offer, with the result that we went to its office. The lady whose job it was to interview us said she had received our letter, but had put it in the 'too hard' basket. She then went on to say there were only two places we could possibly go, one was Papua New Guinea and the other Melanesia. When Anne said, 'Where is Melanesia?' the answer was, 'Down Kennington Road.' It turned out that she was referring to the Melanesian Mission office which at that time was located there. Since the Papua New Guinea Mission office was at Eltham, and we had travelled to London by train, we decided to go down Kennington Road, it being only a short bus ride away.

We had never associated Melanesia with Solomon Islands, even when John Mullett, the Rector of St Saviour's Church in Birkenhead, where we worshipped when we spent the weekends in Morpeth Dock, had told us that was where we ought to go. We had checked the possibility of being able to make the voyage and, after many exhaustive trials, I was confident that we could complete the long passage of three thousand miles between the Galapagos Islands and the Marquesas and still arrive with sufficient fuel in our tanks for a further one thousand five hundred miles. My policy was to end every voyage with sufficient fuel to travel a further distance of at least fifty per cent of each leg. This was in case of any unforeseen problems, such as exceptionally heavy weather.

The Melanesian Mission office was telephoned and advised that we were coming and down to Kennington Road we went. As the door was opened the secretary almost grabbed my hands off and asked for my National Insurance card, or whatever was in force in those days. He hauled us into his office with the question, 'When can you start?' Apparently the engineer in Melanesia had left the previous week. It was, of course, almost a year before we could sail, there being the small matter of a service contract to be honoured and the fact that Guy, our youngest son, who was to sail with us, was still at school with A-levels ahead of him.

We thus had nearly a year to complete the preparations for such a long voyage and it is no exaggeration to say that this time was fully occupied. But the careful planning which went into the voyage paid off in no uncertain terms and made the whole voyage a relatively simple one; although the very small matter of fitting a little key into a pulley on the engine would have prevented a major breakdown the very early stages of the actual voyage.

Every time the motor of the deep freeze, which ran off the 24 volt system, started, it gave such a kick to the system that the alternator driven by the engine felt it. This in turn caused the driving pulley to slip and the retaining bolt, which I had fitted to keep the pulley on the short driving shaft, tightened, so that eventually the pulley was driven hard up against the engine casing. I had not appreciated this when it happened on our voyage to Amsterdam, as can be read later. I then thought I had not tightened the pulley sufficiently and it had merely moved into the engine casing (it had a taper-lock fitting, one which has a bush tapered on the outside fitting into a similarly tapered hole in the pulley; the bush is forced into the pulley by means of bolts, so that it grips the shaft on to which the pulley goes). In actual fact the prime cause of this failure was that the manufacturer of the deep freeze compressor unit had given me the incorrect starting current for the 24 volt motor. It was not the 45 amperes I had been told; the needle of the ammeter went hard over, past the 150 mark (which is as high as the ammeter went) every time the deep freeze motor started.

During our negotiations with the Melanesian Mission office in London, we had not been told that the Diocese of Melanesia was well advanced in its plans to become a separate Province in the Anglican Communion. We both went through a fairly intensive vetting process by a large and formidable committee of about twenty members before we were formally accepted. We later learnt that Bishop John Chisholm, the Bishop of Melanesia, who was in England to attend the meeting of the Anglican Consultative Council in Dublin, would like to meet us personally. On our way to Amsterdam for Gillian's wedding we stopped off in Ramsgate and took a train to London to meet him at a garden party held at the Melanesian Mission. He suggested that after we had arrived in Melanesia, we might act as the delivery crew for the *Fauabu Twomey III,* a ferro-cement vessel being built in Australia to replace an earlier one which had gone the way of most small ships in that part of the world. As can be read later *Fauabu Twomey III* met the same fate as its predecessors.

17

1973

Before the Voyage

Since the Diocese of Chester wanted to give us a formal send off with a Eucharist celebrated on board *Ebb Tide,* it took some time to make the necessary arrangements. Eventually our departure date was fixed for September 8th, 1973, and our destination was Honiara, the capital of the Solomon Islands, so we now knew when and where we were going. There was obviously a considerable amount of work to be undertaken before the following September, but there was another more pressing matter to be attended to first – the wedding of our youngest daughter Gillian to Hanns, the Dutchman she had met during the 1971 Pavillon d'Or in Cologne. She was then living and working in Holland, so the obvious thing was for us to go there for the wedding. Since *Ebb Tide* was almost as much a home as Springhill in Tarporley, we took our home to Holland so that she could be married from it.

In 1971 we had moved *Ebb Tide* from Acton Bridge to Morpeth Dock at Birkenhead. Making weekend passages was becoming more difficult due to the road bridges and locks on the River Weaver being unmanned at weekends as part of British Waterways cost-cutting, this move enabled us to get out to sea most weekends and we had some enjoyable short trips, as well as some when adverse weather forced us to turn back while we were still in the Queen's Channel. We later moved on to the RNXS mooring in order to have power available and save running the generator on the weekends when we were working on board. You can imagine our horror when, one Friday evening, we went aboard to see that *Ebb Tide* looked somewhat different. A close inspection showed that her stem post had been pushed back and broken. This was due to *Puttenham,* who was moored ahead of *Ebb Tide,* having gone astern when she had left for a weekend trip. She had hit *Ebb Tide* with some force since even slow astern was pretty dramatic; she had two 1300 hp engines and was about a hundred and thirty five feet long! On our return home I immediately wrote to the Admiralty and put in a claim for damages. They sent a surveyor who agreed the cost of necessary repairs with Cubbins' shipyard at the far end of the dock. I also received a letter from the Ministry of Defence accepting full responsibility.

Over the next few months we had a battle to get the damage repaired at the Ministry of Defence's expense. It was a long battle and some pretty acrimonious words were exchanged with the Commanding Officer of the RNXS when I tackled him during a visit he was making to the Birkenhead unit. He said he knew nothing about *Ebb Tide.* I said some pretty harsh things to him including calling him an unwholesome prevaricator (but in more basic and gory English). I was fully justified in this since his side-kick had told me only the same day over the telephone that, since the Admiralty had originally sent me a letter accepting full responsibility, they would authorize the repairs. My use of some pretty basic English to the Area Commander prevented my promotion to 'officer' rank when I later took charge of the Birkenhead afloat section.

We then took *Ebb Tide* to Cubbins' shipyard in Birkenhead to have a new oak stem post fitted. I went with their shipwright to a timber yard in Wem, Shropshire, where he selected a piece of oak which had grown to the approximate shape required. We also took the opportunity of having a new propeller shaft made and fitted, using metal to the original Admiralty specification, so that we hoped we would not have any more trouble from this direction. It is somewhat interesting to comment that the cost of the propeller shaft made in 1973 was considerably more than a replacement one made in Australia in 1978. Cubbins' lost a lot of money making the shaft. It 'sprung' every time a cut was taken in the lathe and it was over a week in the making. It was unfortunate that after only a couple of years in Solomon Islands the seasoned English oak disintegrated and a large portion had to be replaced. I could pull out chunks by hand.

It was almost the end of June before we were ready for a shake down cruise. This took place on the 25th when we went as far as Llandudno and anchored off the pier for a couple of hours to check everything over, before we returned to Birkenhead. We were back on our berth by 9 pm and all had been well on this short cruise.

We set off for Amsterdam on July 3rd, after collecting our youngest son, Guy, by car from Rossall, only hours after he had completed his A-level examinations. Our first stop was Dunmore East in the Republic of Ireland to see our eldest daughter and her family. We only spent ten hours there before setting off for our next port of call, Newlyn. The whole time the weather was as near perfect as it could be so the passage was pretty smooth. I discovered that I had not completely cured some of the engine's oil leaks, so we had to stop on the way to refill the sump and fix a leak. We arrived in Newlyn late evening the following day and spent a day there before setting course up Channel for Ramsgate.

On this leg of the passage the weather broke and the wind increased to a Force Five, so soon after leaving we hoisted our sail. The wind being from the north, the sail steadied up *Ebb Tide* and made the passage more comfortable. It was on this leg that the stern tube, which had been removed and re-fitted by the shipyard in Birkenhead, suddenly decided to spring a large leak, and the red lead they had used to seal it into the sternpost was spewed into the bilges. We thought that professionals would have made a better job than yours truly, but we learnt otherwise. Luckily I had a pressure grease gun on board and was able to force some mastic into the space between the stern tube and stern post, which stopped the leak. We made Ramsgate without any further problems and entered in the early morning of July 8th.

I must mention here that it had taken fourteen men in the shipyard to remove the rudder and propeller shaft. Anne and I used to do it ourselves in the little dry dock on the River Weaver – but then we did not have unions with their demarcation restrictions to worry us.

We had planned to have time in hand before the date fixed for Gill's wedding so that we could travel to London to meet the Bishop of Melanesia. *Ebb Tide* spent a full day in Ramsgate before we rejoined her and then headed for IJmuiden in the evening. The weather had improved so that it was back to almost calm conditions. We arrived at IJmuiden at midday, cleared Customs and made our way along the Nordzee canal to Amsterdam where we secured in the little yacht basin by the railway station.

The wedding took place in the Amsterdam Registry Office (all weddings on the Continent have to be civil ones first, with the option of a church one afterwards). Gillian spent her last night 'at home' on board *Ebb Tide* and then we went to the Registrar the following morning. The ceremony over, the reception was held on board. It was quite a squash, Hanns had broken his ankle a short time before and was sitting in a wheel chair with one leg sticking out. He had to be brought aboard, and he was no mean weight! The wedding could not be postponed due to the departure date for Solomon Islands being a 'fixed feast'. The guests followed and sampled an English wedding reception. Anne made the cake and had it iced in Tarporley with strict instructions that the icing should be firm, to withstand the journey. It certainly was firm. When the time came to cut it, Hanns and Gillian were unable to do so. Anne almost had to take an axe to break the icing. We don't know what the Dutch contingent thought, but they were very polite.

The wedding over, we refuelled and three days later set off on the return voyage. On our arrival at IJmuiden we had to wait for the tide to rise sufficiently for the locks to open, so that it was early the next morning before we were back in the North Sea. Soon after breakfast the battery charging alternator decided to cease charging. All my efforts to make it work were unavailing and this caused some delays, so that in the end I had to fit the spare one we carried. It was also the first time that the trouble, which almost ended our voyage to the Solomons, occurred. While I had been dealing with the faulty alternator I discovered that the engine pulley which drove it had slipped on its shaft and was hard against the engine casing. As I wrote earlier, I had wrongly assumed that it had just come loose on the engine shaft and the bolt I had fitted at the shaft end to keep it on, had tightened and forced the pulley in. It is always so much easier to solve problems with hindsight. Apart from this, the passage was pretty well perfect and we arrived in Newlyn fifty-three hours after leaving Holland. On both the outward and inward passages I ran the engine at the speed I planned to use on the major voyage. This was so that I could make a final check on the fuel consumption and speed.

While we were in Newlyn I arranged with the local shipwright to make a new hatch cover for the lazarette and fit it in September before we finally left England. We spent five days there. Simon, our eldest son, then lived at Brixham so he and his family paid us a visit. We then set off for Dunmore East in the Republic of Ireland to report on the wedding to our family there. After staying for the night we set off the following morning for the final leg back to Birkenhead. This was accomplished without meeting any further problems and we arrived back at our mooring early the following morning.

We were now getting close to our sailing date, fixed for September 8th, but still had time for a couple more trips. On August 18th we went to the Isle of Man to say farewell to 'Bungy' Williams and his wife Marion. Bungy and I had met in the RNXS when he was skipper of *Puttenham* and he and his wife had become firm friends. Incidentally, Bungy was one of the eight survivors from the *Royal Oak* which sank in Scapa Flow in the early days of the war. Both he and Marion gave us considerable help when we were hunting for a house in the Isle of Man by telephone from the Solomon Islands in 1977, and that was no easy task with the antiquated telephone system unloaded by the British Government on one of its 'colonies.'

Our last trip was to Tal-y-Foel in the Menai Straits over the weekend of August 24/27th, just over twelve days before the big voyage. We left Morpeth Dock early evening and arrived at Tal-y-Foel in time for breakfast. We spent the weekend there and set off back to Birkenhead after breakfast on the 27th. On the return passage we tried out our sails, but it was almost calm. Another unsuccessful attempt was made to fish. And finally we picked a large wooden cable drum out of the water when we were off Rhyl, North Wales, before stopping at the Princes landing stage to drop off Barbara, the 'extra' hand who started out with us. Then it was just a matter of locking into Morpeth Dock, just over twelve hours after leaving Tal-y-Foel.

During the time from June 25th to August 27th we managed to put another 1,942 miles under our keel. Before we commenced our voyage to Solomon Islands we had logged some 32,405 miles since we purchased *Ebb Tide* in 1960 and we are pretty confident that this distance has not been bettered by any amateur motor yachtsmen.

We spent many months 'bottoms up' on the floor of our sitting room at Tarporley studying charts of the various areas we would be travelling through, together with the appropriate Admiralty Pilots and the large American Naval publication *Ocean Currents of the World,* kindly given to us by Tim Kendall, another member of the Cruising Association. We decided that the only practicable route was:

> Birkenhead – Dunmore East, in the Republic of Ireland –Newlyn, in Cornwall;
> Newlyn to the Canary Islands;
> The Canary Islands to Madeira;
> Madeira to Cape Verde Islands;
> Cape Verde Islands, across the Atlantic to Barbados;
> Barbados to Cristobal, the eastern entrance to the Panama Canal;
> Through the Panama Canal;
> Balboa at the west end of the Panama Canal to the Galapagos Islands;
> The Galapagos Islands to Nuku Hiva in the Marquesa Islands;
> Nuku Hiva to Apia in Western Samoa;
> Apia to Honiara in Solomon Islands, our final destination.

Our departure time was governed to a great extent to hopefully miss the hurricane season in the Caribbean and arrive in Solomon Islands before the cyclone season began.

During preparation for the voyage Anne's responsibility was for the victualling (in between working as a painter and engineer's, carpenter's and electrician's mate). She worked out how much food she considered we would require for a three month voyage, both fresh and dried or tinned. She boned out about thirty chickens and compressed them into cubes to make the most of the space in our little deep freeze. Through the good offices of a butcher friend we were able to purchase meat from the Liverpool Smithfield so we bought a whole side of beef. Anne, with the assistance of Neil and Guy, then boned it all and cut and forced it into suitable sizes, as she had done with the chickens. Neil was extremely popular with his current crop of girlfriends when they received the bones for their dogs. Even a 20lb turkey was treated in the same way. All the canned food was labelled, logged and stowed under the bunks. A gross of eggs was coated with vaseline and stowed under one of the bunks in the saloon. We had read that this was the best way of ensuring that they would keep for a long period. All engine, electrical and seamanship spares were stowed under our berth in the aft cabin.

One of the members of Acton Bridge Cruising Club very kindly donated our medicine chest, the contents having been specified by our local doctor in Tarporley. This was put to a good used several times during the voyage. I unfortunately suffer from a heart condition which entails living on pills. Before sailing I had a comprehensive medical check-up in Liverpool. I did not want to be an encumbrance should the condition worsen, but I was given a clear bill of health. For many years I had suffered with varicose veins in one leg. I felt that these should be attended to before we went to live in the tropics so, to be on the safe side, I had them removed in Chester Royal Infirmary.

During the last few days before sailing we purchased the vital stores 'duty free' (in those days whisky was 70p and gin 50p a bottle). Anne had to cross the Mersey on the ferry from Birkenhead to visit the Customs in Liverpool to obtain the necessary authority to purchase from a ship chandler. When she told them of our plans she was informed that a letter from the skipper would be necessary, so she returned to Birkenhead with this news. On our return home that night I wrote the necessary letter and the next day Anne took it back to the Customs in Liverpool. This time she was met with, 'I have worked out the entitlement for your voyage.' When she saw it she nearly fell down with surprise. The amount was so great that we could not get it all on board. If my memory serves me correctly, it was something like a hundred and twenty bottles of spirits and goodness knows how many pounds of tobacco, part of which could be taken as cigarettes or cigars. The merchant navy 'duty free' allowance is pretty liberal.

1973 Before the voyage – Morpeth Dock Birkenhead

1973 The crew before the voyage - Birkenhead Dock

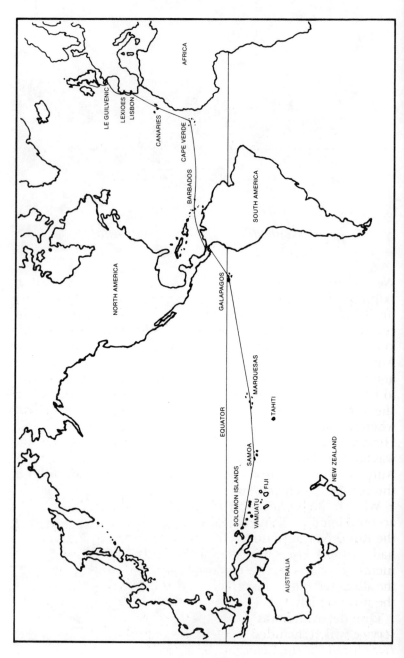

1973 - Route of 'The Voyage'

18

1973

The Voyage – Part 1
Birkenhead to the Panama Canal

We commenced the voyage with a crew of five: myself as skipper; Anne as mate; Neil as navigator (he was on leave from the RFA); Guy as engineer, and Barbara, who had asked if she could join us. We had agreed to this since we thought that we knew her pretty well and she would be female company for Anne and could also alternate between being a 'galley slave' and a watch keeper. Unfortunately this did not work out due to her health problems. We became a little suspicious when she went to the English hospital in Lisbon for a check up, but when she said that she had a clean bill of health we accepted it. However, when we were in Barbados she told Anne that she was liable to have a duodenal, so we sent her back to England. Anne was not prepared to cope with this on the major part of the voyage which was still before us.

We left Birkenhead on Saturday, September 8th, 1973, accompanied by XSV *Puttenham*, the inshore minesweeper of the Royal Naval Auxiliary Service which a few months earlier had pushed *Ebb Tide's* stem post back. Anne and I were members of this service for some years and I was in charge of the afloat section of the Birkenhead unit for a short while up to the time we left.

Our departure was preceded by a very moving farewell service which included a celebration of the Eucharist on *Ebb Tide's* foredeck, the Celebrant being the Bishop of Birkenhead, the the Rt Rev Eric Mercer, assisted by several clergy from the

191

Chester Diocese, and about three hundred friends and well wishers. The band of the Birkenhead Boys Brigade provided the music which was appreciated by all present. The media were present so that our departure was shown on the evening news. We were a little loath to have this coverage since not so many years earlier we had seen a converted lifeboat set out from Fleetwood for Australia. Their voyage did not take them out of the Irish Sea. However, this publicity was some help in overcoming the problems we met with the radio manufacturer later on.

Since we were in Birkenhead Docks, we had to lock out into the River Mersey and so were at the behest of the tides. After the formal send-off we slipped our moorings at midday and made for the lock. Having read several articles in yachting magazines which told of problems caused by unwelcome intruders, and in addition, should one of us be unfortunate enough to fall overboard in shark infested waters, I had ordered a Lee Enfield .303 rifle and a .22 automatic pistol from a gunsmith in Liverpool and arranged for them to be placed on board before we sailed. The arrangements, however, went somewhat astray and we tarried in the lock until the lock keepers advised us that we would have to lock out or miss the tide. So early afternoon we locked into the Mersey and set course downstream, line astern of *Puttenham*. All went well until we were abeam of the 'Q5' buoy in the Queen's Channel, when I noticed that the engine oil pressure had dropped. A quick check revealed that the main oil pipe to an extra lubricating oil filter I had fitted earlier, had cracked. The whole filter was quickly removed and twenty minutes later we were under way again. *Puttenham* accompanied us until we were well clear of the Queen's Channel, then she turned back to catch the afternoon locking. We waved farewell to my sister, the crew, and other friends who were on board, courtesy of the RNXS authorities.

My sister told me later that when we had engine trouble in the Queen's Channel the skipper of the XSV *Puttenham* said, 'Whatever happens, we are not taking them back into Birkenhead after that send off.'

We set our course to clear Anglesey and when we arrived off South Stack, the lighthouse on the north west corner of the island, another alteration was made to take us to Tuskar Rock, on the south east corner of Ireland. There we would make another alteration to take us to Dunmore East in the Republic of Ireland, our first port of call. This was so that we could say farewell to our eldest daughter Vivien and her husband who lived there, also to our youngest daughter Gillian and her husband who had come over from Holland to stay with them for this purpose. After a smooth passage we arrived the next day at midday. We had a slight contretemps with the Irish Customs when Guy gave his tape recorder to his sister. It was a slightly embarrassing moment, but all ended well. Family farewells having been said, we left the harbour early evening and set course for Land's End on our way to Newlyn in Cornwall. Once again the passage was smooth and un-eventful.

It was the first opportunity I had of testing out the high frequency band of the powerful transceiver which had been installed for the voyage. Earlier we had been too close to Portishead radio station (high frequency radio will not normally work at short range). During the transmission I noticed that one of the crystals had been fitted for an incorrect frequency. I immediately telephoned the manager of the manufacturer's Liverpool office who promised that he would send an engineer to Newlyn with the correct crystal and fit it (this was only the first of the problems we had with this transceiver). During this passage I realized we were not making our planned speed in spite of all our previous tests, but I put it down to the fact that we were loaded down to our marks with over three month's rations and a comprehensive set of spares and tools. We had also some personal belongings of sentimental value which we had withdrawn at the last minute from the auction of all our furniture and other effects which was to take place after we had departed.

We arrived at Newlyn mid afternoon on September 10th. The new hatch cover, ordered during our previous visit, was fitted to the lazarette. The weather forecasts were not encouraging so we took the opportunity of carrying out several maintenance tasks which had been left unfinished before we had sailed. They were not vital ones but, since we were being delayed by bad weather, it was the obvious thing to do to complete these before commencing the long voyage ahead. We also had to wait for the radio engineer to arrive from Birkenhead with the correct crystal for the transceiver. Simon, our eldest son, and his family also took the opportunity to come and say farewell. We were interviewed by the local newspaper and TV, the voyage having received a certain amount of unsought publicity, the result of a fellow club member informing the media.

To our surprise the local Customs officer appeared carrying our armoury which, as I said earlier, had been left behind at Birkenhead, and as far as I was concerned had been written off. I had previously suggested to the radio manufacturer's manager in Liverpool that these should be given to the engineer to bring with him when he brought the replacement crystal, but this did not happen. From the engineer's point of view it was a good thing since he had been stopped and searched on arrival at Euston. The amount of electronic equipment he was carrying made him an IRA suspect! If he had been carrying a couple of weapons and ammunition as well, his arrival at Newlyn could have been somewhat delayed!

The radio modified, the hatch cover fitted, and other small jobs completed, we were ready to sail. However, all the weather forecasts gave southerly gales for the Biscay area; our route was more or less due south to Cape Finisterre on the north coast of Spain, so we delayed our departure in the hope of an improvement. After a few days we began to think that we would never get started.

'But timorous mortals start and shrink
to cross the narrow sea,
and linger shivering on the brink,
and fear to launch away.'

The verse from the hymn, *There is a land of pure delight* had been sent to us some years earlier by Allan Pettigrew who had sailed with us on some of our winter cruises, and we had pasted it in the front of our log book. We took courage from this and set off in the evening of September 16th, enjoying an uneventful passage, and arrived at Brest late the following morning. The wind strength had never risen above Force Five in spite of the adverse forecasts.

We spent the whole of the day listening to weather forecasts which were still not encouraging. We had planned to arrive in Honiara by Christmas and realized that we were going to have to meet many adverse weather conditions on a voyage of that magnitude, so if we sat about in harbours listening to weather forecasts we would never get there. To a certain extent the notorious reputation of the Bay of Biscay held us back. We therefore decided to take George Dick's dictum to 'go and have a look' and make for Cape Finisterre the next day. We left Brest the next morning, September 18th. The weather appeared to be fairly good and we had hopes of having a reasonably comfortable passage. Some three hours later we passed through the Raz de Seine and found that the sea conditions were not as favourable as earlier and very soon we were heading into a south westerly gale.

With the wind on our head, our steadying sails were not a lot of use in these conditions, so the passage was pretty uncomfortable. However, our morale was greatly improved when a small cargo ship appeared out of the gloom and flashed us up on her Aldis lamp to ask for her position. Having kept a plot of our position on the chart, we were able to oblige and passed it on by VHF radio.

Eventually the wind ceased and we were making good progress again, until just before midnight an 'expensive' noise, accompanied by a smell of burning, came from the engine. I made a quick check to find that all was not well. The engine would run, but only under protest, which was made evident by the screams of tortured metal. The decision had to be made whether we should carry on for the Spanish coast, some thirty-six hours away, or make for the French coast. I decided to do the latter and altered our course for the fishing port of Le Guilvenic, which was then almost due east; we both knew it well from our years of sailing up and down the Atlantic coast. I called Land's End Radio to tell them of our predicament and advised them that we did not need any assistance. I also gave Portishead Radio a call, since we were acting as a weather ship; unfortunately during this transmission the transmitter gave up the ghost so we had lost our only means of long distance communication. We still, of course, had the VHF radio, but its range was limited.

We were able to make way at a greatly reduced speed in the hope that we would be able to make the port, and continued on the easterly course.

Eventually the loom of the *Echmuhl* light, on the Pointe de Penmarch, appeared well to the north so we altered course to head slightly to the south of it which would take us to the entrance of Le Guilvenic; the time was now 4 am. Two hours later the engine gave a despairing groan and stopped dead. A further inspection revealed that it was seized solid and all my efforts to turn it were in vain.

We were still about twelve miles from the coast with an unserviceable radio and engine. All the sail we had was raised. Luckily there was still a fair amount of wind so we were able to make our way in the required direction. About four hours later the wind dropped completely and, when we were about four miles off Le Guilvenic, we were left with our sails flapping. The only course open to us was to try to tow *Ebb Tide* with our little ten foot launch, which was propelled by a 3hp engine. We had previously seen a dinghy, fitted with a Seagull outboard engine, acting as a tug in Ilfracombe harbour when it pulled a small coaster off the wall, so we felt that our little launch could at least tow *Ebb Tide* which was a considerably smaller vessel. The launch was lowered and the tow began, but after half an hour we realized that our efforts were useless, so another solution to our problem would have to be found. there was only one. Someone would have to go in the launch to Le Guilvenic and find a boat to tow us in. This task was delegated to Anne and Neil, and they set off with strict instructions to be sure to agree the towage fee before finalizing any towing arrangement.

Aboard *Ebb Tide* we saw the little launch disappear into the distance and sat down to wait. It was not long before we realized that the tide was taking us south, but we could do nothing about it, it was too deep to anchor, our anchor chain only being sixty fathoms long. The depth sounder showed that the sea bed was considerably deeper than this and, in any case, for an anchor to hold, the chain has to be approximately three times the depth of the water. After what seemed an age, we saw an open fishing boat appearing and, when it was finally close enough to see details, we were all more than relieved to see Anne and Neil on board. When it was secured alongside, Anne reported that she had been unable to make any financial arrangements with the owner; either he was too drunk to reason, or else she could not understand his patois. We had no option but to accept the situation and were taken in tow. However I made sure that our rope was used for this purpose. Under maritime law it is possible that salvage can be claimed if the tow rope belongs to the towing vessel, even though a tow had been requested for reasons other than being in distress. We made our way into the harbour, which was by then about five miles away. The fisherman took us 'his' way which resulted in our keel being bumped on the rocks on each side of the entrance channel.

As we entered the harbour the fisherman cast off our tow rope and of course we had no control over our movement. Boats do not have brakes and at such a low speed our rudder, large as it was, became useless, so we ended up bumping into the wall below the fish market, breaking one of the flukes of our Danforth anchor in the process; but this was a small price to pay in the circumstances. We then saw three gentlemen standing on the quay looking rather like the Gestapo in their long dark mackintoshes. As soon as we were secured they came aboard. We learned later that Land's End Radio had passed our message on to Brest Le Conquet Radio, who in their turn had notified the French Customs.

As our visitors came aboard they started muttering the word 'sauvage'. This was the only time during the whole voyage that I felt any butterflies in my stomach; we were not insured. The premium quoted was so high that we decided if disaster did strike us we probably would all be lost, so that any insurance money would not be a great deal of help. What I had of course completely overlooked was the possibility of any salvage claim, and here we were, hardly a week out, having to face just that! After some considerable discussion, during which Anne showed them a leaflet about the Melanesian Mission and explained what we were going to do, the Customs officials were convinced that we were not the yacht which had sent out a distress message. I was thankful that a continuous plot had been kept on the chart with our DR (dead reckoning) position being marked on it every hour. The chart was subjected to a close scrutiny, which obviously satisfied them and finally they left us in peace.

That was problem number one out of the way. The next was to agree the towage charge. The fisherman proved to be more amenable than many we had met in the past, and honour was satisfied through the medium of a bottle of whisky and a box of cigars! He was, however, a minor problem during our stay. He kept bringing friends on board to show them the yacht he had towed in. The level of our visible whisky bottle was rapidly lowered and when it was evident that it was empty the visits ceased.

We still had two more problems to solve: an unserviceable engine and an unserviceable radio.

To solve the first we dismantled the engine. After the crankshaft episode in the Bay of Biscay earlier in our career, we always carried a chain block and strong-back for lifting the engine. When the engine was in pieces we found that the teeth of the timing gears had been broken off. Luckily this was the only damage, since the valve timing having been lost, the valves could well have been hit by the pistons or vice versa. Anne went to the local General Motors agent in Quiberon to obtain spares, but when she got there she was told that he only kept General Motors motor car spares. We then telephoned Ernie Hewett in Cardiff who had supplied spares in the past and in this instance proved to be his usual helpful self. Unfortunately when the replacement timing gears arrived we found that General Motors had changed the design since our engine had been built, so more spares had to be obtained which caused a further delay. But this was not too important, we were still waiting for the radio.

The second problem was the most difficult one to solve. The radio manufacturer proved to be extremely obtuse and many reversed charge telephone calls took place. During one they offered to return our money for the transceiver, full stop! During another one they said that if we went to Bordeaux they would arrange for service to be carried out. Finally, after repeated threats that I would contact the Sunday newspapers, they agreed to send out a replacement set if we went to Concarneau to meet their engineer (they claimed that they could not find Le Guilvenic on the map). Needless to say I readily agreed.

As soon as the engine had been reassembled and tested we bought a local chart (all our charts of France had been left in England to make room for the large number we were carrying) and made for Concarneau, where we arrived on

October 3rd. Knowing that we would have to wait for a few days for the radio engineer to arrive, we took the opportunity to scrub *Ebb Tide's* bottom. This operation took two tides with her lying against the harbour wall so that at low water we could scrub. We were more than surprised to find over a quarter inch of shell on the copper sheathing in spite of having scrubbed her in June, under three months before. We had never had this problem before. Birkenhead Docks must have been more alive under the surface than they appeared to be on top!

The engineer with the new radio transceiver, having motored across France from Calais, finally arrived one evening. Further delays then had to be faced, the Customs at Concarneau were closed. It was after 'office hours' so the local officer would not permit it to be cleared. In the meantime the engineer repaired the original set. The fault had been the failure of one small transistor! However, to be on the safe side, and having carried a heavy transceiver from Liverpool, he quite rightly insisted on fitting it, and on October 8th this was done, tested and passed as serviceable.

On October 9th we then re-commenced our interrupted voyage, leaving Concarneau and heading for Cape Finisterre. This leg of the voyage was a welcome change from our earlier experience in Biscay. There was little or no wind, the sea was flat calm and now that her bottom was clean, *Ebb Tide* made her expected speed. Cape Finisterre came abeam on October 11th and we altered course due south to make for Leixoes in north Portugal, where we could top up our fuel tanks. This was a new port for us, so we reduced our speed in order to arrive off Leixoes early the following morning. The chart showed a sunken breakwater which somewhat deterred us from attempting a night entry. As we made our way down the coast the weather deteriorated and, by the time we were off the harbour entrance, the strong southerly winds had raised a terrific swell, causing it to be enveloped in clouds of spray. We were glad we had not attempted the entrance in the dark! We waited until it was fully daylight and had no difficulty in entering.

This was the dirtiest harbour we have ever visited, worse than Bordeaux, and that is saying something. Furthermore, as the result of the southerly wind, all the oil was being blown onto the only spot where we could moor. In a very short time our hull and mooring ropes were oily and black. We completed the necessary formalities and then moved over to the refuelling berth where we took on five hundred gallons of diesel. A fishing boat close by gave us a bucket of sardines in exchange for some of our cigarettes which made a welcome addition to our supplies.

The weather now worsened and we were storm bound, together with several other yachts which were on passage, both north and south. During this enforced stay, we realized that our original plan of reaching Honiara by Christmas could not be fulfilled. We therefore decided to call in at Lisbon and look up some friends there. On October 16th both the forecast and current weather had improved so we left harbour in company with another southbound yacht. The wind was south Force Four, but by lunchtime it had veered south-west and increased to Force Six. Our companion decided that this was enough and returned to Leixoes, while we carried on. After a torrential rainstorm, the weather improved and we were eventually sailing in comparative comfort.

During the time we were in Biscay we heard on the radio that the Arab/Israeli war had broken out and, though we did not realize it at the time, this was going to have quite an effect on the rest of our voyage.

We were still experiencing a certain amount of trouble with our radio transceiver. Due to the stray radio frequency currents which were floating about every time we transmitted, all the electrical equipment became alive. Looking into the radar display was quite unpleasant as the viewer received a faint tingle from the screen visor. The fluorescent tubes in the wheelhouse also lit up! I made a radio telephone call to the manufacturers in Essex who promised that their agent in Lisbon would look at it on our arrival.

We arrived at Lisbon on October 16th and secured to a pilot boat. Later we moved up the river to Doca do Bom Successo, a small harbour under the Salazar Bridge across the Tagus, and then contacted the radio company's agent.

The radio engineer who came aboard was emphatic that the problem resulted from *Ebb Tide* being a wooden hulled vessel, and this made effective earthing for such a powerful transmitter very difficult. He asked if we had any copper sheeting on board. Fortunately we were carrying a supply of spare sheets, *Ebb Tide* being copper sheathed. He told us that he could soon put matters right and we could go ashore and meet our friends, which we did. On our return after lunch, to our horror, we found the wheelhouse in a complete shambles. He had cut the copper sheets into foot wide strips and soldered the pieces together to make a massive earth strap. This had been run from the transceiver earth terminal to the earth connection in the engine room, which had necessitated part of the furniture being dismantled. The operation took until late afternoon of October 18th, so we decided that it was too late to sail that day and to make an early start on the following morning. We also lost the bulk of our spare sheathing to make the earth strap. I still cannot understand why the wide copper strip, which was only connected to the outer copper earth plate by three half inch diameter bolts, could improve the earthing, but it certainly did. Although there was still some stray radio frequency current about during transmissions, it was not enough to cause us any worry and the transceiver worked extremely well for the remainder of the voyage.

On October 19th we made our way down to the mouth of the River Tagus with the intention of following the route we had originally planned, ie. to call at Madeira. However, when we were out at sea a northerly Force Five on our beam made life rather uncomfortable, so we tried altering course for the Canaries. This proved to be much more comfortable, so we set our jib and mizzen sails and maintained the new course. The weather was reasonably kind the whole of the way with the wind being northerly.

Before we left England we had enrolled as a weather reporting ship. This entailed taking the sea temperature, assessing the wind strength, cloud types and their approximate height every six hours and then sending coded reports by radio in 'plain language' – that is, not using Morse code. We now commenced transmitting these reports to Portishead Radio and continued to do so the whole of the way to the Panama Canal. On one or two occasions when Portishead could not be contacted, we sent the reports to Dutch and German coastal stations. In fact we only missed sending reports once or twice during the entire voyage, and made contact with American, Australian and New Zealand radio stations when we could not make contact with Portishead.

The leg to Teneriffe was fairly straightforward – our first experience of ocean cruising. We arrived in Santa Cruz late at night on October 22nd. It was dark and we had some difficulty in finding a suitable berth alongside, so we dropped our anchor more or less in the middle of the harbour. The following morning we were able to secure alongside, which naturally made getting ashore much easier.

Anne's birthday was on October 24th so we decided that she should spend it on terra firma. The intervening day was spent shopping to top up our perishable stores and to do some sightseeing. The birthday party was held in a local restaurant and after it was over we sailed the same night, setting course for the Cape Verde Islands. This leg of the voyage was pretty well plain sailing with light winds all the way. We caught our first flying fish but, after trying them, decided that our rations were adequate without this form of supplement. It was always possible to know that a flying fish had come aboard, its presence was indicated by a strong smell. Once or twice some came in through the open wheelhouse doors and landed inside, some on me while I was asleep!

We did, however, meet a slight mechanical problem on this leg. A few days after leaving Teneriffe, an ominous knock developed. This appeared to come from the propeller shaft, however it was not bad enough to cause any real worry, but was obviously something to be attended to before we commenced the Atlantic crossing. It seemed to me that the propeller had become loose; I knew that it could not fall off because a locking screw, with an opposite handed thread, had been fitted to the main propeller nut to prevent it coming undone.

We collected a hawk which sat on the winch for a couple of days, apparently for a rest, before it disappeared as mysteriously as it had arrived. By this time we were getting near to Cape Verde Islands.

We arrived at Porto Grande on October 29th and secured alongside the main wharf to attend to the necessary formalities. We had the dubious honour of bringing rain to the island for the first time in six years. It was quite amusing watching the young children making their acquaintance with it. Our priority was to make arrangements to slip *Ebb Tide* so that our propeller could be inspected. The port official directed us to the naval workshop which turned out to be a completely open air one – quite a change from what we were used to in England. Understandably the rain was not appreciated by the workers. The officer in charge was most helpful and promised to send a diver down to carry out the necessary inspection. We were grateful for this offer which we were sure would be far less expensive than putting *Ebb Tide* on a slip and arranged to move over to the base the following morning. We also made arrangements to refuel for the ocean crossing, which would be our longest non-stop passage so far. As I said earlier, we had obtained weapons as the result of advice we had read in various articles in yachting magazines, so that night we kept a deck watch. In actual fact we received nothing but kindness from everyone during our stay.

The next morning, October 30th, we moved over to the naval base and secured alongside the wharf. Shortly afterwards a skin diver appeared and dived to inspect our propeller. He had small sharks swimming round him all the time. When he surfaced, he said that the securing nut was slack (as I said earlier, it could not have come off) and went ashore to obtain a small sledge hammer and a large spanner. Then he went down again, gave the offending nut a half turn to harden it up, and all was well. I then visited the OC to settle the bill. He told me that all that was necessary was to send a postcard to say we had arrived safely in Barbados. What more could one wish for? I thanked him profusely. We then moved over to the refuelling wharf and topped up our fuel tanks. Anne also took the opportunity, as she did at every port, to top up our supply of fresh fruit and vegetables. We were somewhat amused when the ship chandler, who could not supply the cabbage Anne had ordered, made it up by including a flagon of wine. Since it was Vino Verde we were not averse to the substitution. We then cleared Customs and made all the necessary preparations for the ocean crossing before moving back to our original mooring to wait for evening.

We left harbour late the same day and set course for the southern end of Barbados. The weather was almost perfect for the whole passage with the wind from the north and east,

Force One to Four. The steadying sails certainly paid dividends and our midday gin and Scrabble game was only upset once or twice. There was still a certain amount of vibrations apparently coming from the propeller shaft, but I finally cured it by fitting a few shims under the bearing on the intermediate shaft.

This was to be the longest leg of the voyage so far. It took ten days or so. The time passed far more quickly than we had anticipated, and the many games of Scrabble and books helped considerably. The off-watch periods soon went and the next on-watch periods seemed to come round extremely rapidly.

Late on November 9th we sighted land on our radar screen, which told us that it was seventeen miles ahead; a little later on it was visible to the naked eye. We all sighed with relief that our first ocean crossing had been completed without incident. We were, however, slightly too far to the north and had to alter course to the south to clear the island. We rounded the southern end without any problems, thanks to our radar, and in the early hours of November 10th finally anchored in Carlisle Bay. As soon as it was daylight we moved into Bridgetown Harbour to complete the usual formalities. Here we met the most unco-operative officials. They showed their country's recent independence by keeping me waiting as long as possible every time I had to approach them. I, on my part, was not going to show any signs of impatience, which would have no doubt given some satisfaction to the official concerned.

In Barbados we met the brother of the previous Malpas Rural Dean, Tudor-Jones (incidentally Tudor had been the unconscious agent of my re-involvement in church work). He had worked for Cable and Wireless but was retired and living there. He proved to be a great help, especially over re-fuelling, which was now becoming a problem as the result of the Arab/Israeli war. We also visited the coastal radio station, which had been very helpful on our way across the Atlantic. Although at times making contact had been quite a problem. Radio waves behave in very different ways in different places. In one place or time of day, contact with a close station is comparatively easy, while in another it can be almost impossible.

In order to try to reciprocate the kindness and help our

new-found friends had given us, we decided to take them for a short cruise and then have a picnic on the beach just to the north of Bridgetown. When we dropped our anchor at the chosen spot, I thought it would be a good opportunity to have a look at the propeller again, to make sure that the nut was still tight. We had been unable to slip *Ebb Tide* in Bridgetown, as we had originally hoped, and the water here was considerably clearer and more inviting than in the harbour. Our guests went ashore, leaving the male members of the crew on board. The propeller shaft was then locked solid by the simple expedient of applying a Stillson wrench to the intermediate shaft and engaging the 'ahead' clutch. I then nipped over the side and found that the propeller nut was still tight. Since by now time was running out, we then rushed ashore to join the rest of the party. The little matter of removing the Stillson and disengaging the 'ahead' clutch had been completely overlooked.

We had been warned at Bridgetown that entry to the harbour after dark was prohibited, but we had been enjoying ourselves so much that time slipped away unnoticed. We suddenly realized that we ought to be making our way back to harbour so we rushed back on board, hauled up the launch, then started the main engine. As usual it started at the first touch of the starter button, but then suddenly stopped. This caused a little head scratching until we remembered that the Stillson wrench had been left on the intermediate shaft, and the 'ahead' gear had been left engaged. By then, of course, it was too late, the damage had been done.

The engine was fitted with a Twin Disc gearbox and starting it with the gear engaged and the propeller shaft locked solid had caused the 'ahead' clutch plate to overheat and thus distort. The result was that we had both ahead and astern engaged at the same time, rather the same as on our first passage down the Bristol Channel in 1960. It was little wonder that the engine had stopped! I tried various dodges to free off the offending clutch and was eventually successful. We then made our way back to harbour with the gear lever held in the 'ahead' position and finally entered just as darkness fell.

We now had a major problem to overcome. Holding the gear lever in was good enough as an emergency measure for a short time, but that was all. There was no way we could continue on our voyage in this condition, so we had to set to and remove the engine and gearbox – and their combined weight was nearly eight hundredweights! My original diagnosis had been correct and when the gearbox was dismantled I saw that the 'ahead' clutch plate had become saucer shaped, so that it was not surprising that both clutches had been engaged. I telephoned Ernie Hewett in Cardiff, who immediately air freighted a replacement.

During our efforts to lift the engine and remove the gearbox, the generator for the revolution counter was caught by one of the large spanners we used and broken off. This was an essential instrument as the whole strategy for the voyage was based on running the engine at predetermined speeds. In my anxiety I had completely overlooked this when I ordered the new clutch plates. However, we were able to solve this particular problem in a quite unexpected way.

While we were in Barbados, Princess Anne had been married and was flying out to Barbados to join *Britannia*. As always the Royal Yacht was accompanied by a frigate and a Royal Fleet Auxiliary vessel. On this occasion it was the *Blue Rover*, and Neil had served on her at one time. He was able to arrange for me to use her workshop facilities so I was able to make an adaptor for the revolution counter drive, which saved the day. For obvious political reasons, *Blue Rover* was naturally unwilling to refuel us in Barbados, we arranged to make contact with her in the Galapagos Islands where we could then   replenish our fuel tanks. Unfortunately the gearbox repairs took so long that by the time we arrived there she had left.

While all this was taking place, Anne who had been the Enrolling Member for the Malpas Deanery Mothers' Union, heard that an Enrolling Service was to be held in Barbados Cathedral. She attended and was amused by the very young Dean who in his address strongly recommended the members to 'make themselves attractive, look after their figures, and wear corsets, so as to keep their husbands from straying when they visited the local grog shop.'

We took the opportunity of topping up our 'duty free' stores while in Barbados. We had experienced the joys of a local rum cocktail and ordered two gallons of rum to help us on our way. The Customs officer was highly critical of the quantity we were taking and made no bones about it. I think that he was a staunch teetotaller.

We left Bridgetown on November 23rd, setting course for the island of Bequia, which was on our way to the Panama Canal and where a fellow member of my club in Chester had a holiday resort. It was with regret that we said farewell to Barbados. Our stay there had been so pleasant. As I said earlier, we parted company with Barbara here and flew her back to England.

We arrived at Bequia some twelve hours later and anchored in Admiralty Bay. We saw a yacht flying the Cruising Association burgee, so paid her a visit. We found a lone occupant whose only company was a tame snake. We had a drink with him and he presented us with two sharks' teeth for good luck. We then made our number with my club member who entertained us royally, after which we repaired on board and slept the sleep of the just.

The next day, November 22nd, we left Bequia for Cristobal, the Atlantic entrance to the Panama Canal. This leg of the voyage took us six days and was comparatively peaceful. The wind never exceeded Force Five but it was always from a northerly direction and so was on our beam. Here again the steadying sails proved their worth. Before we left we were warned that we could meet some high seas in this part of the world, and the warnings proved to be correct. there were heavy rain squalls and enormous seas. I think the waves were the highest we had ever seen, but they were mostly behind us and *Ebb Tide* always enjoyed a following sea, even if her crew became a little fed up living in a large corkscrew. I had previously had thoughts about putting in to Caracas to refuel but the passage was so uncomfortable that it might have been a little dangerous to attempt to enter yet another strange harbour. Also I was not sure about the political situation, or the chance of obtaining fuel there, so the thoughts were not followed up.

One of the penalties of lying alongside in a commercial harbour, especially in the tropics, is that unwanted animals can be collected. Our brief stay in Barbados was no exception and we discovered that we had collected a rat. We were aware of this before we left and one of our friends, who was the local agent for Flick gave us several cakes of a green rat poison which he assured us would kill any rat tempted to sample it. The sampling certainly took place, tooth marks were evidence, but that was all. During the whole voyage, when we were under way, I always slept on a bunk in the wheelhouse, and on many occasions when I opened my eyes I would see Mr Rat sitting at the top of the companionway from the forward saloon and galley. The poison continued to collect tooth marks, but in spite of many searches, no dead rats could be found.

On November 28th, when we were nearly at Cristobal, I decided to contact a ship's agent who was going to help us. He was a 'friend of a friend' who had kept his boat astern of us on the River Weaver. I tried to raise Cristobal Radio, which was about a hundred miles off, but to no effect. I then contacted Portishead Radio and made the phone call from England by landline! At the end of our conversation the Portishead operator asked if I wanted to be advised of the cost of the call. I declined the offer.

We arrived at the entrance to Cristobal Harbour in the early hours of the next morning and piloted ourselves to the anchorage area, marked 'F' on our chart, while we waited for a canal pilot to make contact. In *Ebb Tide* we always seemed to make strange harbours in the dark!

When daylight came our 'Q' flag was seen by the Customs, health and immigration authorities, so a launch came out bearing the respective officials. Customs and Immigration were no problem since we were regarded as being in transit. I notified the health officer that we were 'a rat infested' ship. He said that the necessary action would be taken and I was a little apprehensive about just what such action would be. I thought that we might by put ashore while *Ebb Tide* was gassed to kill the unwanted animals.

Eventually a pilot came aboard who informed us that the harbour rules did not permit the use of a launch engine within the harbour limits. He also told us that if we wanted to visit the yacht club we would have to row, a mere three miles! However, our agent soon came aboard and smoothed things over, with the result that later in the day, we were able to move to the yacht club pontoon under the direction of a pilot of course. Having an agent proved to be a great asset and made life considerably easier, especially since there had been a canal pilots' strike just before our arrival, and commercial ships were being delayed up to a fortnight. We were, however, given some degree of preference and made the canal passage on December 2nd, after a delay of only three days.

On our arrival at the yacht club, as the result of our report, the de-ratisation officer came aboard. He produced two oversized 'mouse' traps baited with meat and set them. About a quarter of an hour later we heard a loud 'snap' and, lo and behold, a large plump rat had been caught. We thought that it would be a good idea to reset the trap just in case and to our surprise, within another quarter of an hour, a second rat met its end.

We were rat free until the next time we went alongside, which was in Samoa. In fact those two traps formed part of our assets, for the whole of our time in Solomon Islands, some eight and a half years, proving their worth many hundreds of times.

While we were waiting our turn to make the canal passage we refuelled and topped up our water tanks. Fuel had begun to be a slight problem as the result of the Arab/Israeli war, but once again having an agent proved its worth. One of the yacht club rules was that refuelling could not be carried out at the club pontoons. We overcame this problem very simply by securing *Ebb Tide* at an angle to the shore and just off the pontoon. The tanker, which was parked in the yacht club grounds, then ran a hose to *Ebb Tide*. Another rule was that shoes would be worn at all times in the club. Neil walked in barefoot with us and was politely told that he could not enter. He returned to *Ebb Tide*, put on his flip-flops and then rejoined us, kicking them off as he sat down. No comment was made!

The distillation plant, which used waste heat from the main engine, worked fairly well most of the time, but really needed the engine to be running at full power. We only ran at under half power in order to get the maximum range from our fuel. We thus took the opportunity of topping up the fresh water tanks whenever we could, and Cristobal was no exception. This was an error of the worst type – the local water was so chlorinated as to be almost undrinkable and was hardly preferable to the brackish water our plant had a habit of producing at times.

209

Canal rules are that yachts have to have a crew of four members in addition to a skipper. Since we were only four in total we had to 'borrow' an extra hand. Luckily a girl from another yacht which was waiting to make the passage offered her assistance. All this help cost us was her rail fare back from Balboa to Cristobal. Before we commenced the passage, the pilot told us that in the locks two crew members had to stand at the forward end, two at the stern and, under his direction, handle the ropes so as to keep *Ebb Tide* in the middle of the lock. We were somewhat amused by the way he continually had a slender cigar in his mouth and kept sucking it in and out while smoking it, so that the outside was continually wet. Maybe his cigars lasted longer with this treatment!

The whole canal set-up is most impressive and efficient and everything went like a well oiled clock. But it is also bogged down by rules and regulations. The dues were only $14 plus a measuring fee of $16, the latter being necessary in order for the dues to be calculated. The authorities have their own system of measurement as the particulars in a vessel's Certificate of Registry are not accepted. A measurement certificate is then issued (this is now hanging on the wall at home in Malpas under an oil painting we had had done of *Ebb Tide* in Solomon Islands when she was anchored in the M'Boli Passage, the view we had from our first house). The pilot told me that the canal dues had been fixed when the canal was built and had remained constant, although I believe that they have been increased since 1973. They were rather a change from what we have paid in the UK: £9 for the Crinan Canal and about £15 for the Caledonian Canal, are two examples which stick in my mind, plus of course the 1/9d British Waterways had tried to charge for 'passing the port of Grimsby' and £1 per bridge on the Gloucester/Sharpness ship canal.

For those who have not made the passage through the Panama Canal, I feel that a few words about it will help them to appreciate what a marvellous engineering enterprise it was, and still is today, some seventy-six years after it was built.

Before the canal was constructed all ships when on passage from one coast of America to the other, had to sail round Cape Horn, a somewhat dangerous enterprise. The idea of a canal across the isthmus was originally suggested by a Spaniard in

1530 but it was 1825 before any surveys were undertaken. A concession to construct a canal was granted to a French company and work was commenced in 1881 by a company with de Lesseps (of Suez Canal fame) at its head. However, the construction proved far more difficult than had been anticipated (shades of the Chunnel?) and a new company was formed in 1894, but the work was given up in 1900. The probable death toll was over twenty thousand, mainly as the result of malaria and yellow fever. In 1902 the United States was authorized by Congress to purchase the rights and property of the French company, but the Colombian government failed to ratify a treaty with the United States. This led to the secession of Panama in 1903. In 1904 the United States army resumed work on the canal and ten years later it was completed after a further loss of approximately ten thousand lives.

The canal is 83.33 kilometres long with three set of locks at each end, which are in duplicate so that ships can be locked both ways at the same time; this saves water as many canal cruisers will appreciate. The locks raise the canal level up to eighty-five feet above sea level as this is the level of the Gatun Lake, which is fed by the Gatun River and provides the water necessary to fill the locks. Big ships are pulled through the locks by electric 'mules', one attached to each of the four corners of the ship. These mules keep the ships in position so that they do not catch the lock walls or gates when the water is being let in or run out, which takes place extremely quickly. For the same reason we had to have a crew member at each corner of *Ebb Tide*.

At the time we went through, it was cheaper to move goods from Seattle to New York by sea through the canal than across America by rail.

1973 Going through the Panama Canal

1973 Galapagos – Anne trying to make friends with a seal

19

1973/4

The Voyage – Part 2
Across the Pacific to Solomon Islands

The passage through the canal took nine hours from the time we slipped our mooring at the yacht club in Cristobal until we anchored off Balboa. The pilot took us by the short cut, which is over the route of the early railway built by the French when they commenced construction of the canal, and is now flooded to its level. When we arrived at the Pacific end the pilot told us that we could not go ashore at Balboa because we had not obtained the necessary permit before we left Cristobal. This was no hardship since we had all we needed on board; he then directed us where to anchor and left.

It was then that we appreciated the information we had read in one yachting magazine; that it was advisable to obtain entry permits for the Galapagos Islands before leaving England. We had taken this advice and were more than glad we had when we were told that yachts applying for permits at Balboa were having to wait for up to sixty days. Without a permit entry was forbidden. Entry has to be made at Wreck Bay. We heard tales of how vessels in distress had been refused entry because they did not have a permit – which could not be obtained from the Galapagos Islands.

The volunteer crew member and the pilot having left, we now settled down to a good night's sleep before commencing our voyage across the Pacific. It was a little formidable to realize that at this stage, some three months on, we still had the major part of the voyage ahead of us.

At dawn the next morning, December 3rd, we weighed anchor and piloted our way out of the Gulf of Panama through flocks of pelicans, until we set our course for the Galapagos Islands. This leg of the voyage was somewhat uncomfortable as the sea was on our beam without sufficient wind to make the steadying sails effective. Occasionally it was southerly Force Four but most of the time it was either calm or variable Force One to Three. We also experienced some navigational difficulties due to the weather being overcast most of the time. This made it impossible to take any sights with our sextant. Our DR plot, coupled with the use of the aircraft radio beacon on the Galapagos, and our own radar, proved their worth. We eventually made our landfall some thirty miles north of the intended one, so had to make a thirty degree course alteration to the south to take us to Wreck Bay on the island of San Cristobal. This is the official port of entry for the whole of the Galapagos Islands, and we entered on December 8th. The ocean current atlas is pretty vague about this part of the world. To add to our problems the Admiralty Pilot stated that 'large magnetic anomalies can be experienced', which did not add a great deal to our confidence.

It was on this leg that we crossed 'the line', so Neil insisted that we all went through the initiation ceremony associated with this event. He, of course, had been through this ritual in the Royal Fleet Auxiliary and had brought some blank 'crossing the line certificates' with him, so all we uninitiated underwent the usual formalities. At least we were not toppled into the sea during the process.

At Wreck Bay we met our first real example of officialdom. We had anchored and run up the 'Q' flag in the usual manner, then waited for something to happen. Nothing did, but later we saw someone on the shore apparently waving to us, so we lowered our launch and went to see what it was all about. We were met by one of the islanders (later engaged to be our guide) who could speak some English. He explained that we must go to the Port Captain's office in order to make our entry; so we went, but it was closed and we had to return later. On our second visit the office was open and we obtained the necessary clearance at a cost of £15. We were somewhat shattered at this. The official explanation given was that we had entered during an overtime period and so had to pay

214

overtime rates! We were also informed that should we leave the harbour for any reason we would have to make another entry and pay the same fee, It seemed to us that overtime was all the time!

Having cleared inwards the first task was to arrange to be refuelled. The Port Captain told me that the inter-island ship from Ecuador would be calling later in the day and would oblige. I was greatly encouraged by this since I had been unable to obtain any information about the supply of diesel fuel in the Galapagos. I knew that there must be a supply of some sort, but that was all. Late in the afternoon the ship duly arrived but our hopes were rapidly dashed to the ground when our request for fuel was met with a blunt refusal. Our spirits were somewhat low at this point since we certainly did not have sufficient fuel to cover the next leg of three thousand miles to the Marquesa Islands. Although our range could be some six thousand miles, I always planned to arrive at every port with sufficient fuel to go a further distance of at least half the previous leg, but we had not been travelling at our most economical speed from Panama, the passage was so uncomfortable that our only wish was to get it over as quickly as possible without worrying too much about fuel consumption.

Pedro, our guide, suggested that we should go sightseeing and we formally engaged him for what to us was a small sum, but which to him was a small fortune. He could not have been more helpful. He took us, plus two of his daughters, to the Franciscan Friary which was also the local radio station and was blaring out pop music to the population at large, as well as transmitting it for others to pick up on their radios. We visited a colony of frigate birds which were so tame that we could go to within a couple of feet of them. Neil was a keen photographer and took many close-up photographs, but unfortunately the processing company lost his films of the whole voyage. We also went tunny fishing outside the harbour limits but, because Pedro was with us, port dues were not levied.

When we had our fill of sightseeing and fishing, we had another discussion with the Port Captain. He suggested that we would probably be better off at Caleta Aeolian on the island of Baltra where we could probably obtain all the fuel we needed. Incidentally, there had been an American seaplane base there during the last war. We moved north on December 11th, passing the Plaza Islands on the way. These islands are featured in the tourist brochure we had obtained from the Ecuadorian Embassy in London when we were getting the entry visas both for ourselves and *Ebb Tide.* From them we obtained the impression that we would see huge iguanas peering over the cliff of the island, but we saw nothing and, since it was impossible to anchor and go ashore to look around, contented ourselves with fishing instead.

We arrived at Baltra after a passage of ten hours and anchored in Caleta Aeolian, the bay forming the harbour. We had some difficulty in inducing our anchor to hold at first, but after several attempts were satisfied that it was secure. We then went ashore and once again had to pay clearance fees. This time we found that officialdom was more sympathetic. We learned that the young Port Captain had only been married for a short time, so we took the opportunity of entertaining him and his bride to a sumptuous dinner on board. This turned out to be a good move, as it had been intended to be, and he became most helpful. He waived the need for us to pay harbour dues each time we left and returned to the harbour, providing that we told him what we were going to do.

We enquired about the possibility of obtaining fuel here. Although we could have made Tahiti we had heard over the grapevine (or coconut news) that yachts were being refused fuel there as the result of the Middle East conflict. The Port Captain was most helpful and told us that in due course a vessel would come from Ecuador and we would be able to fill our fuel tanks from her. He said she was due in about a fortnight – maybe.

He gave us permission to visit other islands in the area and we took the opportunity of visiting Seymour Island on December 13th, the round trip taking about six hours. On our return we carried out various maintenance tasks and enquired again about the progress of the fuel tanker. We were informed that she was due to leave Ecuador on December 15th – maybe. The next day, December 16th, we decided to visit San Salvador. The Port Captain had told us that we would see plenty of iguanas and fur seals there. We left early in the morning and some nine hours later arrived at James Bay where we anchored and went ashore. We found a family of beautiful brown fur seals sitting on the rocks. They did not show any fear when approached, so Anne put out her hand to stroke one, but it snapped and belched fishily at her. Needless to say her hand was quickly withdrawn! We have an excellent photograph of this incident which is one of our treasured memories. We then climbed to a plateau where we found a flock of vultures feeding on the carcass of a goat. We walked over to the cliff edge to have a look at *Ebb Tide* anchored in the bay below.

To our absolute horror we saw that she was dragging her anchor and gradually edging out to sea. Nothing could be done about it from where we were. To our great relief her anchor eventually seemed to hold, and we continued our exploration. There were myriads of red crabs scuttling about over the rocks at the water's edge, and also iguanas. We were somewhat disappointed at our first sight of these creatures; they were only about eighteen inches long, very different from what we had been led to expect. We also saw an old bull seal sitting at the back of one of the caves in the cliffs, but we did not attempt to approach him. We then returned to *Ebb Tide* and spent a peaceful night on board, then returned to Baltra the next day, December 17th. The return passage only took seven hours since we did not tarry to fish.

While we were at Baltra there was only one other vessel in the anchorage. It was apparently a Spanish fishing boat which had been seized for 'fishing in Ecuadorian waters' and had been at Baltra for nearly six months waiting for the fine to be paid. We were told by an American couple we met later that when American fishing boats were seized, the American government paid the fine and then simply deducted the amount from the next year's American aid.

At Baltra we made the usual enquiries about the progress of the tanker and were told that hopefully it would arrive before Christmas - maybe.

While we were at San Salvador a catamaran, crewed by a young American and his wife, arrived at Baltra. We made contact with them and in order to fill in the time before 'Christmas - maybe' arrived we offered to take them on a fishing expedition. We moved off to the island of Santa Cruz, where we anchored, lowered our launch, and motored up a small creek lined with mangroves. The roots were a breeding ground for oysters and by hacking roots we harvested a goodly supply, then returned to Baltra. The American wife made a large oyster pie which was delicious and greatly appreciated by all. After the dishes had been washed up we heard a lot of noise outside and were surprised to see a large armed tug coming alongside the wharf. We were told that this was our fuel 'tanker' and that we would be refuelled the next morning. The opportunity was then taken to move *Ebb Tide* over and anchor alongside. During the evening a live pig was taken on board the tug. It protested most vociferously and continued to do so for some considerable time – then there was silence. No doubt pork featured on the crew's menu that evening!

Early the next morning we were able to fill our fuel tanks to the brim and we also purchased two forty-four gallon drums of fuel which were secured on deck, the first time we had done this on the voyage. We felt that if we met further re-fuelling problems in the Marquesas we would have sufficient fuel to carry on to Tahiti and take a chance on being able to purchase fuel there. We also took the opportunity of filling our water tanks from the large storage tanks on the wharf. The Americans were a little dubious about this and suggested that it could be contaminated with all sorts of things. Where the water came from we did not find out, but it was more than welcome since we had not been using our main engine enough to distil any significant quantity of sea water.

It was now getting close to Christmas, so we decided to spend it on the Galapagos Islands rather than at sea. On the advice of the Port Captain we moved to Academy Bay on the island of Santa Cruz. On arrival we had to go through the whole gamut of paying entry dues again, at overtime rates as usual, and then anchored astern of the other visiting yachts.

Christmas was still a few days away so we took the opportunity of visiting the Darwin Research Station where we saw a few tortoises. We were not impressed with what we saw and felt that the whole place was over-rated. We also visited a museum run by a German called King Gus. Before we left England we had read in a Sunday newspaper colour magazine about his museum and it certainly came up to our expectations. We spent quite a few pleasant evenings in his caves looking at the relics he had accumulated since his arrival; he had opted out of living in Germany in the 1930s. He certainly was a character and we sat on whale vertebra while he regaled us with stories about whales which were reputed to attack yachts. We must admit it was with some trepidation that we sailed from the Galapagos, especially after the Robertson's experience some two years earlier. Their yacht had been sunk by a whale attacking it and, before being rescued, they had spent several weeks adrift in their rubber liferaft. They had written a book about their experience and were on one of the stands at the Boat Show we attended in January 1973, but we did not make contact.

A couple of Swiss who were circumnavigating were moored astern of us, so we invited them aboard. The owner was estranged from his wife who had stayed behind in Switzerland. He made a Christmas telephone call to her through our transceiver, but it did not sound as affectionate as one would have expected (for those who do not know the procedure for using a coast radio station to make a telephone call, both sides of the conversation can be heard by anyone who happens to be close to the transceiver, as in a yacht). We had managed to keep in touch with Portishead Radio and made the phone calls through this radio station. They were most surprised that a small yacht could do this and told us that they always had extreme difficulty in keeping in touch with the *Oriana* when she was in that area. Anne nearly burst the buttons on her blouse when she was making a routine call with the weather report and Portishead said (to the world at large), 'Hold on *Oriana*. I will take *Ebb Tide* first.'

The research vessel *Beagle* returned to her base at Academy bay for Christmas and I was asked to try to repair her radar but I was unable to sort out the problem.

On Christmas Eve the staff of the naval base received a visit from Santa Claus who arrived standing up in the stern of a dinghy. We were somewhat saddened to see all the local children being kept apart with their noses hard up against the strong wire fence surrounding the base. We had not become inured to the effects of cultural differences then and were probably experiencing a certain amount of cultural shock ourselves. Our first contact in this direction had been on the

Cape Verde islands where the Europeans lived in well-built houses while the locals lived in houses built from flattened oil drums.

We invited the crews of the other two yachts to join us for a traditional Christmas dinner. Anne lived up to her reputation as a gourmet cook by producing a traditional 20lb turkey Christmas dinner, with all the necessary trimmings. She had been jealously guarding the turkey in the deep freeze for this occasion. As I said earlier, the turkey had been boned out and then squashed into a symmetrical block to freeze; when the time came to cook it, Anne pulled it into shape and stuffed sausages into the wings and legs to put some shape into them before roasting it. We ended up with a succulent Christmas pudding which she made on the spot.

On Christmas night we were invited to an American owned hotel which was minus guests. Apparently the Ecuadorian officials would not grant entry permits to visitors unless they stayed in government-owned hotels. They had to be full up first. We had a first class party which went on into the early hours of Boxing Day. Among others at the party was a professor of snails, who had a very young and attractive girl with him. We took her to be his daughter and so suggested to our two sons that they might 'entertain' her. Luckily we realized just in time that she was his wife. The professor was very cynical about other snail scientists and said that every time they met a snail with a slightly different shell marking and at a different altitude, they would classify it as a completely different species. He was firmly convinced that this was unethical.

Christmas and Boxing Day over, the time had come to move on and tackle the longest leg of the whole voyage – three thousand miles to the Marquesa Islands. We obtained the necessary clearance and set off on December 27th. As predicted by King Gus, we met a school of whales almost exactly where he said that we would, approximately two hundred miles west of the Galapagos Islands. Thank goodness they kept well away from us, which caused sighs of relief all round. During the night watches large phosphorescent objects could be seen swimming round under water and we presumed they were whales. We decided the noise from our propeller kept them from making too close an inspection of the large object moving above them.

On this leg of the voyage a peculiar smell began to pervade the ship. Our investigations led us to the eggs which we found to be covered with small grubs and flies which had previously been feeding on the vaseline. Although the eggs appeared fresh enough when opened, we decided that the safest course was to put them over the side and so fed nearly a gross to the fish.

Twelve days out, the 'thump' which had occurred off the coast of Africa reappeared. This time I knew that the propeller must have come loose again. A new one had been fitted before we had left England, but the taper of the propeller bore must have been slightly different from that on the shaft. We carried a spare propeller and securing nut on board, just in case. It was with some trepidation that I went over the side armed with the necessary large spanners and a hammer, all being attached to my waist by lanyards. The nut took another half turn to harden it up. This was not an easy operation as *Ebb Tide* was heaving about in the ocean swell while I remained comparatively stationary. The number of cuts I received from the growth on her hull were a painful reminder that the time was approaching for another bottom scrub. It was a somewhat eerie feeling to know the sea bed was some two thousand fathoms below and, if I dropped any of the tools, there would be no diving to reclaim them. The tightening operation being completed, I broke surface to see Neil, the second mate, standing on the aft deck with the .303 rifle at the ready. 'In case of sharks,' was the answer to my query.

Apart from this incident, the passage to the island of Nuku Hiva in the Marquesas was uneventful. We cruised at six knots to obtain the maximum range from our fuel, in case we were unable to top up at the Marquesas (at this speed we could travel approximately four thousand miles). During the whole of this passage the wind never rose above a Force Four, always from the east or south. The steadying sails were always filled and once again proved their worth from a comfort point of view, although they made no contribution whatsoever to our propulsion. The fuel consumption was exactly the same each day, our fuel meter reading to the nearest one hundredth of a gallon. We met another slight problem when the governor of the diesel generator decided to fail, so that the engine ran away with itself. Anne noticed this when she was cooking and realized that the cooker had become much hotter than usual. When I was investigating the cause I saw that the needle of the voltmeter on the AC system was showing 'hard over,' past the maximum reading of 300 volts, instead of the normal 240. In order to reduce the heat from the galley we usually had the air-conditioning unit switched on during cooking times. Since the speed of an electric motor on an AC system is dependent on the frequency of the supply (usually fifty cycles) and the frequency of the supply is governed by the speed of the alternator, when the engine ran away, the frequency of the ship's mains also went haywire. The result was that the fan in the air-conditioning unit over-speeded and lost a few blades in the process. When I dismantled the fuel pump of the generator engine I discovered that the governor diaphragm had split. This was one spare it had never entered my head to carry. I had never known a governor diaphragm fail before. However, I was able to make a replacement from a piece of rubber insertion which was carried in the spares locker, and all was well again, although our meal was delayed by some twelve hours. The replacement was still in place when we left Solomon Islands nine years later!

On January 14th our log had the following entry made in the second mate's handwriting and copied exactly as written: 'Dear mother was hereby rewarded one tot of gin for her powers of observation – namely sighting land and observing the green flash with father for the first time.'

No doubt 'father' also had an extra ration!

We arrived at Taihoae Bay, Nuku Hiva, on January 14th, after a passage of seventeen days and seventeen hours. This was one and a half days better then expected; obviously the following current was stronger than we had anticipated from the information given on the ocean current chart.

When we left the Galapagos we had reported in to the American Coastguard safety organization AMVER. On our arrival at Nuku Hiva I had great difficulty in inducing the American coastal radio station, KM1, in San Francisco, to accept a reversed charge call to report our safe arrival. It was only when I told the operator, unless the call was accepted the American Coastguard would probably institute a full scale air/sea search that she eventually accepted it.

Since Nuku Hiva is part of the French Pacific Territories we cleared the inward Customs and immigration formalities in much the same way as we had been used to when cruising in French waters; that is, with little formality. We then made enquiries about a supply of diesel fuel but the officials there were most unhelpful. It is worth remarking here that before we left England we had tried all possible sources for information about the Pacific, but no-one would give us any information at all, let alone any about fuel supplies. We held two credit cards from major oil companies but they had expired at the turn of the year, quite apart from being useless in that part of the Pacific anyway. We asked one of the 'yachting experts on the advice stand at the 1973 Boat Show for information about the Pacific area. The only recommendation he could give was to take plenty of matches – we took a gross of boxes for good measure. Someone who had seen a newspaper article about our voyage wrote to us before we left and recommended that we took a sack of onions with us but this advice was disregarded.

While we were at Nuku Hiva we learnt that Herman Melville, the author of *Moby Dick* had lived there, native fashion, for some years. I must admit that if I had not been going to work in Solomon Islands I too would have been very tempted to have stopped there, although no doubt when the novelty had worn off boredom would have set in.

While at Taihoae Bay we met several American and Canadian yachts. One of the American ones told us that a local entrepreneur, Maurice, had several drums of diesel hidden away from the French. He used this for his generator, but it was out of commission. We tracked him down to his lair and discovered that he was a half breed whose mother or father originally hailed from Birkenhead; we never found out which. Anyway I offered to look at the offending generator and found that the main bearings were worn out so that, other than obtaining replacements, nothing could be done. Maurice was, however, grateful for my efforts and offered to sell us ten drums of diesel which he had hidden away from the French authorities. I gathered that they would only pay the price he had originally paid for it well before the Middle East war. He laid down the condition that we must take the diesel aboard in five gallon jerricans so that the French would not see that he had some. Obviously he had denied that he was holding a supply. He thought that he was making a goodly profit by charging 17 pence a gallon. In fact this was less than we had paid at the dockside in Panama. It was also more than we had paid in the Galapagos where it had been 11.2 pence a gallon. However we were both well satisfied with the deal.

The task of getting it aboard then began. The first day we managed to transfer the contents of five drums by emptying them into five gallon jerricans which were then ferried aboard. This was an extremely laborious procedure so we had a further discussion with Maurice who relented, and agreed that the next day we could float the drums out to *Ebb Tide*, then haul them aboard. This operation, however, proved to be easier said than done. We had anchored fairly well out and, in order to avoid having to make five trips, decided to rope the five drums together and tow the lot with our little launch in one fell swoop. We rolled the drums to the water's edge and roped them together with a few feet of rope. Unfortunately, every time the first barrel was pushed into the water a wave would come and begin burying it in the sand. At one time we had five drums half buried and began to think that we would lose the lot, but eventually we were able to disinter them and commence the tow. Everything else after this was child's play! We hauled each drum onto the aft deck by using the boom of the mizzen mast which was fitted with a three and two block and tackle. The contents of the drums were transferred in no time at all and getting them back ashore proved to be considerably easier than towing them out.

During our brief stay we were visited on several occasions by locals who were using outrigger canoes. These were the first we had seen and we were naturally intrigued. The natives of the Marquesas are Polynesians, and so use Polynesian canoes, as opposed to the natives of the non-Polynesian islands, such as the Solomons, who are Melanesian, or some of the other islands who are Micronesians.

We had made friends with the crew of an American yacht when it entered the harbour and anchored close by. It was crewed by three couples who told us that they had met in a bar in Los Angeles and decided to sail round the world. When they made their first landfall at Nuku Hiva, tensions aboard were running high. We had had enough problems taking an

224

extra hand with us and we thought that we knew her well enough to fit in. What the six Americans met on their first long cruise, living in the confined space of a small yacht, even for a fortnight or so, can be imagined; we were not surprised. We left before they did, so we never found out if they abandoned the attempt or carried on, We also met a delightful Canadian couple who were crewing their own yacht. They were just wandering around the Pacific, going where and when as they pleased, without any deadlines to keep.

As noted earlier, the underwater excursion I had made to tighten the propeller nut had very forcibly drawn my attention to the fact that *Ebb Tide's* bottom, in spite of being copper sheathed, was getting in need of a scrub. The opportunity was now taken of careening her (that is, driving her ashore and then waiting for the tide to go out when she would lie on her side and be more or less dry) so that we could give her a good scrub and scrape. This operation took two days, one side each day. I was somewhat disconcerted to find at the end of the first day that most of the main engine's sump oil had emptied itself into the bilges when she had been lying on her starboard side. Quite apart from the mess this made, our stock of lubricating oil was by now getting low.

A French destroyer entered the harbour while we were carrying out the bottom scrub. We were told that it was carrying the French Minister for the Pacific Territories who was making one of his routine visits. Later that evening we suggested to Neil that he should go aboard the destroyer and extend an invitation for some of the officers to come aboard *Ebb Tide* for a drink. He was away for a long time and finally returned with an invitation from the officers to join them for drinks on the destroyer. Needless to say, we accepted with alacrity and had an excellent evening which ended up with flambé bananas, more flambé than bananas! During the evening we gravitated towards one officer who seemed to be a little out of things. Apparently he was the only reservist on board and thus was looked down upon by the regulars. He told us that the whole point of the party had been to get the three women from the American yacht on board. In this they succeeded, but they also got the husbands - which had not been anticipated. However, a good time was had by all.

The next evening a Pacific feast was held ashore for the

Minister, so we went and stood with the rest of the local population who were eyeing the delicacies being set out on the tables. It was not long, however, before our reservist friend saw us and quickly invited us to join him at his table. It was a memorable evening and our first experience of a Pacific feast, very different from the many we later attended in Solomon Islands. The dancing was as portrayed in films we had seen of the South Pacific. It was particularly interesting since apparently it was the first time the dancers had performed the 'long pig' dance for a very long time. The title of the dance indicated that it used to be performed round the body of the luckless human who was to provide the meat for the feast at the end of the dance.

We learnt that the island was inhabited by goats and cattle and they were available for hunting, the only stipulation being that a hunting permit should be obtained from the French Resident's office. Anne duly obtained one and we took the Canadian couple with us round to the west of the island, where we anchored in Bay Marquisenae. Neil and the male half of the Canadian couple went ashore armed with the .303 rifle. They eventually returned with a great carcass which made a welcome addition to our stock of fresh meat and did not taste like goat at all. Whether this was due to the meat or Anne's cooking I don't know, but it was very good.

When Neil returned aboard it was obvious that he was unwell and not from any connection with the goat hunting. Anne took his temperature to find that it was 103 degrees. On our return to Taihoae Bay, she consulted the French doctor at the little hospital there who advised that the trouble was caused by an infected wisdom tooth, probably from some dirt getting in his mouth during the bottom scrubbing. The doctor said that he could not improve on Anne's treatment so we decided to tarry awhile until the infection had cleared up. Fortunately our extremely comprehensive medical kit included a good supply of antibiotics. This was put to good use.

It was therefore, January 24th before we weighed anchor and set course for Apia in Western Samoa. This passage was uneventful, taking just over eleven days with almost perfect weather conditions, the winds ranged from Force One to Five, and until the last two days, were always astern, which meant

1974 Nuku Hiva – towing the fuel out to Ebb Tide.

1974 The one we threw back – Marquesas to Samoa.

that our steadying sails made the passage pretty comfortable. We ran through several tropical rainstorms and were able to fill our freshwater tanks by fitting hosepipes to the drainpipes from the wheelhouse roof and leading them into the water tank fillers on the deck below. We tried fishing with a line trailed out astern and caught a dorado but, since we did not recognize it we merely took a photograph of Neil holding it up on the deck, before returning it to its habitat. It was on this leg that we saw the only vessel from the time we left Panama until we reached Honiara. We only 'saw' it on our radar screen since it was night. We believe that it was a Japanese fishing vessel returning to Nuku Hiva to collect a crew member who had been left in the hospital there.

We had slight mechanical problems on this leg. The solenoid valve (which actuated the steering) was controlled by the automatic pilot and it decided to leak, but this only necessitated fitting new oil seals and was a simple repair. It was hardly surprising that the leak occurred; the valve was actuated many times a minute, especially during rough weather and must have moved backwards and forwards many million times since it had been installed. The propeller shaft stuffing box also followed suit, but this was cured by fitting a different type of packing. The automatic pilot, however, steered us so accurately that, at the end of a two thousand mile run, we were only twenty miles north of our planned track.

We arrived at Apia during the early afternoon of Sunday, February 3rd, and secured to a tug lying inside the main wharf. We ran up our 'Q' flag and waited in vain for the Customs to come aboard, making uncomplimentary comments about the Customs service the while. Late in the afternoon a young girl approached us and invited us to her house. It turned out that she was Dutch and her husband was working for one of the many United Nations organizations operating in the developing countries in the Pacific. She contacted the harbourmaster on our behalf, as he lived close by. He told her that we would not be able to obtain clearance until the next morning. On Monday morning as soon as it was obvious that the Customs office was functioning, I presented myself in order to obtain our inward clearance. Of course the first thing asked for was our outwards clearance from the

228

Marquesas. This had been completely overlooked; we had become so accustomed to the informal approach we had always met when visiting France that I had adopted the same attitude when leaving French territory. We had so enjoyed our stay at Nuku Hiva, I had completely forgotten to obtain an outwards clearance certificate before we left. A long conversation took place. It eventually turned out that the official in question was a Seventh Day Adventist and when he realized that we were going to work for the church in Solomon Islands, he relented and gave me the very necessary piece of paper. It was one of the more uncomfortable half hours of the whole voyage.

It was here that we had a further encounter with 'Mr Rat'. Unknown to us, one had slipped aboard during the short time we had been there. Luckily we had kept the two traps we obtained in Cristobal and set them whenever we were alongside. We were sitting on board when we heard the bang of a trap and I saw a semi-conscious rat running round in circles at the foot of the companionway. He had set off the trap but other than being knocked semi-conscious by the spring had not been trapped. I quickly picked him up and consigned him to the deep.

The next problem was to obtain fuel, for which purpose the local BP representative was approached. He was very co-operative, but explained that, due to the Middle East crisis, he had to obtain permission from his head office in Wellington, New Zealand before he could supply fuel to a yacht. He duly sent a cable requesting the necessary permission and advised us to return in a couple of days.

During this intervening period we were well entertained by the United Nations staff. In fact one couple later turned up in Honiara where they were instructing the staff of the 'international hotel' there. It was also in Apia that we met the only con man of the whole voyage. He claimed to know everyone, or be related to them, and promised huge quantities of fruit and vegetables. Needless to say they did not materialise and when we pressed him, he eventually produced a miserable selection, dramatically different from his earlier promises. Part revenge was obtained later after we had met an American whom he had apparently conned out of his camera. He was on board with us when the con man paid one of his frequent visits. We had quite an amusing half hour while we enjoyed his discomfiture. Honour was at least satisfied in part.

We decided to dispose of the two forty-four gallon fuel drums here. We did not want to arrive in Honiara with the deck looking untidy, so we gave them away. It was only when we had been in Solomon Islands for some time that we learnt the value of oil drums in the Pacific. They were, in fact, cut in half to make cooking pots, bread ovens, or even water tanks to collect rain from house roofs.

We had no use for the .22 automatic and knew that together with our rifle it would be confiscated on our arrival at Honiara. During our time in the Pacific we learnt the value of .22 ammunition having received many offers for it, but not for the automatic. When we were talking with the harbourmaster he said that he was interested in purchasing it. I agreed to sell it and accepted his offer after the usual bargaining of course. We learnt later from the UN couple who came to Honiara that he then shot his girlfriend with it and ended up in gaol.

We kept in touch with the BP representative who had not received any reply to his cable. We explained to him that we were hoping to reach Honiara before the Queen arrived on February 19th and in order to do this would have to leave Apia by the 9th at the very latest. He was very sympathetic and promised that if he did not receive a reply by the next day he would make a decision. He would not say what the decision would be, but gave indications that it would be a favourable one. The next morning we presented ourselves at the BP office and were told that the decision was a favourable one. I then had to visit the depot and make the necessary arrangements with the refuelling staff. Before any discussion could take place, I had to partake in a local custom. This necessitated sharing in a drink of 'kava' with the staff. Some people might like this essentially Pacific refreshment, but a bottle of beer would have been far more welcome. However bad any beer could be, it could not be any worse than that particular brew of kava. After this, refuelling was accomplished without any further difficulty and we took eight hundred and fifty gallons on board at, what was then to us, the exorbitant price of 20.25 pence a gallon. During the time we were waiting in Apia the two boys paid a visit to 'Aggies' famous hotel. Anne and I stayed close to the harbour so we did not visit Stevenson's grave, or do any other sightseeing. We were more concerned with con men and obtaining a supply of diesel.

Having now refuelled, there was nothing further to delay our departure so we rushed round and said farewell to the friends we had made. This time I made sure that the necessary outward clearances were obtained, and in the afternoon of February 9th set course on the final leg of our voyage – Samoa to Solomon Islands.

This passage took nine days and, like all our passages in the Pacific, proved to be uneventful. The weather was kind to us and, when there was any wind at all, it was from behind. Occasionally we met a Force Five on the nose, with the usual associated squalls and torrential rainstorms. We had problems with the distillation plant which kept passing brackish water into the freshwater tanks. A friend in England had made a 'saline detector' which rang a bell if there was any salt in the water from the distillation plant. This was happening so often that I began to disbelieve it and at our peril ignored its message. The problem was pretty well overcome by fitting a different pulley to speed up the sea water cooling pump which provided the vacuum to the distillation plant by means of an ejector, as well as cooling the main engine. The 24 volt alternator which charged our batteries also gave up the ghost, but this was a comparatively minor problem; it was only a matter of fitting the spare one we carried for such an emergency.

Neil and I had a slight difference of opinion on this leg when he took a morning fix and reported that we had only averaged five knots over the previous day. The ocean current charts showed that we could expect favourable currents in the area at this time of the year and the engine revolutions were set to give us eight knots. The log reading confirmed that we had been steaming at this speed. We could only assume that the current was not as shown on the chart and had been in fact against us. The fickleness of the ocean in this part of the Pacific was confirmed when we were sailing round Solomon Islands at a later date, also when we were taking part in several air searches for missing ships and planes which often appeared in places well away from those which had been calculated by the Marine Department in Honiara.

During this last leg we continued to transmit weather reports, as we had done during the whole voyage, but as we moved further west the American coastal radio station was not keen on accepting them. In the end they told us not to send any more but from time to time we managed to keep in touch with Portishead Radio and also Sydney.

On one occasion, to our great surprise, we were able to raise Auckland Radio on 2.182khz (the international distress and first contact frequency) at midnight ship's time, in spite of the fact that we were over two thousand miles away. This surprised Auckland as much as it did us and we made contact several times. We were able to send a message to a priest in Auckland with a request that he pass it on to the Bishop of Melanesia. We had been unable to raise Honiara Radio to pass our estimated date of arrival to the Bishop, who had been expecting us for nearly two months. When we were in Solomon Islands we discovered that the watch-keeping at Honiara Radio left much to be desired. On one occasion *Ebb Tide* had gone on to a reef not far from Honiara, the bosun's distress message was picked up by Sydney Radio and eventually relayed to Honiara, but of course this could have been due to the propagation of radio signals in the tropics.

Land was sighted on February 15th and it turned out to be the island of N'deni, one of the Eastern Outer Islands group, some three days sailing from Honiara. We found that we were slightly north of our required track and had to alter course five degrees to port. Apart from course alterations to make life more comfortable for Anne when she was working in the galley, or in order to avoid heavy squalls, this was the first alteration made for navigational reasons since leaving Apia. After passing the Outer Islands we were in the open sea again and our next sighting took place on February 17th. Then the island of Ulawa appeared on our port side instead of being well to the starboard. A thirty degree course alteration was necessary, and again we realized that the ocean currents in this part of the Pacific do not follow the predictions given in the various pilot books and ocean current charts.

We arrived in Honiara, the capital, early in the evening of Sunday February 17th, and were met by John Chisholm, the then Bishop of Melanesia who immediately offered us baths and introduced us to the harbourmaster, whose only interest was to get us off the wharf; the port having been closed during the afternoon in preparation for the Queen's visit the next day. After clearing Customs and immigration and having our rifle confiscated, we were graciously given permission to lie alongside until 8 am next morning. Early that morning the harbourmaster appeared and banished us to the farthest part of the anchorage, which was crowded with all the little inter-island trading ships which had come in from the islands to see the Queen.

Our welcome was not a very exciting one after making a voyage of 13,807 miles. It was very different from the wonderful send-off we had had in Birkenhead just over three months earlier. I had planned the voyage to take sixty-seven days sailing time; in actual fact we took only nine days longer.

We had thought that Prince Philip, a keen yachtsman, might have been informed that a little yacht had just arrived from England, but it was not to be. Neil, however, saw one of the Rover class of RFA ships, which was acting as tanker to *Britannia*, (*Blue Rover* having left due to engine trouble), so he called her up on our Aldis signalling lamp with the message, 'Who is on board?' To our great surprise he was answered, and the conversation then moved to the VHF radio. Several of the *Grey Rover's* officers were known to him and we were invited to the party which was being held on board that evening. A jolly good time was had by all. Neil then invited three of the officers for lunch aboard *Ebb Tide* the next day, somewhat to Anne's chagrin, the Queen had proclaimed a two day public holiday so all the shops were closed and we had been at sea for some time. However, Anne rose to the occasion in her usual inimitable manner and the entertainment aboard *Grey Rover* was well repaid.

20

The Years in Solomon Islands

Almost before we had bathed on our arrival, the Bishop asked me to take on the office of Diocesan Secretary as apparently the current incumbent was leaving the following week. I refused on the grounds that I had come out to Melanesia to look after the workshops and ships and also that we had moved into a completely different culture of which we had no experience whatsoever. So the first year was spent on the island of N'Gela about twenty-five miles, or three hours sailing, from Honiara. During this first year I was responsible for overseeing the completion and delivery from Bowen, in Queensland, Australia, of a ferro cement vessel named *Fauabu Twomey* (she was in part paid for by the Leprosy Trust Board in New Zealand, hence the name 'Twomey'); salvaging one of the other ships *Baddeley,* which was virtually high and dry on a reef at Sikaniana; and travelling round the islands carrying bishops, priests and cargo as the occasion demanded.

When the *Fauabu Twomey* was eventually completed, we took her to Solomon Islands. I said earlier that when we met Bishop John in London he had suggested that we might act as delivery crew but was sure that she would have been delivered well before we arrived; but she was far from being complete.

For this purpose Anne and I took five Solomon Islanders to Bowen in Australia. It was the first time all but one of them had been in an aeroplane, let alone to a major city. On our arrival at Brisbane airport we were well and truly 'gone over' by the Customs officials, mainly because we had so much equipment with us, plus the fact that all the Solomon Islanders had 'seaman' in their passports. Anyway all was

234

eventually well and we spent the night at a motel in Brisbane. It was the first time any of our crew had seen television and Anne turned on the set in one of the rooms. A football match was in progress and Joshua stood with a suitcase in each hand and just gaped; hardly surprising! The next morning we flew up to Rockhampton and were then conveyed by a special bus to Bowen. The cost of the bus was more than the total air fare, but the airline had to keep the route open in order to retain their licence.

It took us the best part of three weeks hard work to complete this little ship. I could write a whole book on this saga alone! At last all was complete and we took her through the acceptance trials. For this purpose the insurance company would not accept my 'Master Solomons' ticket and insisted that a local pilot be on board. The one selected did not even know the rules of the road and I had to tell him which side of a buoy we had to go. Anyway all was well and since the vessel had not been formally named we arranged for a 'launching ceremony' to be held. We went inside the Barrier Reef to Townsville and then to Cairns, which is further up the coast. This was at the insistence of the insurance company.

After finally filling the hold with all the diesel we could carry (it was considerably cheaper in Australia than in Solomon Islands) we set off for Guadalcanal. On this passage, which took five days, I had to pilot our way through the Barrier Reef, which was quite a thrill, having read so much about it in the past. Once through the reef we set course for the northern tip of Guadalcanal and five days later, after only one course alteration, we arrived off Cape Astrolabe. There we turned south east and made our way down the coast to Honiara.

We had Joshua Makai, the master of *Southern Cross* with us and he was an expectant father. His face was a picture when we received a radio message from our headquarters to say that not only was he a father, but his wife had presented him with twins. While we had been in Brisbane he had been trying to buy napkins, but had to call on Anne for her assistance since he did not know the Australian name, which was 'diapers' and he was asking for all sorts of things. Anne took him up elevators and was somewhat alarmed about the possibility of him getting his toes caught in the mechanism since he was barefooted.

The Solomon Islanders could not understand why 'paw paws' in Australia should cost up to two dollars each; at home they simply picked them off a tree. It must have been quite an experience for them to move into a completely different culture.

While we were still living on the island of N'Gela and I was in Bowen, supervising out the completion of *Fauabu Twomey*, Anne was called by the matron of the little church hospital, which was just below our house, to take an expectant mother across to Honiara in *Ebb Tide*, so that she could be admitted to the Government hospital, there being some complications with her delivery. The saloon was converted into a delivery ward and the expectant father was sitting apprehensively in the wheelhouse. From time to time matron would come up the companionway and shake her fist at the poor father, saying in pidgin, 'It is all your fault for having an argument with your wife,' before retreating below again to see how the mother was progressing. He had to endure this for nearly three hours, but got his own back by pinching matron's umbrella on arrival! 'Pay-back' is an important part of the culture there.

The Marine Department rules and regulations were that a single engined vessel could not go beyond certain fairly well defined limits. The Eastern Outer Islands were outside these limits. A little church vessel, *Charles Fox*, of about thirty-five feet, and with a single Gardner 6LW, had been refitted at Taroaniara and was ready for delivery just about the time we arrived. I was told that a twin screw vessel would have to be chartered to escort her back to her anchorage on the island of Santa Cruz. I decided that rules and regulations were all very well in their place but we would act as escort without telling the Marine Department. We took a Melanesian, Andrew, with us as an extra hand and he asked if we could call at the island of Santa Anna on our way so that he could arrange to collect his wife on our return. We duly went into the little bay on the island and he went ashore. He was away for an appreciable time and we began to wonder if he ever would return. He did, so we continued on our way as escort.

The delivery trip having been successfully completed, we took the opportunity to have a look at the church school on the island. By our standards it was pretty basic, but we were new at that time and did not appreciate that schools there were not housed in solidly built classrooms. Our visit over, we set off back for Santa Anna. It was dark on our arrival and Andrew went ashore to collect his wife. We waited and waited and waited, but no sign of Andrew. He eventually appeared over the side and asked me to go ashore with him to talk to his wife's father. Somewhat hesitantly I agreed, and we went ashore in our dinghy. It was my first visit to a Melanesian house and I was somewhat surprised to find it in almost complete darkness, the only light coming from a very dim hurricane lamp. The father and two of his sons were sitting in the gloom dressed only in loin cloths. I was told that the sons were government officers and were on leave. The conversation was carried out in Pidgin, which of course I could not understand, so the sons translated into the local language for the father. I am pretty certain that the father could understand what I was saying, or the sons were deliberately mis-translating. The upshot was that Andrew could not have his wife back; either he had not paid the correct bride price or had broken custom in some way, but I was unable to find out.

We then went back on board with a very dejected Andrew, weighed our anchor and set off for Taroaniara, bumping the reef in the process. The reef clearly showed up on our radar, but it was a very black night and I am pretty certain that the reef was just below the surface. The rest of the trip home was uneventful and we made Taroaniara about twenty-four hours later.

On another occasion I had the job of taking recently ordained deacons from their ordination in St Barnabas Cathedral back to the island of Malaita. All went well and the first batch were dropped off at Auki and then we made our way down the coast to the island known as Small Malaita (it was separated from Malaita by a narrow passage but to all intents and purposes was a separate island with its own customs). We left Auki late evening and I went off watch and below to our cabin. Anne was left on watch and at about dawn she called me up to say that she thought that she was lost since she could not see any land. Once again the fickle currents had been active and while *Ebb Tide* had faithfully steered the course, the currents had not run as had been expected. At this time the radar was out of commission; it did not like the tropics! The Malaita men were telling her that she was in a different place while she was confident that she was on course. I came up to the bridge and saw that we were well away from the coast, not close in as we should have been. I could, however, see some islands on the horizon so took a compass bearing on them and plotted our position on the chart. As soon as I had done this I realized that we were in fact far from where we ought to have been and gave a course alteration of a hundred and twenty degrees to port. The Malaita men thought that I was mad and made no bones about saying so, but I was right and some three hours later we arrived at Small Malaita where we dropped more of our passengers before continuing round the island to drop off the rest at their villages.

I had been 'volunteered' on to the Diocesan Council and was more than pleased when, at its last meeting before independence from the Church of New Zealand, a telegram was sent to a priest in New Zealand urging him to accept the position of provincial secretary, no other suitable persons having come forward. I felt that the pressure which had been put on me had now been removed. However, the offer was not accepted (the priest concerned is now an archdeacon in New Zealand). Later, due to a chain of events almost similar in many ways to how we came to be in Solomon Islands, I finally accepted the position of provincial secretary. This necessitated our moving over to Honiara in December, 1973, in time for the independence of the new born Church of the Province of Melanesia, when it separated from the Church of New Zealand on January 25th, 1974. This meant giving up sailing around the islands, although for the first year or so in my new job I was able to go over to Taroaniara on N'Gela pretty well once a week.

One Saturday morning in November, while we were still based at Taroaniara, I said to Anne, 'Let's go over to Honiara to join the farewell party for David Hastings.' He was the printer whose contract had ended and he was returning to New Zealand. We rushed down to the wharf, boarded *Ebb Tide* and set course for Honiara. The passage took about three hours and we arrived at the printing works to find that the party had ended; nothing unusual in this, most Melanesian 'feasts' were of comparatively short duration.

Bishop John, as he then was, took me aside and said, 'Basil, come and have a cup of tea with me at home.' The three of us went to his house and after tea he said, 'Would you like to see the house I have bought for the provincial secretary?' I replied in the affirmative and we walked over to the house, which was next door. It was about fifty feet from the edge of the sea and in between the house and coral reef there was a small swimming pool. It was this latter which proved too hard to resist as I had often thought that a swimming pool would be rather nice to have in the garden. Bishop John suggested that I could anchor *Ebb Tide* outside the reef, but of course this was completely impracticable. I had to give the offer very careful consideration as the decision whether or not to leave Taroaniara and all the staff, with whom we had built an excellent relationship, was not an easy one. However, in the end I realized that I could probably contribute more to the work of the church as provincial secretary than simply just looking after the ships, and finally accepted Bishop John's offer.

During the time we lived on N'Gela, Guy, our youngest, who had accompanied us in *Ebb Tide* and originally had planned to join Anne's sister on her farm in West Australia, agreed to spend a year or so working for the Diocese as a volunteer. He was put in charge of the stores in Honiara after the previous incumbent had returned to Australia. Guy has an outgoing personality and this was reflected in his work. He had been allocated a house at Diocesan headquarters in Honiara and was in the habit of inviting all the stores employees and some of the office staff to lunch in his house. A shipment of rice had arrived from Australia with several burst bags, so he told the stores staff to collect up the spilt rice and take it to their quarters, using buckets to carry it. He also told them to get a move on and return for lunch as quickly as possible. In the event he ended up with just one of the office girls alone with him in his house. He did not realize that this would be construed as 'breaking custom,' a pretty serious offence in that part of the world, especially as she came from the island of Malaita.

He soon learnt about it, however, when the girl's father and brother entered the house and savagely attacked him, nearly biting off one of his nipples in the process. He was rescued by other staff members and Franciscans who lived close by. Anne and I were away in *Ebb Tide* at the time and on our return to Taroaniara found him waiting for us. He was obviously pretty shaken up by the whole episode, since the 'offended' father would still be looking for 'payback', and could well attack him again. Malaita people are among the most fierce in Solomon Islands and have the reputation of carrying a grudge, real or imagined, to the grave. We were able to send him to New Zealand on the next plane. He has settled there and is now married with two children.

When I agreed to take on the position of provincial secretary I did so because I knew that I would have the Archbishop to guide me. Three months after the inauguration, when we were on leave in England, we received news that he was in hospital in Melbourne suffering from cancer of the throat. I decided that we must return to Honiara via Melbourne. When we arrived at the hospital we saw the Archbishop in his hospital bed, from which he gave me instructions and said that he was confident that he would be returning to Honiara to develop the spiritual life of the young church, now that he had me to assist him with the administration. This had occupied a lot of his time since his appointment as Bishop, some six or seven years earlier; he was the architect of the Church of Melanesia becoming an independent Province in the Anglican Communion.

We returned to Honiara and the next time I saw the Archbishop was a fortnight later when I opened his coffin so that he could lie in state in the cathedral for people to pay their respects. Little did I realize just what a task I had taken on! There was no more time for sailing, other than when on official business. There were just not enough hours in the week to complete all the tasks which came my way.

When the new Archbishop, who was a Melanesian, was elected, the whole of the administration of the Church of Melanesia was left to me. This necessitated visiting all the four dioceses, one of which is in Vanuatu (which used to be called the New Hebrides before its independence in 1979). For one visit to Vanuatu we travelled in *Southern Cross,* and since I had been given a 'Master Solomons' ticket (Anne has a 'Mate Solomons' ticket and is probably the only woman to hold one), I acted as skipper. I did not realize that the radar was unserviceable. If I had, I would probably have let one of the other skippers take charge. The weather was overcast the whole way. It is about a three day voyage and I was only able to obtain one position line from the sun. This convinced me that we were going too far to the south and so would have to get to Santo by going round the southern end of the island. The mate and most of the crew were convinced that we were on the correct track, so I took their advice. In due course the island appeared and we were bang on track for the north of the island. I never learnt how they navigated; there are many theories including one that the shape of the waves are used for a guide.

Following the independence of the Church of Melanesia, the Diocese of Ysabel held its own independence celebrations. The Bishop was also the paramount chief of the island, so these celebrations were on a pretty large scale. Very many invitations were sent all around the country. I had been on a visit to the New Hebrides with the accountant, who came from Auckland, together with one of the Provincial Office staff. Both were Europeans since at that time there were no Solomon Islanders qualified in this field. For this purpose we travelled in *Southern Cross,* the eighty-five foot church ship. On our return to Honiara it was quite by chance that I decided to take the accountants to Ysabel in *Ebb Tide.* The decision was made on the grounds of economy, in preference to taking the larger *Southern Cross.* No-one had thought to tell me that *Southern Cross* was required to carry a full load of passengers from Honiara to Ysabel!

After we had made our inspection at the Diocesan headquarters, situated in the Marine lagoon on the north east side of the island, we went to Sepi where the independence celebrations were to take place. I discovered that once again, no arrangements had been made to collect invited guests. Invitations had been sent to church members on the island of Malaita, so I offered to take *Ebb Tide* to collect them. On our return with a full complement of passengers I was on watch and as usual worked on the theory that the shortest distance between two points is a straight line. I knew that there was a small rocky islet between the two islands and was certain that I could clear it.

Suddenly, in the dark, I saw breakers dead ahead and had to

quickly switch off the automatic pilot and put the wheel hard a-port. We missed the rocks by the skin of our teeth or the copper sheathing on *Ebb Tide's* bottom, I am not sure which. The island was clearly visible on the radar screen but of course the underwater part was not, and this extended much further out than I had realized.

The celebrations were highly organized with a lot of dancing and drama in the form of the re-enactment of the visit of the first missionary to the island, and a celebration of the Eucharist in the open air in 'language', as all the local languages are called. When all was over the problem of transporting the invited (and uninvited) guests had to be faced, but it all went smoothly. I am pretty certain that a blind eye was turned to the official passenger capacity of the ships.

Later, in the following year, the bishops said, 'Basil, you are working too hard and must take a holiday.' For this I was banished to Ontong Java, the largest lagoon in the Pacific and part of Solomon Islands. I was going to take *Ebb Tide,* but when the word went round Honiara that a ship was going there, a steady stream of people came into my office to see if they could come with me. In the end Anne and I travelled on *Southern Cross* as passengers, with Joshua Makai, an Ontong Java man, as skipper.

We had an uneventful passage, arriving at the entrance to the lagoon at first light. It was a wonderful sight. Standing on the wheelhouse roof, the reefs could be seen clearly, changing colour as the water deepened; it was almost out of this world. We continued on our way and dropped anchor just off the village of Lui Nui on the first island.

We were invited ashore (it would have been considered impolite if we had just lowered the launch and gone ashore) and shown around the village. We saw a well, about thirty feet deep, dug in the coral which formed the island, besides rain collected from the house roofs it was the only supply of fresh water. We were taken to the cemetery, where large stones set upright marked the graves. One had a woman sitting alongside and we were told that it was 'custom' for someone to guard a grave, night and day, for six months to prevent evil spirits from entering.

The church on the island was split over the tattooing of

women. The old practice was to tattoo them from top to toe, but the more 'advanced' members of the community disagreed with this. The local priest supported the old view, hence the split. We returned to *Southern Cross* and went to Palau, the second inhabited island further north. Here we dropped off the remaining passengers and cargo, had a good look around and then re-loaded.

Not far north from Ontong Java there is another large lagoon which is in fact part of Papua New Guinea. The islanders do not bother with such things as Customs and immigration and travel pretty freely between the two lagoons, much to the annoyance of the officials of both countries.

On our return to *Southern Cross* the Master asked us if we would like to visit 'Bird Island'. We thought that we would be going to a bird sanctuary and readily accepted. We had to return to Lui Nui to collect the owner, a wizened Polynesian, and had to take him with us. During the short passage, most of which was made outside the lagoon, we passed a whale blowing, which surprised us. We had completely forgotten that whaling had been a major industry in the South Pacific before they had been more or less decimated by over-hunting.

On our arrival at Bird Island, we re-entered the lagoon and *Southern Cross* anchored close to the beach. We all went ashore to see the birds. We had not known what to expect and were to a certain extent expecting some form of bird sanctuary. We were more than surprised to find that there was only one species of bird which looked very similar to a large blackbird. The crew lost no time in shinning up the trees in which the birds were nesting and helping themselves to the eggs, which they put in their pockets, and then to the birds, whose wings they knotted together and slipped them over their arms. In no time at all, they were covered with birds and their pockets filled with eggs.

We were then told that a feast would be held, so a fire of driftwood was prepared and lit. The eggs were put in a large pot of water and boiled. During this time the birds were prepared for cooking by being plucked. Next, bamboos were split and the pieces held apart by placing stones between them. The birds were then thrust on to the spikes thus formed, by pushing them down their gullets, and then held

243

over the fire and roasted. Anne and I tried the birds and were they tough? We were then offered boiled eggs; if they had a chick inside they immediately became 'haute cuisine' and were eagerly sought. We could not face this, so those we had were eagerly taken by others. We did, however, manage to find a few chick free eggs, but they were not particularly tasty. The next day as we left I was presented with a batch of freshly cooked birds as a parting gift. I handed these over to the crew who gratefully received them.

Soon after the independence of the New Hebrides, when the country became 'Vanuatu', an insurrection broke out on the island of Santo, where the Diocese of Vanuatu had its headquarters. I had to fly down from Honiara to sort out some of the problems over land etc. which had arisen there. When I arrived at the airport to return home, I found a large crowd massed around the airport entrance, and an attempt was made to prevent me from entering. They were jabbering away in 'Bislama', the local pidgin, which I could not understand. I kept repeating, 'Solair,' the name of the airline, and gradually forced my way into the departure lounge. After some delay, the pilot appeared and said that there was a problem which could prevent us from leaving. However, a short while later he told us to get on board as quickly as we could, which, needless to say, we did with alacrity. As we took off we could see a large horde, armed with bows and arrows and spears, rushing on to the runway behind the plane. We got off safely and were the last plane to leave Santo until the insurrection had been put down.

Jimmy Stevens, the ringleader, was eventually captured and placed under detention. The insurrection then collapsed and normal communications were established. A few days after this, the managing director of Solair asked me if I would like to fly to Santo with him on the first plane to land there after the insurrection had collapsed. I gladly accepted. On our arrival we found that an immigration office had not been re-established at the airport, so I was taken under armed guard to the police station in the town. I was somewhat amused to see that the guard's rifles had, 'Jesus is Love' stickers plastered over their butts.

Another time in Honiara there was some form of demonstration against the government which took place while I was in the church headquarters office in the centre of the town. Tear gas was used to disperse the mob, but of course this only made matters worse. The office windows were smashed and tear gas was rolling around our offices. I was glad that I only had a few whiffs of it!

We also experienced quite a severe earthquake, the epicentre only about twelve miles away. The office, a steel framed two storey building, rocked like a mad thing, but no damage was done. The Hong Kong and Shanghai Bank suffered some damage which caused it to be closed. Anne was driving our car at the time and said that it went completely out of control, but of course she did not realize what was happening. Luckily she had the good sense to stop before she ran into anything, or before the overhead electric cables came down on her. On our return home we found the bookcase in our living room lying on its face on the floor. The two Staffordshire figures which sat on its top were broken. The clock we had brought out in *Ebb Tide* was also lying on its face, but luckily the domed glass front was undamaged. Our last bottle of brandy was not so lucky and ended up broken on the floor of the storeroom.

Anne for her part was kept fully occupied with Red Cross work. She was appointed Director of the British Red Cross in Solomon Islands soon after we had moved to Honiara. She had been a member before the war and later she served as a VAD in various parts of England and Wales.

She is also an extremely competent needlewoman and was called on many times to make copes and mitres for the new bishops when they were elected. She had the slight problem of finding a suitable stiffening for mitres which would stand up to being wet when carried by canoe. She eventually solved this by obtaining used x-ray films from the hospital and rubbing off the pictures, then putting two at a time in each half of a mitre.

The Diocese of Melanesia had two Diocesan Secretaries at the time we arrived, one in Auckland, New Zealand, and the other in Honiara. Soon after our arrival, the Honiara Secretary having left, Harry Bullen the Auckland one, died. The bishop decided to have all the documents sent from Auckland to Honiara and when they arrived they were dumped in an office. The acting secretary made an attempt to sort them and they ended up in the strong room at the office. The British Government had given an archive building to Solomon Islands as part of its independence gift. I realized that the mass of papers in the strong room contained some priceless documents and managed to get the Provincial Council to agree that the archives, which had accumulated prior to the Diocese of Melanesia becoming an independent province, should be placed in the government archives where they would be properly looked after. I delegated to Anne the task of sorting through the mountains of paper. There were certainly some treasures in them. She found some original letters from Bishop Patteson, who had been murdered on September 20th, 1871, because he was the first white man to set foot ashore on the island of Nukapu in the Eastern Outer Islands Group where 'blackbirders', ie. Europeans who were collecting islanders to work in the cane fields in Queensland, Australia, had called a few months earlier and taken off by force some of the able bodied men. The chief had vowed to kill the next white man who set foot on his island and Bishop Patteson unfortunately happened to be the one. He has naturally become one of the Saints of Melanesia and Bishop Patteson's Day is a church festival. The theological college on Guadalcanal is named in his memory.

Another treasure was a beautifully illustrated book containing the Eucharist, or Communion Service. It was really a pity that it had to be hidden but had it been left anywhere it would have eventually 'walked.'

The headquarters of the Melanesian Mission had been on Norfolk Island, just north of New Zealand, and there were many priceless records relating to that period.

I learnt how few scruples some anthropologists have about purloining or 'borrowing' documents. Bishop John had placed some irreplaceable letters in the conference room and written on the envelope, 'Letters from Welchman – not to be taken away.' I quickly placed them into the strong room when one anthropologist told me about the bad habits of some of his colleagues. We had been in the habit of letting 'ists' look at our archives without any supervision. After this I laid down a rule that permission had to be obtained from the Provincial Council before any archive materials were examined.

I had been highly involved in the election of four new

bishops, the last one having been extremely difficult, so I had arranged to have my leave over the time when the election of yet another bishop was to be held. This was in part to give my successor the experience of coping with the election and all the consecration arrangements. Anne thought that she would get out of having to provide yet another cope and mitre, since our return had been planned to take place a few days before the consecration. Not a bit of it! She was duly requested to make not only a cope and mitre but an alb as well. As usual she 'coped' (no pun intended).

These are but a few of the many experiences we had in Solomon Islands. However, following the country's independence in 1978, it was pretty obvious that the time was nearing for us to leave. I had told the Archbishop that I would stay with him until he retired, when I would be seventy. However, I visited the Secretary of the Anglican Consultative Council when we were on leave in England and put my problem to him. To my surprise (and disappointment) his advice was to hand over to a Solomon Islander as soon as I could. To many people's surprise I did just this at the Provincial Synod in June 1982, having spent nearly seven years training a successor. The Chancellor, a New Zealand Queen's Counsel, also handed over his responsibility to a Solomon Island barrister at the same Synod. We were both installed as Lay Canons of the cathedral as a mark of appreciation for our services. It was with some sadness that we finally left at the end of August the same year.

1974 Baddeley on the reef at Sikaiana before the tow.

Honiara – 'Wild Men' greeting the Archbishop of Canterbury.

248

21

Farewell to Ebb Tide

We eventually handed *Ebb Tide* over to the Church of Melanesia. She had been 'reefed' so often – the last straw when she was holed going aground on Malaita – that the insurance premium would have been astronomical. it was the logical thing to transfer her to the church fleet in which she would be covered by the church's insurance policy which was on very preferential terms. If we had kept her it would have taken at least a year to prepare her for the voyage back to England. So long as the engine would start and run, and the steering would work, a ship was considered to be serviceable by the crews. I am not denigrating the Solomon Islanders in any way. They are excellent seamen, but from an engineering point of view they have had to adjust from a very primitive culture in a comparatively short period of time, and it will probably be years before they have inherited the engineering instincts of the Western World.

Apart from sorting out the mechanical and electrical installation, plus a fair amount of refurbishing the accommodation, the preparations would have included getting rid of the rats and large tropical cockroaches which invaded all little ships. This alone would have been a major problem; we could not have worked at the pace we had earlier when in England. Working in the tropics is not easy as many will know. I did not feel that we could sell her since over the years, when we had lent her to the church, a considerable sum had been spent on her maintenance.

Quite apart from the problem of making *Ebb Tide* seaworthy again, the current price of fuel and charts make it impossible for us even to contemplate trying to complete the circumnavigation under our own steam. We did, however, leave by ship on the *Corabank,* a Bank Line cargo vessel, and strangely enough the first officer had been a pupil on the training ship *Worcester* with Neil and we had previously met him in Newlyn when he had been on his father's boat *Two Boys,* during one of our visits there.

Thus ended a twenty-two year involvement with a little ship which had had such a great influence on our whole family life. And so ends the story in the life of a vessel, built in 1941 for the navy during World War Two, made into a family home, ending her life somewhere on an island in the Pacific, un-mourned by those who had the use of her, but not by those on whose life she had had such an enormous influence.

ADDENDUM

Since writing this book I received an invitation to attend the Opening Eucharist for the eighth meeting of the Anglican Consultative Council held in Llandaff Cathedral, followed by a reception by the Lord Mayor of Cardiff. There we met the present Archbishop of Melanesia who we knew fairly well. We asked him what had finally happened to *Ebb Tide* and he told us that they had tried to sell her, but the sale fell through, (nothing unusual about this in that part of the world) so the engine and all equipment had been removed and the hull sold. The money from the sale had then been donated to the Mothers' Union in Melanesia. We both feel that this was a satisfactory ending to the chapter.

APPENDIX

Statistical Details of the Voyage to Honiara

Date of departure	Passage	Date of arrival	Distance naut mls	Time	Fuel used imp galls	Av. Speed in knots
Sept 8th	Birkenhead-Dunmore	Sept 9th	187	23.25hrs	77.8	8.1
Sept 9th	Dunmore East-Newlyn	Sept 10th	150	20hrs	62	7.5
Sept 16th	Newlyn-Brest	Sept 17th	134	17hrs	55	7.85
Sept 18th	Brest-LeGuilvenic	Sept 19th	128	16hrs	not recorded	
Oct 3rd	LeGuilvenic-Concarneau	Oct 3rd	20	2.5hrs		7.0
Oct 9th	Concarneau-Lexioes	Oct 12th	477	63hrs	172	7.57
Oct 15th	Lexioes-Lisbon	Oct 16th	170	26.25hrs	70	6.3
Oct 20th	Lisbon-Teneriffe	Oct 22nd	720	86.5hrs	259.3	8.1
Oct 24th	Santa Cruz-PortoGrande	Oct 29th	850	4days 9hrs	319	8.1
Oct 30th	PortoGrande-Barbados	Nov 10th	2,040	10days 5.5h	767	8.3
Nov 22nd	Bridgetown-Bequia	Nov 22nd	103	12.5	40	8.25
Nov 23rd	Bequia-Cristobal	Nov 28th	1,100	5days 10hrs	470	8.4
Dec 2nd	Cristobal-Balboa	Dec 2nd	45	9hrs	18	-
Dec 3rd	Balboa-Wreck Bay	Dec 8th	884	5 days	367	7.4
Dec 11th	Wreck Bay-Baltra	Dec 11th	62	9½ hrs	16	-
Dec 16th	Baltra-San Salvador	Dec 16th	44	6.33 hrs	12	-
Dec 17th	San Salvador-Baltra	Dec 17th	44	6.75 hrs	16	-
Dec 21st	Baltra-Academy Bay	Dec 21st	32	5.33 hrs	10	-
Dec 27th	Academy Bay-NukuHiva	Jan 14th	3,040	17days 17½hrs	767	6.4
Jan 20th	NukuHiva-NukuHiva	Jan 20th	22	3 hrs	7	-
Jan 24th	NukuHiva-Apia	Feb 4th	1,875	11days 3hrs	558	7.0
Feb 9th	Apia-Honiara	Feb 17th	1,680	9days 4hrs	780	7.6
	Totals for voyage:		**13,807**	**76 days**	**4,852 gallons**